Against th

Michael Glenny was born in 1927. He learned Russian first at school and continued during his time in the army. At Oxford he read Russian and undertook post-graduate research in Soviet history and politics. He has translated over forty books, including those of Alexander Solzhenitsyn and Mikhail Bulgakov. He is co-author with Norman Stone of *The Other Russia*, an oral history of Russians exiled by the Revolution.

BORIS YE~~LTSIN~~

Against
the Grain

AN AUTOBIOGRAPHY

translated from the Russian
by Michael Glenny

PAN BOOKS
London, Sydney and Auckland

First published 1990 by Jonathan Cape Ltd
This edition published 1991 by Pan Books Ltd,
Cavaye Place, London SW10 9PG

9 8 7 6 5 4 3 2

© Boris Yeltsin 1990

English Translation © Michael Glenny 1990

ISBN 0 330 31767 9

Printed in England by Clays Ltd, St Ives plc

Preface

Over the past two years, several major publishing houses have suggested that I should write my autobiography. I refused to do so, knowing that I would not be able to find the necessary time. I also felt that the time had not yet come for a summing-up.

Meanwhile life in the Soviet Union has gone on, and over the past months and weeks as many stormy and dramatic events have occurred as would, in the past, have taken place over whole decades. We have changed; we have said farewell to an epoch which, one would like to believe, will never return again. At a certain moment I realised that perhaps there was, after all, some point in writing my memoirs. Yielding to these insistent requests, I agreed to write about myself and about the receding past through which I have been fated to live.

As I had expected, work on the book was largely done on Sundays or at night, and were it not for the help of the young and talented journalist Valentin Yumashev, who, in fitting in with my working rhythm, has had to work in his own spare time and for many nights on end, it is doubtful whether this book would ever have been written.

Devoted assistance, given in a spirit of true friendship, was also provided by Valentina Lantseva, Lev Sukhanov, Tatyana Pushkina

– and of course by my family.

To all of them I give my most heartfelt thanks, and I am grateful to fate for placing them by my side.

I wish to donate the earnings from this book to the campaign against AIDS in the Soviet Union. The lack of disposable syringes and of other essential instruments in our hospitals has already led to a number of tragic cases of children being infected with AIDS. I consider it my duty, in so far as I am able, to make my contribution to the fight against this terrible scourge. My royalties will be used to buy disposable syringes and similar necessary equipment. If this is of help to people, I shall be happy.

Finally, I would like to express my deep gratitude to my literary agent, Andrew Nurnberg, who helped to bring this book to readers in dozens of countries.

Boris Yeltsin

Prologue

Chronicle of the Election Campaign

25 March 1989

There would seem to be no more room for doubt. The election of people's deputies[1] takes place tomorrow and in the Moscow no. 1 constituency, where the candidates are Yuri Brakov and myself, the Muscovites (and there are six million of them in this constituency) should elect me as their deputy by an overwhelming majority. All the official and unofficial public-opinion polls, including the American predictions, say so; this is confirmed by the pre-election mood and my intuition simply tells me that all will be well.

For some reason, though, I still can't sleep. Once again I mentally run through all the events that have befallen me during recent months, weeks and days. I try to understand where I made mistakes and where I did the right thing. Mistakes there were, and I am grateful for them; they spurred me on, made me work with twice, three times my usual energy. When analysing situations and events, I ignore whatever went well and concentrate on my shortcomings and mistakes. This is one of the basic traits of my character; I don't know whether it is good or bad. Hence my feeling of permanent dissatisfaction with myself, a dissatisfaction at 90 per cent of what I do.

Tomorrow will be a summing-up of the past eighteen months of my life, in which I have been both a political pariah and holder of several resounding party appointments. I had been out of politics since I resigned from the Politbureau in 1987. In Stalin's time ex-politicians were shot; Khrushchev pensioned them off; in Brezhnev's 'era of stagnation' they were packed off as ambassadors to distant countries. Here, too, Gorbachov's *perestroika* has set a new precedent: a dismissed politician is given the chance of returning to political life.

Mikhail Gorbachov, as general secretary, telephoned and offered me the post of first deputy chairman of the state committee for construction (Gosstroi); I accepted, since at that moment I was indifferent to what my next job might be. At the end of our conversation he told me to bear in mind that he wasn't going to let me back into politics. At the time he evidently believed in what he was saying with all sincerity; it did not occur to him that he had created and put in motion a set of democratic processes under which the word of the general secretary ceased to be the word of a dictator – a word which, in the past, had been immediately transformed into law, binding on the whole empire. Now the general secretary of the central committee of the Communist Party of the Soviet Union (CPSU)[2] might say that he was not going to let me back into politics, but the people might think otherwise and decide that I must be allowed back. And now they can do this: times have certainly changed.

And they will bring us much more that is new! This is one delightful aspect of the present time: but it is also fraught with trouble. Nobody knows either what will happen next, or where the step we have taken today may lead us tomorrow. The huge, lumbering machine of the party bureaucracy (*apparat*) is making clumsy manoeuvres in its defensive attempts at self-preservation, but by so doing it will surely destroy itself all the sooner.

It was given a limited and not particularly complicated task to perform – namely to ensure that I was not elected as a people's deputy. After all, it should not have been a difficult assignment to carry out. It is nothing compared with providing a flat for every Soviet family by the year 2000 or ensuring that the country is decently fed within the current five-year plan. In my case, all they had to do was to deal with one person! And to do this, what's more, they would be aided by a remarkable new electoral law, with its adoption meetings,[3] carefully designed to sift out undesirable candidates; by the excessive powers given to the constituency commissions (all designed by the party bureaucrats themselves) and by control over a vast, obedient propaganda machine, which would say and publish just what they wanted! Yet with all of this available to them, they still managed to fail. All the dirty tricks that have been used against me in the past months – juggling the facts, telling lies and making stern denunciations against me at the plenary sessions (plenum) of the central committee – have had exactly the opposite effect to that intended, and have only brought me the ever greater support of the electorate.

Each time the next piece of stupidity was aimed at me, invariably evoking a surge of sympathy for me from the voters of Moscow, I suddenly became acutely aware of what a morass we had sunk into and how immeasurably difficult it was going to be to haul ourselves out of it. For it is precisely this body of people – the party bureaucracy – which is doing its best to put new obstacles in the way of *perestroika* and *glasnost*; and they are not prepared to surrender to anyone their right to do so. It is at such moments of insight that one is apt to throw up one's hands in despair. Thanks, however, to the fact that during the election campaign I was able to meet my electors almost every day, I imbibed new energy from them and a renewed faith that we would never again live in the way we have lived before. The era of moral slavery is over.

But what if I am nevertheless the loser in tomorrow's election? What will that mean? That the party *apparat* was after all the stronger, that injustice has triumphed? Nothing of the sort. Simply that I, too, am human and that I have a mass of failings. I have an awkward, obstinate character; I have made misjudgments and mistakes, so that it is entirely possible that I may not be elected. But even if the vote goes to Brakov – which is what the party bureaucrats are counting on – it is still a profound illusion to imagine that he will become the obedient tool of those who put him up to it. In today's climate, both he and I – or anyone else – can only fulfil the role of people's deputy by listening to the people and not to the *apparat*, by carrying out the demands of the people and not of the party's bureaucratic 'establishment'.

And yet I believe that the Muscovites will vote for me. There is not long to wait now.

'If you could have October 1987 all over again, how would you have acted?'*

'Boris Nikolayevich Yeltsin! Was your speech at the October 1987 plenum a gesture of despair, or were you hoping for support from one of the members of the Politbureau?'*

By 12 September 1987 I had been a candidate member of the Politbureau for nearly nine months, but during that time my relations with Gorbachov and the other members had grown steadily worse – no doubt due to my difficult character. At the Politbureau meeting on that day, the point was reached at which I clearly could not remain either as first secretary of the Moscow city committee of the party or a candidate member of the Politbureau. After the meeting I went back to my office and took a clean sheet of paper. I collected all my thoughts and began a letter to Gorbachov:

12 September 1987

Dear Mikhail Sergeyevich

My decision to write this letter has been a long and difficult one to reach. A year and nine months have passed since you and the Politbureau proposed that I should head the Moscow city party organisation[4] and I accepted the post. My motives for acceptance or refusal were not, of course, of any significance. I realised that it would be an incredibly hard assignment, and that much more needed to be added to my previous experience of such work, including time on the job itself.

None of that discouraged me. I sensed your support, and I came to the job with a degree of confidence that surprised even myself. I began working with a new staff in a spirit of self-sacrifice, dedication to principle and comradely loyalty.

The first landmarks charting our progress are in place,

* (From questions handed up from the floor at meetings during the election campaign.)

4

although in fact very little has been achieved. But without enumerating any specifics, our chief success has been that the spirit, the mood of the majority of Muscovites has changed. Naturally the circumstances in the country as a whole have had their effect on this; but strange as it may seem, my personal sense of dissatisfaction has only increased.

In the actions and remarks of certain high-level leaders, I have become aware of something that I had not noticed before. There has been a noticeable change from an attitude of friendly support to one of indifference towards matters concerning Moscow and of coldness towards me personally, especially in several members of the Politbureau and some secretaries of the central committee.

Generally speaking, I have always striven to express my own point of view, even when it did not coincide with other people's opinions. As a result, an increasing number of undesirable situations have arisen – or to be more precise: my style, my frankness and my past history reveal me as being untrained for work as a member of the Politbureau.

Nor can I avoid raising certain questions relating to matters of principle. About some of them, especially those concerning personnel, I have already spoken and written to you; in addition, I would like to mention the following points.

First, there is the style of work favoured by Comrade Yegor Kuzmich Ligachov.[5] My view and that of others is that his style is inappropriate, especially now (although I do not want to belittle his positive qualities). And his style of work has also affected attitudes in the secretariat of the central committee. Certain secretaries of 'marginal' committees copy him unthinkingly; but the real point is that it is the party as a whole which suffers. To decode all this: if all this were to be said publicly great harm would be done to the party. Only you personally can change something in this state of affairs and in the interests of the party.

The party organisations have turned out to be lagging behind all the recent, splendid events. Here (apart from the conduct of our foreign policies) there has been practically no *perestroika* at all, with a whole chain of consequences. The result is that we wonder why *perestroika* has become bogged down in the primary [party] organisations. *Perestroika* has been devised and formulated in revolutionary terms. But putting it into effect, particularly in the party, has come down to the same old approach – a lot of inflated language for public consumption, while in reality the implementation has been pettifogging, self-serving and bureaucratic. There has been an abundance of paper (if you spend all your time counting tomatoes, tea or railway wagons, of course there will be no substantial change to report); endless meetings on minor issues; niggling criticisms; careful searches for negative results – all concerned to reinforce the 'authority' of the party *apparat*.

I shall refrain from even mentioning any attempts at criticism from the grassroots of the party. It is very disturbing that people are thinking in critical terms but are afraid to say so. This, it seems to me, is most dangerous for the party.

In my view, Yegor Kuzmich [Ligachov] works in a way that is altogether unsystematic and crude. His constant references to his 'experience at Tomsk' [where he had been first secretary] are getting to be embarrassing.

I cannot describe his behaviour towards me after the June plenum of the central committee and his attacks on me at the Politbureau meeting of 10 September as anything but co-ordinated persecution. The ruling on demonstrations passed by the executive committee [of the Moscow City Soviet] was a municipal matter and was a correct decision. I cannot understand the function of the committee that has been set up and I ask you to correct the situation that has arisen in consequence.[6]

The result of Ligachov's behaviour is that what he creates is not harmony but discord in the party mechanism and I do not want to say any more about his attitude to the events in Moscow. But it is amazing how in two whole years he never once inquired into the state of affairs of the 1,115,000 party organisations throughout the country. The party committees are losing their independence (at a time when collective farms and industrial enterprises have been given more powers of decision-making).

I have always been in favour of demanding high standards, but I do not approve of the fear [of dismissal] under which many party committees and their first secretaries are being made to work. I regard it as the fault of Comrade Ligachov that in relations between the permanent staff of the central committee and the local party committees there is neither an adherence to ethical standards nor the comradely atmosphere that should exist within the party – an atmosphere conducive to creative thinking, self-confidence and dedication to the task. Therein, in my opinion, lies the source of the party's 'go-slow' attitude [to *perestroika*]. The *apparat* must be significantly reduced in size (by 50 per cent) and its structure must be decisively altered. The value of this was proved when I, in my capacity as first secretary of the Moscow party organisation, cut down the *apparat* of the district committees by a half, although this was, admittedly, a small-scale example.

I am personally distressed by the attitude of several of the comrades who make up the membership of the Politbureau. They are intelligent, and therefore they have quickly become supporters of *perestroika*. But is their 'conversion' to be wholly trusted? This suits them, and – if you will forgive my saying so, Mikhail Sergeyevich – I believe it also suits you. I sense that they feel frequently the need to remain silent, when in fact they disagree with something, so that the agreement expressed by some of them is insincere.

I am an awkward person and I know it. I realise, too, that it is difficult for you to decide what to do about me. But it is better to admit one's mistakes now. Later, given my present relations with my colleagues, the number of problems I am likely to cause you will increase and will start to hamper you in your work. And that I most sincerely do not want to happen.

I do not want it because, despite the incredible efforts you are making, the struggle to maintain [political] stability can lead to stagnation, to the state of affairs (or something very like it) that we reached before [under Brezhnev]. And that must not happen. These are some of the reasons and motives that have induced me to address my request to you. I am not doing so out of either weakness or cowardice.

I wish you to release me from the duties of first secretary of the Moscow city committee of the CPSU and from my responsibilities as a candidate member of the Politbureau of the central committee of the CPSU. Please regard this as an official statement.

I do not think it should be necessary for me to submit my request directly to a plenum of the central committee of the CPSU.

Respectfully yours,
B. Yeltsin

I sealed the letter in an envelope and wondered for the last time whether I was right in sending it; might it not be better to wait a little? Then I sharply rejected all thoughts of leaving a loophole of escape; I called my assistant and handed him the envelope. I knew very well that the postal service between Moscow and the general secretary's holiday *dacha* at Pitsunda on the Black Sea was most efficient and that Gorbachov would receive my letter within a few hours.

What would happen then? Would he call me to see him? Or would he telephone me and ask me to stay working steadily at my job as I had worked until now? Perhaps my letter of resignation would help him to realise that a critical situation had developed in the top leadership of the party, and that immediate steps must be taken in order to ensure that there should be a healthy, constructive atmosphere in the Politbureau.

I decided not to try guessing. My bridges were burned, there was no way back. I worked, as usual, from early morning to late at night. Inwardly, I did not admit to myself that I was nervous and suffering agonies; I pretended that nothing had happened and that everything was normal. No one, not even my family, knew anything about what I had done.

Afterwards I was often asked whether there had been any specific reason, any particular impulse that had made me sit down and write that letter to Gorbachov. I have always replied quite definitely that there was not. Somehow everything had accumulated gradually and imperceptibly. Admittedly there had been one particular session of the Politbureau, at which Gorbachov's speech for the seventieth anniversary of the October 1917 Revolution was discussed; I made about twenty separate comments on that speech, which caused him to explode. At the time, I recall, this had shattered me; I was amazed that anyone could react so hysterically to criticism. Even so, that episode had certainly not been decisive.

It had all begun earlier, in my first days as a member of the Politbureau. I could never rid myself of the feeling that I was some kind of outsider – or rather, an alien – among these people; that I somehow didn't belong within the framework of a set of ideas that I found incomprehensible; that the members were accustomed to acting and thinking only according to one man's – the general secretary's – way of thinking. In this, the party's supreme decision-making body, which is supposed to function as a collective, practically no one expresses their own point of view if it differs from that of the chairman, or only expresses it on inessential matters – and that is what is called 'party unity'. I, on the other hand, have never concealed what I am thinking, and in this I was not prepared to change when I started work as a member of the Politbureau. This annoyed many of them, and more than once I clashed with Ligachov, Mikhail Solomentsev [chairman of the party control commission and a full member of the Politbureau] and others. Some of them privately supported me, even sympathised with me to some degree, but never gave any outward sign of it.

A sense of protest at the Politbureau style of work had long been growing in my mind; it was far too out of keeping with the appeals and slogans calling for *perestroika* which Gorbachov had proclaimed in 1985. Naturally the Politbureau does not function as it did in Brezhnev's day. The sessions now last a long time, and more often than not the members sit listening to monologues by the chairman. Gorbachov loves talking in well-rounded periods; he will hold forth at length, complete with preambles and perorations, and he will pass comment on what practically everyone else has said. Thus the semblance of a discussion is created; everyone apparently has their say, but this does not change the essence of the matter: the general secretary does what he wanted in the first place. Everyone, in my opinion, understands this perfectly well, and they all play the game and play it successfully.

But I wasn't prepared to play it and would express my views fairly sharply, frankly and directly. My remarks, to be honest, had little effect, but they profoundly disturbed the placid atmosphere of the sessions. Gradually I came to the firm conclusion that a majority of the Politbureau membership had to be replaced by younger, fresher forces, by energetic people who didn't think in standard clichés. This should accelerate the process of *perestroika*, after which it would be possible, without reneging on one's convictions, to continue working actively and seriously to get things moving all along the line. Either this, or one should resign.

When Gorbachov was on leave and Ligachov chaired the Politbureau, my clashes with him became particularly frequent. He would act self-confidently, mouthing old, worn-out dogmas in a demagogic tone. The horror of it was, however, that one was not only forced to listen to all this, but also to take it as a guide to one's actions – actions that would affect the whole party, indeed the whole country. This was no way to work.

One of my regular skirmishes with Ligachov took place at a Politbureau session on issues of social justice, the abolition of privileges and perks. It was this last skirmish that prompted my letter of resignation to Gorbachov. When Gorbachov returned from his holiday, he phoned me and said, 'Let's meet later.' I didn't understand what he meant by 'later' . . . so I waited. A week, two weeks passed, and still there was no invitation to meet for a talk. I decided that I was therefore free of any obligations to remind him of this; that he had evidently changed his mind about meeting me, having decided to take the matter of my resignation to the plenum of the central committee.

I should like to recall that in my letter I asked Gorbachov to relieve me of my duties as a candidate member of the Politbureau and as first secretary of the Moscow city committee of the party, and I expressed the hope that this request could be granted without my having to refer it to a plenum of the central committee. There was no mention of our meeting after the plenum. Later – that was all. I was sure that he was talking of an interval of two or three days, or perhaps a week at the most. After all, it is not every day of the week that a member of the Politbureau resigns, with a request not to refer the matter to a plenum. A fortnight passed without a word from Gorbachov. By then, quite naturally, I considered that he had decided to refer the question to a session of the central committee plenum, in order to arrange a public discussion with me instead of a private meeting.

The date of the plenum was announced. I had to start preparing to make a speech and to face what would come after it. Naturally, I made no effort, in any way, to organise a group of supporters from among those members of the central committee whose thinking and whose assessment of the state of affairs in the party and its leadership concurred with mine. The mere thought of any such thing struck me then – and still does – as blasphemous. I would never have undertaken the business of briefing other speakers, agreeing on who should say what and when – in other words, weaving a plot. No, no and no again – although afterwards many people said to me that we should have joined forces, made preparations and spoken as a united front. They felt that if we had done that it would at least have created a certain effect; the leadership would have been obliged to reckon with the views of the group, even though a minority, and this would have posed them with more of a problem than a lone individual, whom they can accuse with impunity of anything they like.

I did not take that course. What is more, I had not told a single person that I was planning to speak at the plenum. Even the members of the Moscow city committee of the party who were closest to me knew nothing of my intention, because I did not say a word about it to them. I had no idea, therefore, whether or not anyone might support me. My closest comrades in the central committee were unlikely to say anything either, so psychologically I had to prepare myself for the worst.

I went to the plenum without a prepared speech; I had written only seven headings on a piece of paper. Usually I take a very long time to prepare every one of my speeches, sometimes rewriting the text ten or fifteen times in an attempt to find the most precise and telling words. But this time I acted differently. While I was not speaking entirely impromptu – I had given very careful thought to my seven points – I nevertheless did not write out my speech. Even now I find it difficult to explain why I did not. Perhaps I was not 100 per cent sure that I would speak and I was leaving open a tiny crack in case I decided to retreat, on the assumption that I might not speak at this plenum but at the next one. That thought was no doubt lurking somewhere in my subconscious.

The agenda of the meeting marking the seventieth anniversary of the October 1917 Revolution was known in advance. I was in no way embarrassed by the solemnity of this occasion. On the contrary, I considered it a good thing that we had finally arrived at a healthy attitude that an anniversary was by no means the occasion for nothing but long solemn speeches with orchestrated applause, but that at such times it is useful to talk about our problems too. I was greatly mistaken. Afterwards, the foremost charge against me was that I had allegedly spoilt the otherwise unsullied, upbeat mood of this festive event.

Gorbachov introduced the report in his speech. While he was speaking, a struggle was going on inside me: should I or should I not speak? It was obvious that to postpone it was pointless. I knew I must go up to the rostrum. But I was also well aware of the storm that would greet me after a few minutes, of the torrent of filth that would be poured over my head, of the many unjust accusations of treachery that I would shortly have to hear.

Gorbachov's speech was coming to an end. Ligachov, who was in the chair, was already preparing to declare the meeting closed. Then something unforeseen happened. I had better quote the dispassionate stenographic record of the plenum:

CHAIRMAN, COMRADE LIGACHOV: Comrades, the report is thus concluded. Does anyone have any questions? Very well. There are no questions? If not, the platform wishes to consult for a moment.
GORBACHOV: Comrade Yeltsin has a question.
CHAIRMAN, COMRADE LIGACHOV: Then we will consult the floor. Do we need to throw the report open to debate?
VOICES: No.
CHAIRMAN, COMRADE LIGACHOV: No.
GORBACHOV: Comrade Yeltsin has a statement to make.
CHAIRMAN, COMRADE LIGACHOV: Comrade Boris Nikolayevich Yeltsin, candidate member of the Politbureau of the central committee of the CPSU, first secretary of Moscow city committee of the CPSU has the floor. Please, Boris Nikolayevich . . .

And I went up to the rostrum to make the speech that was to destroy the self-congratulatory atmosphere of that anniversary plenum – and to inform the central committee of my wish to resign from the upper echelon of the party leadership.

I

Chronicle of the Election Campaign

13 December 1988

Rightly or wrongly, I have made a decision: I will stand in the election of people's deputies. I fully realise that my prospects of being elected are far from being 100 per cent, as the new electoral law enables the government and the party *apparat* to control much of the proceedings. There are several hurdles to be surmounted before the voters themselves make their choice. The system of proposing candidates; the adoption meetings to sift out the unsuitable ones; the electoral commissions that are packed with *apparatchiki* of the local party executive committee – all this gives rise to gloomy reflection. If I lose, if I fail to be elected as a deputy at these elections, I can only imagine the triumph and delight with which the party establishment will rush to give me the *coup de grâce*. It would be their trump card: the people didn't want him, the people didn't put him forward as a candidate, the people threw him out. But, in reality, these adoption meetings have no connection whatsoever with the expression of the people's will. This is obvious to everybody, from the rank-and-file voter all the way to Gorbachov himself. They are simply a support to prop up a collapsing system of government, a sop thrown to that mangy Cerberus, the party's bureaucratic *apparat*.

It would be perfectly possible, of course, not to stand for election;

close friends have advised me to keep out of this particular fight, as my situation means that the odds are weighted too unfairly against me. For the last eighteen months the very word 'Yeltsin' has been under a ban; I was alive, but at the same time it was as if I didn't exist. So, if I suddenly re-emerge into the political arena and start talking to the voters and taking part in rallies and meetings, then the whole of the party's immensely powerful propaganda machine will come down on me with a farrago of lies, slander and half-truths.

Furthermore, under the new electoral system, ministers do not have the right to be people's deputies. Consequently, if I am elected I shall have to resign from my post [as first deputy chairman, Gosstroi – a ministerial post] and after that – who knows what may happen? The Congress of People's Deputies, elected under the present system, is more than likely to see to it that I am not elected to the Supreme Soviet of the USSR, and I shall therefore be unable to work in the parliament. So I am faced with the more than real prospect of becoming, at best, an unemployed deputy. As far as I know, not a single minister is intending to give up his job. There are a lot of people's deputies but few ministers.

Telegrams have started to come in from all over the country. Huge organisations, many of them several thousand strong, have been putting me forward as their candidate. They come from so far and wide that one can learn the geography of the Soviet Union from them.

The forthcoming election is going to be a battle, exhausting and nerve-racking. What's more, my enemies will bend the rules and hit below the belt; they will suddenly attack me from behind and use all sorts of illegal but nevertheless effective methods. Knowing all this, am I prepared to set out on the long, hard slog of an election campaign?

As I debate the matter to myself, I have many doubts. I almost persuade myself not to stand. But the most interesting thing of all is that inwardly I have long ago made the decision – perhaps it happened at the very moment when I learned that these elections were now going to be possible. Yes, of course, I am going to throw myself into this crazy maelstrom, and it is entirely possible that this time I shall break my neck; but I cannot do otherwise.

'When did you start to become a rebel?'*

'Whom do you most resemble in character – your mother or your father? Tell us about your parents in a little more detail.'*

'It's said that you used to be a real sportsman and you even played in a championship team. Is that a rumour or is it true?'*

I was born on 1 February 1931, in the village of Butko in the Talitsky district of Sverdlovsk province, where all my forebears had lived. They had ploughed the land, sown wheat and, in general, had passed their lives like all other country people. Among the people in our village there were the Yeltsins, my father's family, and the Starygins, who are my mother's family. My father married my mother there and soon I made my appearance in the world – their first child.

My mother used to tell me the story of what happened at my baptism. The little church with its priest was the only one for the whole district, which consisted of several villages. The birth rate for the area was quite high and even so a baptismal service was held only once a month. Consequently, that day was a more than busy one for the priest, and the church was filled to bursting with parents, babies, relatives and friends. The baptism was conducted in the most primitive fashion: there was a tub full of holy liquid, water seasoned with something or other, in which the baby was completely immersed. The squalling infant was then christened and given a name which was entered in the parish register. And, of course, as was the custom in villages all over Russia, the parents offered the priest a glass of home-brewed beer, moonshine liquor or vodka – whatever they could afford.

Since my turn did not come until the afternoon, the priest, having drunk many toasts, could hardly stand. When my mother, Klavdia

* (From questions handed up from the floor at meetings during the election campaign.)

15

Vasilievna, and my father, Nikolai Ignatievich, handed me to him, the priest dropped me into the tub and, having been drawn into an argument with a member of the congregation, forgot to take me out. At first, my parents, who were standing at some distance from the baptismal font, didn't know what had happened. When they realised what was going on, my mother screamed, leaped forward, and fished me out from somewhere at the bottom of the tub. They then shook the water out of me. The priest was not particularly worried. He said, 'Well, if he can survive such an ordeal it means he's a good tough lad . . . and I name him Boris.'

Thus I became Boris Nikolayevich. I won't say that after that I developed any special attitude to religion – of course not.

My childhood was a hard time: very bad harvests and no food. At that time, everyone was forced to join a collective farm – and all peasants were treated as *kulaki*.[1] To make matters worse, gangs of outlaws roamed at large all around us, and almost every day there were shoot-outs, murders and robberies.

We lived in near poverty, in a small house with one cow. We did have a horse, but it died, so there was no animal to pull the plough. In 1935 the situation became unbearable; even our cow died, and my grandfather, who was over sixty, began going from house to house, stove-building. Apart from being a ploughman, he could also turn his hand to carpentry and joinery; he was a complete jack of all trades.

In order to save the family, my father decided to leave the farm and find work on a construction site. It was the so-called period of industrialisation. He knew that building workers would be needed for the construction of a potash plant at Berezniki in the neighbouring province of Perm, so he moved the family there. We all harnessed ourselves to the cart, loaded it with our few possessions and set off for the railway station – a distance of twenty miles.

After we arrived at Berezniki and my father signed on at the construction site as a labourer, we were housed in one of the communal huts typical of the time – and which, to this day, are still to be found – built of wooden clapboard, through which draughts whistled relentlessly. The hut had a central corridor and twenty small rooms, naturally without any modern conveniences; there was only an outdoor toilet and water had to be drawn from a well. We were given a few sticks of furniture and we bought a goat to supply us with milk. My brother and my sister, the youngest, had already been born by then. The six of us, including the goat, slept on the floor, all huddled together. From the age of six the household was in my charge. This meant looking after the younger children – rocking my sister in her cradle and keeping an eye on my brother to see that he didn't misbehave. My other domestic duties were boiling potatoes, washing the dishes and fetching water from the well.

While my father laboured on the building site, my mother, a gentle and kind woman by nature, would help everyone by sewing clothes for all and sundry – a skirt here, a dress there, for relatives or neighbours. Every night she would sit down with her sewing, never taking money for her work. She was most grateful if someone gave her, say, half a loaf of bread or some other morsel of food.

My father, on the other hand, was rough and quick-tempered, just like my grandfather. No doubt they passed these characteristics on to me. He and my mother would constantly have arguments about me. My father's chief instrument of teaching good behaviour was the strap, and he would wallop me good and proper for any lapses. Whatever happened anywhere in the vicinity – if a new neighbour's apple tree had been robbed or someone had played a nasty trick on the German teacher in school – he would not say a word but reach for the strap. This always took place in silence, except for my mother weeping and begging him not to touch me. But he would firmly shut the door and as he told me to lie down, I would pull up my shirt and lower my trousers. I must say he laid into me with great thoroughness. I always clenched my teeth and did not make a sound, which infuriated him; but my mother would then burst in, snatch the strap away from him, pushing him aside as she stood between us. She always defended me.

My father was forever inventing something. One of his ambitions, for instance, was to invent a machine that would lay bricks. He would sketch it out, rethink, make calculations and then produce another set of drawings; it was a kind of will-o'-the-wisp that he was perpetually chasing. Unfortunately no one else has yet invented such a machine, although even now whole research institutes rack their brains over it. He would constantly describe to me what his machine would be like and how it would work; how it would mix the mortar, lay the bricks, clean off the surface mortar and move forward. He had worked it all out in his head and drawn the general plan, but he never managed to realise his idea.

We lived like this in the wooden hut for ten years. Strange as it may seem, the people who lived crowded together in those conditions somehow managed to be good, friendly neighbours, especially when one considers that there was no sound insulation. If there was a party in any of the rooms – for maybe a birthday or a wedding – we would play an old wind-up gramophone. There were only two or three records, and these were shared by the whole hut; I can still remember one song in particular: 'Shchors the Red Commander, marches on beneath the standard . . .', which the whole hut used to sing. Conversations, quarrels, rows, secrets, laughter – the whole hut could hear everything and everyone knew everyone else's business.

Perhaps it is because to this day I can remember how hard our life was then that I so hate those communal huts. Worst of all was winter, when there was nowhere to hide from the cold. As we had no warm clothes, it was the nanny-goat that saved us. I remember huddling up to the animal, warm as a stove. She was also our salvation throughout the war; although she gave less than a litre a day, her rich milk was enough to enable the children to survive.

In addition, of course, we earned money on the side. Every summer my mother and I would go out to a nearby collective farm. We would be allotted several acres of meadow-land, and there we scythed the grass, stacked it and generally prepared the hay, half of which went to the collective farm and the other half to us. We would then sell our half and buy a loaf of bread for r.100–150, or sometimes as much as r.200.

That, broadly speaking, was how my childhood was spent. It was a fairly joyless time. There was never any question of sweets, delicacies or anything of that sort; we had only one aim in life – to survive.

At school, I stood out from my class-mates by my energy and drive, and from first grade to last I was elected class-leader, even though I went to several different schools. I did well at my studies, gaining top marks in exams. My behaviour, however, was less praiseworthy; more than once I was on the verge of being expelled. In all my years in school I was always the ringleader, always devising some prank. In fifth grade, for instance, I made all the class jump out of a first-floor window, and when the class-mistress came in (we all disliked her) there was no sign of us; the class-room was empty. She immediately went to the school porter at the main entrance, who told her that no one had left the building. Alongside the school was a small yard, where we would gather to tell each other all sorts of stories, and so we hid there. After a while we returned to the class-room where we were given a '1'² for the subject in question – just like that: the day-sheet of the class-record was produced and marked, '1, 1, 1, 1' all the way from top to bottom. We protested. We said, 'Punish us for bad behaviour, but test us on the lesson – we've learned it.' The headmaster arrived, organised a special session and questioned us for about two hours. We, of course, had learned everything by heart, and all of us, even the weak pupils, answered every question correctly. In the end the '1's were cancelled, although we were, admittedly, given a mark of only '2' out of '5' for behaviour – the lowest possible mark for this.

Another of our pranks involved the local stream, the Zyryanka. In spring it would overflow its banks to become a real river and logs were floated down it. I invented a game which involved seeing who could run across the floating logs to the far bank. The timber tended to flow in a fairly tight mass, so that if you judged it carefully there was a chance of being able to get across – although to do so you needed to be extremely skilful. Step on a log and if it gave the slightest sign of rolling over and you delayed for a second, you would be under water; so you had to move really fast from one log to another, keeping your balance all the time and leaping briskly in order to reach the far bank. The slightest miscalculation and it was splash! into the icy water, with nothing but logs above you, which prevented you from pushing your head between them and gulping a lungful of air, not sure if you would come out of it alive. Such were the jolly games we devised.

We also used to have fights – district against district, with between sixty and a hundred boys at a time fighting with sticks, cudgels or fists. I always used to take part in these fights, although I got well and truly clobbered. When two solid walls of opponents clashed head-on, however strong and nippy you might be you would always end up with several bumps on your head. To this day I have a broken nose like a boxer's, from when someone caught me a whack with the shaft of a cart. I fell, everything went black and I thought it was the end of me. But all was well; I came to my senses and was carried home. There were no fatalities in these fights, because, although we fought enthusiastically, we still observed certain limits. It was more in the way of a sporting contest, though a very tough one.

One day I was expelled from school. It happened at the end of our seven years of primary schooling. About 600 people were gathered in the assembly hall – parents, teachers and pupils – in an atmosphere of cheerfulness and elation. Everyone was solemnly handed his or her certificate. Everything was going according to plan when I suddenly stood up and asked permission to speak. No one doubted that I would simply stand up and say a few words of gratitude; my exam results, after all, had been excellent, nothing but top marks in every subject, and for that reason I was allowed up on to the stage. Naturally I had some kind words to say to those teachers who really had given us a great deal of valuable instruction that would stand us in good stead in our lives and who had developed in us the habit of reading and thinking. But then I declared that our class-mistress had no right to teach or educate children because she crippled them mentally and psychologically.

That teacher was an awful woman. She might hit you with a heavy ruler, she might stand you in the corner, she might humiliate a boy in front of a girl and vice versa. She made us clean her house. The class had to collect food scraps from all over the district to feed her pig. It was endless, and naturally I couldn't bear any of this. Some of the children refused to do as she told them, but others nevertheless submitted to her.

Briefly, at that solemn gathering I described how she used to mock her pupils, destroy their self-confidence and do everything possible to humiliate every one of us – no matter whether he or she were good, middling or poor at school work, and, giving some fairly glaring examples, I went for her hammer and tongs. There was an uproar. The whole event was ruined.

Next day the school's staff council sent for my father to tell him that my certificate was being withdrawn and instead I was to be given a so-called 'wolf's ticket': a little scrap of white paper which at the top testified that I had attended the required seven years of primary schooling, but stating below it that I was 'deprived of the right to attend secondary education throughout the territory of the USSR'. My father came home furious and reached for the strap – but at that moment, for the first time, I gripped him by the arm. 'That's enough!' I said, 'From now on I'm going to educate myself.' And never again was I made to stand in the corner all night and no one ever took the strap to me again.

Obviously I refused to accept the decision of the staff council and started to take my case to every level of the education authorities: first to the district and then the city education department. I think this was the first time that I discovered what a local party committee was. I succeeded in getting a commission of inquiry set up, which examined the work of that teacher and dismissed her from the school. She got exactly what she deserved, because she was totally unfit for teaching work; and I got my certificate back, although under the heading 'discipline' the word 'unsatisfactory' glared out from the line of '5's.

I decided not to go back to that school and instead I entered the eighth grade at another school, the Pushkin school in Sverdlovsk, of which I still have the fondest memories: the staff were excellent, and in Antonina Khonina we had a superb class-mistress. That was really good teaching.

It was then that I began taking an active part in sport. I was at once fascinated by volley-ball and was quite prepared to play it for days on end. I liked the way the ball obeyed me, that I could catch even the most impossible ball with an unbelievable leap. At the same time I also took up skiing, gymnastics, light athletics, decathlon, boxing and wrestling; I wanted to try my hand at them all, to do absolutely everything well. In the end, volley-ball got the upper hand and I started playing it seriously. I kept a ball with me all the time, even putting it beside my pillow when I went to bed, and when I fell asleep my hand would still be resting on it. As soon as I woke up I would start training by myself; I might practise spinning the ball on one finger, or bouncing it off the wall and the floor. But because I was missing two fingers on my left hand, I had difficulty in catching a ball and I therefore worked on my own method of holding my hand in a special position, with the result that I have a unique, non-standard way of catching.

This is how I lost my two fingers: it was wartime; every young man was hastening to the front, but being too young we were naturally not allowed to go. We made our own pistols and rifles and even a cannon. We decided to find some grenades and take them apart in order to learn what was inside them. I undertook to break into the local church, which was being used as an ammunition store. At night I crept through three layers of barbed-wire fencing and, while the sentry was on the other side of the building, I filed through the lattice-work on a window and climbed inside. There I took two RGD-33 hand-grenades with their fuses and was lucky enough to make my way back unharmed (the sentry would have fired without warning). We went to a forest about four miles away and there we decided to take the grenades apart. I persuaded the other boys to take cover about a hundred yards away; then I put the grenade on a stone, knelt down and hit it with a hammer. Out of ignorance I had forgotten to take out the fuse. There was an explosion – and two of my fingers were mangled. Luckily, the other lads were unharmed. I lost consciousness several times while they took me to town. Having obtained my father's written permission (gangrene had set in), the hospital surgeons operated on me and cut off the two fingers.

Every summer during my school days I worked to earn pocket money, but apart from that I used to organise the others into taking long hikes. Each trip had a special objective: either to find the source of some river or to go to Denezhkin Rock, or something of that nature. It usually involved camping, hiking a few hundred miles with rucksacks and living in the taiga for several weeks.

It so happened that one summer, after ninth grade, we decided to find the source of the River Yaiva. We spent a very long time climbing up through the taiga, having found out from the map that the source of the river was somewhere near the crest of the Urals range. The food that we had taken with us was soon finished and we fed ourselves on what we could find in the forest. The Urals forest is very rich; one can survive there for a considerable length of time. We ate nuts, mushrooms and berries. Far away from any roads, for a long time we tramped through the virgin woodland of the taiga. Occasionally we came across a little hut used by hunters, where we would spend the night, but more often we built our own brushwood shelter or simply slept in the open.

We found the source of the river – a spring of natural hydrogen sulphide. We were delighted; we could now turn back. We descended a few miles to the first little village, by which time we were pretty worn out. We would need a boat to travel further. We collected whatever each person could offer: a rucksack, a shirt, a belt, more or less everything we had – to trade for a boat. Then we went into a cottage, where we gave all these things to the owner and in exchange asked him to lend us a little boat – a wooden, flat-bottomed punt. In this punt we floated downstream, no longer having the strength to walk. The landscape was beautiful – indeed it still is, because it has not yet been spoiled by human hand. As we were floating along, we suddenly saw a cave in the hillside above us. We decided to stop and explore it. The cave led us on and on, until it suddenly opened out and brought us to a point somewhere deep in the taiga. We scouted around, but could not make out where we were. We were lost and we had lost our boat too. We wandered in the taiga for almost a week. We had brought nothing with us, and unfortunately the region turned out to be swampy, with nothing but stunted saplings and undergrowth. It provided us with barely enough to eat, but absolutely no fresh water at all. We collected the murky swamp-water and sodden moss in a shirt, squeezed it out and drank the liquid that dripped out of the shirt.

In the end we managed to make our way back to the river, where we found our boat and were able to estimate our position, but the dirty water we had drunk gave us all an attack of typhoid fever. Everyone including myself had a temperature of over 40°C,[3] but in my role of organiser, as it were, I stayed on my feet. I carried all the other lads down to the boat, laid them in the bottom, and exerted my last ounce of strength to prevent myself from losing consciousness. I could then more or less steer it as it drifted downstream. I had only enough strength left to give the other lads some river-water to splash over their faces, as they were all burning with fever. They lost consciousness and soon I, too, began passing out. When we reached a railway-bridge that crossed the river, we decided that someone would notice us, so I moored up to the bank and collapsed unconscious. We were seen, picked up and driven back to town; the school term had already begun a month ago, and everyone, of course, was searching for us.

Typhoid fever kept us in the hospital for nearly three months. They had no special medicines for dealing with it. We were now in the tenth grade – our last – and I had missed practically all the classes so far. My companions on that dramatic expedition had decided to skip tenth grade that year and to stay on at school for an extra year. Half-way through the school year, however, that is in the spring term, I began studying again at home on my own. I undertook the whole tenth-grade syllabus and read and learned a great deal, working literally day and night, and when the final exams began I went to the school to take them.

When I arrived at school, I was told this wasn't allowed, that there was no provision for external students in the final year. Once again, helped by the fact that this path was already familiar to me, I set off on a well-beaten track: all the local education departments, the executive committee of the Soviet and the city committee of the party. By this time I was already a member of the city's volley-ball team; fortunately, I was also known as junior city champion in several sports and champion of Sverdlovsk province at volley-ball. In the end I was allowed to take the exams as an external student. Admittedly, I did not get top marks in all subjects; I was given a '4' in two subjects, but got a '5' in all the others. So that was my baggage for the onward journey to higher education.

As a boy I had dreamed of studying at the Institute of Ship-building. I had studied ships and tried to understand how they were built, reading a number of standard textbooks on the subject. But gradually I began to be attracted by the profession of civil engineer. This was no doubt because I had already done a bit of work as a builder's labourer and because my father was also in the construction business.

But, before I could enter the faculty of civil engineering at the Urals Polytechnic Institute, I had to pass one more test, admin-istered by my grandfather. He was over seventy by then, a most impressive old man with a long beard and a quirky, original cast of mind. He said to me: 'I won't let you go into the building trade until you have built something with your own hands. You can build me a bathhouse. A small one, in the back yard, complete with a changing-room.'[4]

In fact, we had never had our own bathhouse; the neighbours had one, but we did not. Although it is traditional in Russia, circum-stances had always prevented us from building one. My grandfather went on, 'But only on these terms: you must build the walls and the roof, doing it all yourself. My only contribution will be to get the local office of the State Timber Trust to allot you some trees in the forest; from then on you must do it yourself – fell the necessary pine trees, prepare moss for caulking the walls, clean it and dry it; you must carry all the logs here yourself – two miles – to the place where you're going to build the bathhouse; you must make the foun-dations and do all the joinery yourself, all the way up to the roof-tree. That's it. And I,' he said, 'will not come anywhere near you.' He was a stubborn old man, obstinate as they come, and he never once came within thirty yards of me. Nor did he lift a finger to help me, even though I found the work incredibly hard, especially when I had to raise the upper roof-beams. I fastened them with a rope and hauled them up. Then I had to trim them neatly with an axe, set the roof-tree in place and number each beam. When it was completely finished, the whole thing had to be dismantled again and then reassembled, this time after inserting an insulating layer of dried moss, all of which had to be rammed into place in the proper way; this can only be done when the roof timbers have been cut to size. Well, I spent the whole summer on this job, leaving only just enough time to go to Sverdlovsk and to take the Polytechnic entrance exams. When I had finished my grandfather solemnly announced that I had passed the test and I now had his full permission to enter the faculty of civil engineering.

Although I hadn't done any special preparation for the entrance exams, because I had been building that bathhouse, I passed them comparatively easily, with two '4's and '5's for all the other papers. So began my student days, which were to be hectic and interesting. During my first year I plunged into extra-curricular work. I became president of the sports association, which meant organising all sporting activities. By then, I was playing volley-ball at a fairly high level; I was in the city's volley-ball team and after a year I was playing for Sverdlovsk in the senior league, where we played against the twelve best teams in the country. Throughout my five years at the Polytechnic I played, trained and travelled all over the Soviet Union with the team. The strain, on top of my studies, was enormous. Though we only reached sixth or seventh place in the league, and we never became the champions, everyone took us seriously.

Volley-ball has definitely left a big mark on my life, since I not only played it later, but I also trained four teams, including the men's and women's second teams of the Urals Polytechnic Institute. Altogether, volley-ball took up about six hours of my day, and I could only study (no concessions were made to me on that account) late in the evening or at night. I had schooled myself to do without much sleep and I have somehow kept to that regime ever since, sleeping for no more than three and a half or four hours a night.

Until I entered the Polytechnic, I had never seen anything of our country; I had never seen the sea and, in general, I had never travelled anywhere. Therefore, as soon as I had finished my first year I decided to make a journey around the USSR. Without a copeck in my pocket and with a minimum of clothing – track-suit trousers, trainers on my feet, a shirt and a straw hat – I left

Sverdlovsk. I admit that I also had a tiny little suitcase of artificial leather, eight inches by twelve in size. It contained one clean shirt, and if I ever managed to buy food on the way by doing odd jobs, I would put it in there too. The trip was, of course, quite an unusual one. I began it in the company of a fellow first-year student, but after a few days he realised that he wasn't up to completing our journey and he turned back for home. I went on.

My basic means of transport was to ride on the roofs of passenger carriages, sometimes on the open platform at each end of a carriage, sometimes on the running-board, sometimes hitching a ride on a lorry. More than once I was removed by the police, who would ask me where I thought I was going. I would say that I was going to see my grandmother in, for instance, Simferopol in the Crimea. 'In which street does she live?' Since I knew that every Soviet town has a Lenin Street, I was never wrong in giving that as my grand-mother's address and they would let me go.

I would travel at night and when I arrived in some town – I naturally chose big, well-known places – I would spend the whole day, sometimes two days, exploring it. I would sleep either in a park or at a railway-station before setting off again on the roof of a passenger carriage. From each new town I wrote a letter to my friends at the polytechnic.

And this was the itinerary that I managed to complete: Sver-dlovsk – Kazan – Moscow – Leningrad – Moscow again – Minsk – Kiev – Zaporozhe – Simferopol – Eupatoria – Yalta – Novorossiisk – Sochi – Sukhumi – Batumi – Rostov-on-Don – Volgograd – Saratov – Kuibyshev – Zlatoust – Chelyabinsk – Sverdlovsk. I did that journey in a little over two months. I returned home, of course, in rags. My trainers had lost their soles, and I was only wearing them for form's sake: I was actually barefoot, but it looked to everybody as if I was wearing trainers. My straw hat, too, had worn to tatters and I had had to throw it away. You could see daylight through my track-suit trousers from every angle. When I had set out I had also possessed a big old-fashioned watch, a present from my grandfather. But I had lost that watch, along with all my clothes, in a game of cards – literally at the very start of my trip when I had just left home.

It happened thus. Just at that time an amnesty had been declared and many newly released prisoners were returning home on the roofs of railway-coaches. One day several of them joined me up there and they said, 'Let's play *bura*.'[5] This was a card game of which I knew absolutely nothing; I had never played cards in my life and to this day I can't abide them. In the circumstances, however, I could not refuse. They proposed playing for clothes and very soon they had stripped me down to my underpants. They had won everything I had. Finally they said: 'Now we'll play for your life. If you lose this time, we'll throw you off the roof of this coach while the train's moving. We'll choose a spot where you'll land good and hard. But if you win, we'll give it all back to you.' I still find it hard to understand what happened then, as I gradually began winning, first my hat, then my shirt and finally my trousers: either I had already grasped something about the game of *bura* because I had gained experience or they suddenly felt sorry for me and some human feelings awakened in them. There were murderers among those released prisoners, since the amnesty was very broadly applied. There were plenty of such prison camps in Sverdlovsk province. In the end, I finished the winner. They gave everything back to me, except my watch. After that game they never bothered me again and even started to respect me. Whenever they went to fetch hot water at a station to make tea, they would share it with me. One of them even gave me a hunk of bread. They all left the train before we reached Moscow, because they knew they wouldn't be allowed to travel through the capital. After that I was usually alone on the carriage roof.

In Zaporozhe, when I was nearly starving, I remember that I chanced upon a colonel in the army, who said to me, 'I want to study at the local polytechnic, but I don't understand a damn thing about mathematics. Will you give me some intensive coaching in maths, so that I can pass the entrance exam?' He had been through the war and clearly managed to bring home a considerable amount of loot, because, for a mere colonel, his flat was richly furnished. I made it a condition that apart from three or four hours of sleep, we should work for twenty hours out of twenty-four. The colonel doubted whether he could keep up such a pace, to which I countered that otherwise it would be impossible to prepare him for the entrance exam within a week. My other condition was that he should feed me – and feed me well. His wife did not work, so she strove with all her might to keep to the bargain. The colonel carried out our agreement fully and honourably. I ate my fill for the first time since leaving home and I even put on weight. The colonel proved to be a dedicated student, a man of strong character and he survived the pace of instruction that I had set him. I continued my journey. Later I heard that he passed his maths exam and was accepted into Zaporozhe polytechnic.

Back at the Urals Polytechnic, my studies went well. I got nothing but '5's in my exams, although volley-ball, training and travelling to matches took up a lot of time. And, unlike today's practice in this respect, I was allowed no concessions on the academic side for my successes in sport. If anything, it was the reverse: some of the lecturers were harder on me than on others in the [oral] exams, as they resented my enthusiasm for sport and considered that volley-ball was distracting me from serious work.

One day, during an examination on the theory of plasticity, Professor Ragitsky proposed that I should answer a question straight off, without preparation. He said: 'Comrade Yeltsin, take the piece of paper with the question written on it and try to answer it unprepared. You're a great sportsman, why should you need any preparation?' Everyone had notebooks on their desks, because in the theory of plasticity there are certain formulae which take more than a page to write out and are impossible to learn by heart, so we were allowed to refer to textbooks and notes. The professor had decided to try out an experiment on me to test my knowledge to the utmost. We argued over the question for a long time; but he only gave me a '4' all the same, which was a pity. Yet he generally treated me well. One day I solved a very difficult problem for him, which in the previous ten years none of his students had been able to master, and for that reason he developed a real affection for me. All the same, that was how I got my one and only mark of '4'.

On one occasion my beloved volley-ball all but brought me to the grave. At a certain point, both training for six to eight hours a day and studying at night (because in my final report I wanted to get no assessments less than 'excellent'), I evidently over-exerted myself. As a result, I fell ill with quinsy; I had a temperature of 40°C, but I still went on training and my heart wouldn't stand it. With a pulse of 150, I collapsed and was taken to hospital. I was told that if I stayed in bed there might be a chance that in a minimum of four months my heart might recover – otherwise I would develop heart disease. I discharged myself from hospital after a few days. My friends fixed up a sort of rope for me made of sheets, I lowered myself down it

28

from the top floor of the hospital and took the train to my parents at Berezniki. There I began slowly to recover, although whenever I got out of bed I would sway from side to side and if I stood upright my heart would start pounding. Soon, however, I began finding my way back to a gymnasium; a couple of minutes on the volley-ball court, picking up the ball a few times, was all I could manage before collapsing again. My team-mates would carry me to a bench and I would lie down. There appeared to be no way out of my situation; it seemed that my heart might be permanently damaged and my days as a player would be over. Nevertheless, I decided to keep going and fight this thing. I began by going on to the court for only a minute at a time, then for two minutes, then five, and after a month I was able to last out a complete game. When I returned to Sverdlovsk, I went to see my doctor and she said, 'Well, even though you ran away from us, your condition is such that you must have been in bed all the time without getting up. Your heart is in excellent shape.' I had felt that I shouldn't spare it but should, on the contrary, force it into working properly again by very gradually increasing the strain on it. I knew I had taken a colossal risk, because I could have done permanent damage to my heart.

When it came to writing my graduating dissertation, I had only one month in which to do it instead of five. I was away on tour the whole time, because the national championships were in full swing and our team was travelling from city to city. When I returned to the Sverdlovsk campus, there was only a month left before I had to submit my dissertation. The topic of my thesis was the television tower. In those days there were practically none of them, so I had to go out and find all the necessary material myself. To this day I don't know how I managed to do it. The amount of mental and physical energy that I expended was unbelievable. What's more, there was nobody who could offer me much help; the topic was a new one and nobody knew anything about it. I had to do everything myself, from beginning to end – all the drawings, all the calculations. Even so, my dissertation was accepted and marked 'excellent'.

So my student years came to an end; but our class made an agreement – we were a very close-knit, mutually supportive group made up of splendid boys and girls – that every five years we would all spend our holidays together.

Since 1955, when we graduated, thirty-four years have passed and not once has this tradition been broken! On one occasion we even brought our children with us, and no less than eighty-seven people came to that gathering. There was never any question of going to a sanatorium or a hotel for our joint holiday. In one way or another, we have always roughed it: we have hiked across the taiga; through the Urals; around the Golden Ring.[6] Once we sailed down the River Yenisei in Siberia as far as Dixon Island, a large island in the Arctic Ocean, off the mouth of the River Yenisei. We have always thought up new variants and they have always been fun. To this day we are still very close to each other, and are now planning to spend our holiday together in 1990. Each time we set up an organising committee, which prepares our next regular gathering. For the first three five-yearly occasions I was chairman of the organising committee, but when I became first secretary of the Sverdlovsk provincial party committee my friends decided to release me, since I then had more than enough on my plate.

Over the years relations between us have become amazingly close, warm and heartfelt. And here I would like to record one fact. When I found myself in the dramatic situation that followed the October 1987 plenum of the central committee, they all responded to it by offering me their support. One can safely say that these are real friends.

2

Chronicle of the Election Campaign

19 February 1989

A start has been made. I have succeeded in passing through the sieve of the adoption meeting; now my election depends on the people. I was proposed as a candidate in nearly two hundred constituencies and this support for me has come largely from big factories and other organisations that are thousands strong. These figures need no comment.

But such proposals still count for nothing. The adoption meetings, which are organised, conducted and controlled by the *apparat*, allow it to get rid of any unsuitable candidates. A majority of these meetings, made up of so-called workers' representatives, were largely packed with party secretaries, their deputies and members of workers' groups who have been 'instructed' to the point of intimidation. It was naturally no problem to manipulate such an audience and from all corners of the country protests have come pouring into the central electoral commission, declaring that the adoption meetings were usurping the people's right to hold real, meaningful elections. The authors of the scenario of this show called the Election of People's Deputies, USSR only rubbed their hands, delighted that their carefully devised plans had been so successfully put into effect.

Even so, they have miscalculated. Their plan has not been successful everywhere. They had somehow failed to realise that even a secretary of a party committee might defect and vote as his conscience dictated; that even an obedient member of a workers' collective might leave on his voting-slip the name of a candidate which was not the one for which he had been told to vote.

The first adoption meeting in which I decided to take part was in the town of Berezniki in Perm province. I had once lived in that town and there are people there who still remember me – and the name Yeltsin, too – since my father had worked there for a long time. Therefore my chances of passing the selection process there were good – provided the party organisation did not succeed in completely stifling the true wishes of the adoption meeting.

I decided to make a somewhat unusual move. After the last flight had left Moscow for Perm, I flew to Leningrad, where friends and supporters were waiting for me. In turn, they drove me out to the military airfield, where some more of my devoted helpers were waiting. Thence I flew to Perm in a propeller-driven transport aircraft, which roared and rattled so loudly that I was almost deafened for life, and in which I spent the journey embracing something that was either a Cruise missile or a bomb. We landed at Perm early in the morning; there, too, I was met by trusted people and very soon I reached the adoption meeting just in time for it to begin. My appearance was a shock to the organisers, since no one from the local provincial committee of the party had yet arrived. I made a speech in which I gave my programme, answered oral and written questions, and everything went splendidly. When the voting on candidacies began, I honestly had no worries about the outcome. It was evident from the whole atmosphere of the meeting that I would succeed in overcoming the first obstacle on the way to being elected. I received an overwhelming majority of the votes, and I could go back to Moscow to continue the election campaign.

After that, the adoption meetings began in the capital. Despite my success at Berezniki, I decided to take part in the adoption meetings of the Moscow region. I wanted to feel their atmosphere, to try and learn something about the mechanism by which the powers that be exert their influence on people. I found it an excellent school.

I should mention that I made a point of withdrawing my candidacy in constituencies where it would have competed with someone whose honesty and competence I respected. In the October district of Moscow, for instance, Andrei Sakharov was on the list of would-be candidates; I telephoned him and told him I would withdraw my candidacy in his favour. Admittedly, he was ultimately elected through being a member of the USSR Academy of Sciences one of the 'social organisations' [entitled to nominate their own deputies to the Congress of People's Deputies; other such 'social organisations' include the Communist Party and the trade unions].

Each constituency adoption meeting provided me with some new experience. Where the mood of the audience was particularly alienated, I even found it all the more interesting to intervene on its behalf. I could almost literally see the audience overcoming its almost hypnotic state of fear and trembling in the face of the [local party] leadership and the presidium, which was controlling it like a conductor controlling an orchestra.

In this respect, I remember, the adoption meeting of Moscow's Gagarin district was a revelation. Among the aspiring candidates were some very strong figures – the writer and commentator on current affairs, Yuri Chernichenko, General Dmitry Volkogonov, the military historian, the film director Eldar Ryazanov, the cosmonaut Alexei Leonov, and others – ten in all. In his speech, each one of them asked the assembly to confirm all ten applicants as candidates, so that at the election the voters themselves should be able to decide for whom to vote.

Since each candidate's speech was powerful, emotional and convincing, the audience began to show uncertainty, to fragment and in the end it was prepared, almost in its entirety, to dispense with its right to sift out unsuitable candidates.

And then it began! The presidium simply mocked the public, thinking up one trick after another to prevent them from accepting the proposal to nominate all the candidates. The ever-cheerful, optimistic Eldar Ryazanov was ready to explode with anger, some of the selectors ran up to the microphone and called shame on the presidium, while others were almost chanting in chorus to demand that all the candidates be registered. This insulting treatment of the selectors, the struggle between the public and the brainwashed, programmed presidium lasted until two o'clock in the morning – until finally the public won. All candidates were included in the electoral list for the constituency. I left that Saturday with a feeling of relief that after all fair play and common sense had prevailed – but at the same time I was horrified at what a terrible, pitiless machinery of power hangs over us all – a monstrous, highly refined instrument, created by Stalin and Stalinism.

———

'Tell us – Is it true that after you had graduated you went to work as a labourer on a building site? Why did you have to do that?'*

'It's said that you were once put on trial in Sverdlovsk. Tell us what happened.'*

An hour after the oral examination for my dissertation, I was sitting in a train bound for Tbilisi to take part in the national volley-ball championships. Thus it happened that I spent the whole summer of graduation travelling all over the country to play in matches – either for the national championships, the inter-university tournament or the national league cup in Riga. I returned from the tour on 6 September and went to start work at Uraltyazhtrubstroi (Urals Heavy Pipe Construction Trust), the organisation to which I had been assigned on graduation.

I had been offered – as is every new graduate – a job as foreman on an industrial building site, to which I replied that I was not yet prepared to work as a foreman. While a student, I had come to the conclusion that although the teaching at the Urals Polytechnic Institute was of a high quality, some of the professors and lecturers were nevertheless remote from industry and taught their subjects in excessively academic terms which bore little relation to real life. I therefore considered it a great mistake to go straight into a job that put me in charge of men and construction work, without ever having acquired direct experience of such work myself. I knew for certain I would find life very difficult if any work-team leader could – deliberately or not – twist me round his little finger, since his practical knowledge of the job would be so much greater than mine.

For my own sake, therefore, I decided to spend a year learning

* (From questions handed up from the floor at meetings during the election campaign.)

the twelve basic trades in construction work. I would spend a month on each one. Thus I laboured for a month on an equal footing with other workmen in a bricklaying team, where I learned the techniques, starting first with the simple methods and then the more complicated ones. I did not work for just a shift at a time but one and a half or two shifts in a row, in order to accumulate experience more quickly. Even though the workers laughed at a young graduate's enthusiasm for getting his hands dirty, they nevertheless helped me, encouraged me and generally gave me moral support.

After a month of working at a particular trade, the appropriate official body would grade me according to my skill, usually awarding me grade 3 or 4. I soon acquired professional standing as a bricklayer and a concrete-maker. Incidentally, I found the latter trade particularly hard to learn: although I am considered physically strong, pushing a wheelbarrow-load of liquid concrete along narrow, high scaffolding is a very tricky job. If you allow the barrow to tilt, the centre of gravity immediately shifts, and there were times when I fell down several yards with the wheelbarrow: fortunately it never ended in disaster and in time I managed to acquire the necessary skill. I then learned the trade of carpenter, followed by a month driving loads of concrete in a ZIS–585 tipper-truck. Once there was a nasty moment when I was driving a loaded tipper (at the time I still didn't have a driving licence), and that ZIS – it was far from new, already having more than 300,000 kilometres on the clock – stalled right in the middle of a level crossing. I could hear a train coming and what's more it was obviously travelling fast. The level crossing was ungated and unmanned. At any moment the train was likely to come pounding along and smash both the truck and me into smithereens. Then, luckily, I remembered the starter-motor. When you engage the starter, the truck will jerk forward a little. By the time I had made a few feverish jabs with the starter, the train was already hooting and its brakes were squealing, but I sensed that it would not be able to pull up in time: the huge mass was already heading straight for me. All the while I was still jabbing at the starter, making the truck lurch forward a little each time, until it finally rolled a few inches off the track as the train passed by, missing me by a hair's breadth.

I got out of the cab, sat down on the edge of the roadside ditch and waited a long time before getting my breath back. In spite of it all I delivered the concrete safely and told the men how I had almost been killed. They said, 'Well done! You did exactly the right thing.' The alternative would have been to jump out, but then I would have been held responsible for the expensive loss of the truck and I had no savings. I had none then and, by the way, I still have none. There are five roubles which I deposited symbolically in a savings account during my student days – and that is all.

After that came the other trades – joiner, glazier, plasterer, painter – all of which were not, of course, easy to learn, but I saw no alternative to my chosen course.

While working as a driver on a tower-crane, I experienced another incident that strained my nerves almost to breaking-point. We were building a block of flats for Uralkhimmash (Urals Chemicals–Plant Trust). The crane was a BKSM5–5A and I thought I'd checked everything when I switched off the electric current. But I had missed one check. When you finish work, it is essential that the crane should be fastened to the rails with special hooks. I did not do this. Either I forgot, or had not yet been taught to do it; it is hard to say which was the case. That night it poured with rain and there was a terrible wind. I woke up and remembered the crane with horror. We lived right next to the construction site and looking out of the window, I saw the tower-crane moving – slowly, but definitely moving. Just as I was – in nothing but my underpants – I bounded out of doors, ran to the crane, found the knife-switch in the dark and switched on the current. I climbed feverishly up the narrow steel ladder, while the crane was rolling inexorably towards the end of the rails. If it had rolled off, it would have crashed over and been a total loss. I heaved myself into the driver's cab, which was pitch dark. Unable to see anything, after a moment's desperate thought I reckoned – correctly – that the first thing to do was to release the brake holding the jib. It immediately swung round with the wind and stopped acting as a sail. The crane's speed was slightly reduced, but even so it continued to move forward along the rails. I then switched the crane's propulsion motor into full-speed reverse. As I watched, the crane began gradually to slow down and its wheels stopped a few inches from the end of the rails. It was an awful moment, but I stayed up there, having decided to try and save the crane at all costs. I stopped the huge juggernaut, climbed down and fastened the hooks in position. Of course I could not sleep again that night and for a long time I used to have nightmares in which I would climb up a tower-crane and crash down to the ground with it.

So that was how I worked for a year to learn the twelve special-ised trades in the construction industry. I went to my section boss and told him that I was now ready to work as a foreman. I was sent to a number of sites. I helped build machine shops for the Ural-khimmash; a plant producing reinforced concrete; workshops for a factory at Verkh-Isetsk; subsidiary factory buildings; blocks of flats; a palace of culture; kindergartens; day-schools and boarding-schools – in other words, a lot.

I found the job as foreman relatively easy, although, of course, a number of problems did arise. I was obliged, for instance, to combat pilfering, which is very persistent. Unfortunately, the building workers had got into this habit, until I started strictly checking every bricklaying job – measuring the amount of mortar and other materials being used – and troubles arose as a result. Gradually, though, the matter was brought under control and people began to realise that I was in the right, for the 'worker's conscience' is not an empty phrase and the problem was eventually solved.

While working as a foreman I encountered more than a few difficult, funny and complicated situations. There were times, for instance, when we worked with convicts. I decided to break with the tradition by which these men were paid at the rates they demanded instead of what they had earned at normal rates. At the end of the first month, I calculated the volume of work which they had done against the pay they should have had at the correct rates. It turned out to be two and a half times less than the amount they were used to getting.

Soon a hulking giant of a man came into my little foreman's office, carrying an axe which he raised and held over me saying, 'Are you going to pay us at the proper rate like they always paid us before you came along, you puppy?' I said, 'No.' – 'In that case,' he countered, 'just you remember that I've got nothing to lose. I'll smash your skull before you've even had time to squeak.' I could see from the look in his eyes that he might easily split my head open without batting an eyelid.

I could have dodged him, of course, or tried somehow to tackle him physically, although it was a cramped little room and the axe was already poised over my head. So I decided on an unexpected move. I have a very loud, powerful voice, and, with great effect in that tiny room, I gave a sharp, full-throated roar of 'Get out,' while

37

looking him straight in the eye. He suddenly lowered his axe, dropped it, turned around and went out in silence, his back bent in submission. Exactly what went on in his mind at that moment is hard to say.

Incidentally, it was not an occasion for using bad language, which, in any case, I have never used in my life. At the polytechnic people even used to bet on whether I would avoid swearing or using bad language for a whole year, and I always used to win the bet. So I am simply not accustomed to it, and to this day I never swear – nowadays, of course, even less than I might have done before, though there is often greater cause for it.

I was once sent as section chief to a quite unique site – a half-built worsted mill. It was a huge seven-storey building, consisting of only a framework of reused steel girders that looked like a skeleton. It had been there for a long time and was all rusty, but instructions had come from above to develop light industry, and it had been decided to complete the building. I was put in charge of this complex site. I was living in a hostel belonging to the Chemicals-Plant Trust, so I had to walk from there to the site every day, a distance of about eight or nine miles. I would leave at six in the morning and was usually on the job around eight.

Up to a thousand men were working on this site, and when the city authorities weighed in with an increased labour force, the numbers reached nearly two thousand. The work went on practically around the clock. That winter they were building a water-tower: it was to be made of concrete, unique in itself, including the water-tank at the top. The concrete-pouring could not be stopped for a single hour: we were working with concrete that had to be heated during the mix and I never left that water-tower for days on end. I worked on this site right up to the point at which we signed the hand-over documents, transferring the mill to the worsted-spinning enterprise.

When the whole job was handed over and the plant began to work, the buildings suddenly began to shudder and the whole massive metal frame, together with the reinforced-concrete cladding, started moving – all in one direction. The spinning looms had to be stopped. I went straight to Professor Bychkov at the polytechnic. Together we surveyed and recalculated every element in the construction, coming to the conclusion that there was a basic flaw in the design. The plinths supporting the cladding were quite inade-

I had just become the head of a construction enterprise. The man who preceded me in the job was appallingly slovenly in his work and a drunkard. Any job which could be ruined, he ruined, including the building of a boarding-school. In the September, when I took over his job they were still only laying bricks for the first floor, and there were supposed to be four floors. The site was obviously doomed in advance and there was no hope of it being handed over by the end of the year. At the beginning of the following year, new members were received into the party by the district committee and membership cards were handed out in a solemn ceremony. On the next day I attended the city committee of the party when it issued its report summing up the previous year. Suddenly I heard it being said, 'Let's give Yeltsin a severe reprimand to be entered in his records – just to teach the others a lesson.'

I went up to the rostrum and spoke. 'Comrade members of the committee (and there were a lot of them) – only yesterday you gave me my party membership card. Here it is, still warm. And today you are proposing to give me – a communist of one day's standing – a severe reprimand, to be entered in my records, for failing to hand over the boarding-school on time. There are other construction workers here, they will confirm that it was simply impossible to have handed it over on time.' No – they insisted – it was to be a lesson to others. Clearly, Sitnikov had had a hand in this. It was a serious blow to me.

I believed sincerely in the ideals of justice which the party espoused; with equal sincerity I had joined the party, having carefully studied the party statute, the programme and the classics, re-read Lenin, Marx and Engels. And then suddenly this had to happen at the city committee. A year later the severe reprimand was annulled, but the entry remained in my records until the next exchange of party documents.[2] Only then did I have a clean sheet.

It is only recently that we have begun considering the negative role played by the party's interference in economic affairs. In those days, though, both people engaged in industry and, still more, the party officials thought of this as a perfectly normal state of affairs. I thought so, too, and regarded it as quite natural when I was summoned to attend several district committee meetings simultaneously. Admittedly, of course, I tried to wriggle out of attending these sessions, but the fact that they took place – the fact that attempts were made to solve numerous economic and other problems by the application of pressure and the issue of reprimands was all part and parcel of the way the system functioned and it never evoked any questions or objections. The main thing was to keep out of the way of some nagging *apparatchik*, who, thanks to either stupidity or megalomania, could easily make one's life a misery. I remember coming into contact with one Leonid Bobykin, first secretary of a district committee, the same man who was later to become first secretary of the Sverdlovsk provincial committee, and who at the nineteenth party conference [June 1988] was to hand up to the platform a note with a ridiculous attack on Volkov who had spoken in my defence.

One day I got a telephone message from Bobykin ordering me to attend a meeting at a certain time. I was surprised at the tone of it – I don't know whether to call it lordly or boorish – and I did not reply to the message. Once, out of interest, I counted up: it was possible for me to be invited simultaneously to twenty-two separate organisations, beginning with the seven district committees and executive committees in those districts where we were engaged in building work, and ending with the provincial committee party. Naturally it was impossible to be everywhere at once: to some I would telephone and rearrange the meeting; to others I would send deputies – in other words we would juggle with dates and times on a mutually acceptable basis. But now came a summons from Bobykin in this strange, hectoring tone. He sent me two more telephone messages. Finally, he phoned me himself – would I kindly explain why I was not going to turn up at the meeting, which was being conducted by the first secretary of the district committee of the party? I asked him why I should go to his meeting in particular, if at the same time I had meetings in other districts; why I should give preference to him and not to someone else. This made him bristle with fury, 'I'll report you! I'll damn well make sure you come.' – 'After talking to me like that you will never see me at one of your meetings again.' He couldn't do anything to me: he had only wanted to satisfy his self-importance . . . and he hasn't changed to this day.

After that job I was offered the post of chief engineer at a large, newly created house-building firm, with its own sizeable factory and a work-force of several thousand, which subsequently grew even bigger. Soon the general manager of the complex was retired on a pension and I was nominated to take his place. Thus, at the comparatively young age of thirty-two, I found myself running a very large industrial complex.

It was a difficult time. We were simultaneously taking over the factory and introducing new technology, including a system-building technique based on the flow principle to speed up the rate of construction. We also carried out the experiment of building a five-storey block of flats in five days. Then, when we were building a new housing estate made of such blocks, we used tower-cranes one after the other without dismantling them: the tracks were extended from one building to the next, then on to the next and so on, and in this way we saved a lot of time normally needed to dismantle and reassemble the cranes. There were other interesting technical innovations and the complex began regularly to meet its planning targets. We had special overalls embroidered with the initials DSK [the Russian initials of the words House Building Combine] and furthermore we made each suit of overalls to measure for each individual worker, male and female. Our people liked this very much and they began to show pride in their firm. Life was hard, of course, towards the end of a year or the end of a quarter, when we had to work practically around the clock to meet our targets. Often, particularly on the night shift, I used to go and visit the construction teams.

My style of work was generally described as tough. I required my people to behave with discipline and stick to their word once given. Since, as I have said, I never swore and tried not to raise my loud, shrill voice at people, my main arguments in the battle for discipline were my own total dedication to the job, a permanent insistence on high standards, constant checking of work – plus people's faith in the rightness of what I was doing. I believe that people who work better, live better, and are more appreciated. Good, professional, high-quality work never went unnoticed, just as spoiled materials, unnecessary waste and slovenliness didn't go unnoticed either. If you've given your word – keep it, and if you don't keep it – you must answer for it. These clear, understandable attitudes created, I think, a climate of mutual confidence between the management and the work-force.

We had a carpenter named Mikhailishin, an excellent, skilled craftsman. On one occasion I had to ask him to get us out of trouble: the government commission was coming to take over the building the next day and although all the doors had been painted,

43

they needed to be turned around and rehung. Through carelessness the factory had put the hinges on the wrong side of the doors. We would deal with them later, but right then we had to save the situation. As the doors had been painted already, they couldn't be scratched or chipped. You couldn't go at the job like a bull at a gate. What was required was careful, neat, skilled work: the doors should not be marked, the floors should not be scratched. The job had to be done so carefully that early the next morning all that needed to be done was to repaint the hinges. I left him working on the job all night and came back at six o'clock the next morning. As I arrived he was finishing off the front door at the main entrance. I had brought with me my own transistor radio and gave it to him; we embraced, and not another word needed to be said. Do you think he felt any sense of bitterness or offence because I left him to do the job all night?

There were other critical situations; for instance, when the worsted mill was about to be handed over it suddenly emerged – literally only a few days before the hand-over date – that again as the result of sheer sloppiness a fifty-yard passage from one building to another had not been built. Incredible, but true. There was a separate drawing for that passage but it had been mislaid, so at the last moment we discovered that the passage didn't exist! The factory was enormous, visible to the whole city, indeed to the whole country – it was due to produce six million yards of cloth annually. I immediately gathered together the best brains on the project, and we decided, clearly and exactly, how the work should be organised, the whole discussion taking only half an hour. Everything was calculated to the minute: so much time for the excavation work, so much time for the concrete pouring and finishing, putting first one team and then another on the job. An excavator would start digging the trench, immediately followed by another. I stayed on site, never leaving it for a moment. Each person was responsible for their own sector of the work. There was no unnecessary fuss or confusion, everything having been organised with extreme precision. By six o'clock the next morning the asphalt was already being laid on that damned passage way. Soon the whole job was finished: we had made it.

Another point which might seem trivial was that I would go and join one of the women's teams during the night shift and chat to them about this and that, helping to hang wallpaper or paint window-frames. This was a great boost to morale, both for myself and for them. What's more, it was of value for the project as a whole: I was able to identify apparently minor snags which, if the boss was not kept up to date about them, might blow up into huge insoluble problems. Installing mirrors in the women's changing-rooms; lengths of dress-material as rewards for good work; other gifts, bought either from trade-union funds or, sometimes, out of my own pocket: all of this created a wholly new, different atmosphere in the relationship between management and the women workers.

I had worked for fourteen years in the construction industry – and suddenly there came an invitation to head the section of the provincial committee of the party responsible for construction. I was not too surprised to receive this offer; as I had been constantly engaged in party work outside working hours, I accepted it without any great enthusiasm. The work as head of a construction complex suited me: we were regularly achieving our planned targets, and altogether the work was going well, plus the fact that I was getting a decent salary. Nowadays as a member of the Supreme Soviet, I earn less than I did in that job twenty years ago. But I took on the party job all the same. I wanted to try making a move in a new direction. To this day, though, I am still not quite sure exactly where that move has led me.

3

Chronicle of the Election Campaign

21 February 1989

It's strange and I still can't believe it: I have been accepted as a candidate for the Moscow city no. 1 constituency. What the *apparat* so much didn't want to happen and what they opposed so desperately has happened after all. My opponent as candidate for this constituency is Yuri Brakov, general manager of the ZIL automobile factory.

But first to tell the story in sequence. I was supposed to have been blackballed at the adoption meeting. Of the 1,000 people in the hall, 200 were representing the 10 candidates and 800 were carefully chosen, obedient, brainwashed selectors.

Everyone knew how the adoption meeting was supposed to end: the *apparat* had nominated two candidates – Yuri Brakov and Georgii Grechko, a cosmonaut. My only hope was that I might, nevertheless, succeed in breaking the *apparat*'s grip on the meeting and make sure that all three candidates were adopted, thus giving me a real chance. Before the start of the meeting all the would-be candidates, on my initiative, signed a joint letter to the meeting requesting that all of us be adopted as candidates for this constituency. It must be said that they signed this appeal very readily; none of them wanted to take part in a performance whose outcome had been fixed in advance. From the mood of the selectors, however, I sensed that on this occasion this tactic wouldn't work: only two names – Grechko and Brakov – had been firmly hammered into their heads; the lessons of previous adoption meetings had been learned, since even clumsy bureaucrats are capable of drawing conclusions from their mistakes.

After each candidate had made a speech giving his programme, the procedure required us to answer written questions for five minutes, followed by seven minutes of answering verbal questions from the floor. More than a hundred written questions were passed up to me.

I already knew that the hall was packed with people who had been given deliberately provocative questions to ask, and they were only waiting for the signal from the organisers of the show to say their piece. I therefore made up my mind to use an unexpected tactic. Of all the written questions put to me, I purposely selected those that were most unfair, unpleasant or insulting. Candidates usually choose to answer the most potentially favourable questions; I decided to do the reverse.

I began by answering questions such as the following: 'Why did you let the Moscow party organisation down, by your cowardly failure to face up to difficulties?'; 'Why was your daughter able to move into a new flat?'; and so on, all in the same spirit, the only exceptions being that there were no questions asking why I had been questioned by the police or whether I had any discreditable links with dubious figures. The answers that I gave, however, completely ruined the plans of the people who had instigated these moves. Nearly all the hostile questions which they had planned to be asked from the floor had already been aired, so I was able to answer the oral questions easily and calmly. I could sense the audience gradually starting to melt, and it began to look as if it might well end in a way that the organisers had not planned. But we also had another surprise up our sleeves. Before the start of the proceedings, the cosmonaut, Georgii Grechko had approached me and said that he wanted to withdraw his candidacy; he thought it right that I should go forward as a candidate at the election and he did not want to stand in my way. I said, 'All right, but think about it carefully.' He replied, 'I have definitely made up my mind.' That being so, I asked him not to announce his withdrawal until immediately before the voting was due to begin.

Grechko played his part to perfection. In fact, I realised that in

47

him the stage had lost a brilliant actor. Throughout the meeting he looked anxious and concerned, giving every appearance of being sincerely affected by the reaction of the selectors, the answers, the questions and the procedural arguments. Then, finally, just before the votes were cast, each candidate was given a minute to make a final statement. When it was Grechko's turn, he walked calmly up to the rostrum and announced, 'I wish to withdraw my candidacy.'

This was, of course, a shattering blow to the organisers. All of those who had been instructed to vote for Brakov and Grechko were suddenly faced with a real choice, especially since they could vote for me in total secrecy.

Thus it happened that I collected more than half the votes. All the candidates gave me their warm congratulations. A friendly, comradely atmosphere had developed between us, and this, too, greatly influenced the outcome of the ballot.

In fact, the plans of my enemies will always be frustrated because for some reason they think they are dealing with people who are basically bilious and ill-natured. They always base their tactics on an appeal to the rotten apples in the barrel, and there are very few of them. That is why they fail. If they had managed to fill the meeting with people like that, then of course I would have lost. But in all Moscow they could not find 800 people of their own ilk. What bad luck for them.

A new stage in the election campaign now began. Because I had cleared this particular hurdle and my chances of winning had therefore increased, the resistance of those who saw my election as a catastrophe also increased a hundredfold. I represented to them a collapse of faith in the unshakeability of the established order of things. The fact that the established order had long since turned rotten through and through did not worry them. The main thing for the *apparat* was to keep Yeltsin out.

It seems, though, that it was too late for that.

———

'What mistakes did you make when you were working as first secretary of a provincial committee of the party?'*

'Was any criticism directed at you, and how did you react to it when you were first secretary of a provincial committee?'*

'The best years of your work as first secretary of a provincial committee were during the "years of stagnation" [the Brezhnev era]. What are your feelings about this?'*

I worked as a section chief [in the Sverdlovsk provincial committee of the party], after which I was elected as secretary of the committee. Approximately a year later I was sent to Moscow to attend a course at the Academy of Social Sciences, where I studied for about two weeks. At the time, a plenum of the central committee was being held, at which Yakov Ryabov, the first secretary of the Sverdlovsk provincial committee, was elected a secretary of the central committee. Next day, during a lecture, the official in charge of our course came up to the microphone and announced that Yeltsin was invited to report in person to the central committee at eleven o'clock. My fellow students, all of them people of considerable experience, began to cluster around me, wondering why I was being summoned. I had no idea of the reason – although, of course, somewhere deep inside me I sensed what the topic of conversation might be, but I tried not to let it disconcert me. I went to the central-committee offices.

I was told to go first to Kapitonov, the secretary of the central committee responsible for organisational matters. Among other things, he asked me how I was getting on with my studies, and how were my relations with my colleagues in the provincial committee. I replied that everything was going well. He said no more and did not explain why I had been called. 'Now let's go,' he said, 'and see Kirilenko.' There was more general conversation, which again

* (From questions handed up from the floor at meetings during the election campaign.)

ended in nothing specific being said. Next I was taken to see Suslov.[1] This time the tone was slightly less subtle and more to the point: Did I feel I was up to a bigger job? Was I well acquainted with the party organisation in the province? And so on, but there was still no mention of anything definite. This is a funny way of going about things, I thought; what does it all portend? Then I was told that Brezhnev wanted to see me. I therefore had to go to the Kremlin, where I was accompanied by two of the central-committee secretaries, Kapitonov and Ryabov. We went into an ante-room, where an aide said to us, 'Go in, you're expected.' I went in first, followed by the others. Brezhnev was sitting at the far end of a big conference-table. I approached him, he stood up and we exchanged greetings. Then he turned to my 'escort' and said, 'So he's decided to take power in Sverdlovsk province, has he?' Kapitonov explained that this was not so, as I still knew nothing of this proposal. 'How can he not know, since he's decided to take power?' So began our talk, half joking, half serious. Brezhnev said that the Politbureau had held a session and had recommended me for the post of first secretary of the Sverdlovsk provincial committee of the party.

At that time, Korovin was second secretary of the Sverdlovsk committee, but the usual procedure, whereby the second secretary moves up when the job of first secretary falls vacant, was being disregarded. In consequence, a rank-and-file secretary was being immediately promoted to first secretary over the head of the second secretary, who would stay in place. Objectively speaking, of course, Korovin was unsuited for the job of first secretary and everyone realised this.

'Well, what do you say?' Brezhnev asked. The whole matter was a surprise to me; the province is a very large one, with a correspondingly big party organisation. I replied that if the Politbureau and the party members of the province had confidence in me, I would do the job to the very best of my ability. We all stood up, and Brezhnev suddenly said, 'For the time being, though, you will not be a member of the central committee; the party congress is over and so elections to the central committee are also finished.' Naturally I could not raise this point myself, but I felt encouraged by his tone of voice which indicated his approval of me. Then he noticed that I wasn't wearing the red enamel lapel-badge of a deputy of the Supreme Soviet, and said, 'Aren't you a deputy?' I replied, 'Yes, I am.' He looked round with astonishment to the two central-committee secretaries, 'What sort of deputy is he?' Quite seriously I said, 'Of the provincial Soviet.' This, I must say, caused considerable amusement, because at Kremlin level a deputy of a provincial Soviet is not considered to be a deputy at all. On that note we departed. 'Don't be too long,' said Brezhnev, 'in getting him confirmed at the local party plenum.'

Literally within a few days, on 2 November 1976, a plenum of the Sverdlovsk provincial committee of the party was held at which Razumov, first deputy head of the organisation department of the central committee, was present. Everything went off in due fashion; Razumov announced that following upon Ryabov's election as a secretary of the central committee of the CPSU, Yeltsin was proposed as first secretary of the Sverdlovsk provincial committee of the party. I had meanwhile jotted down a few points for a short speech, feeling that this would be required of me. The voting, as usual, was unanimous. After receiving congratulations, I gave my brief speech, outlining my programme for the future. The main idea behind it was extremely simple: we should above all be concerned about people and their welfare, since if you treat people well they will respond with improved performance in whatever their occupation may be. This has remained my credo to this day.

The fate of the second secretary needed to be resolved, because the new situation had made it psychologically very difficult for Korovin to continue working in that position, and after a while he was offered the post of chairman of the regional trade-union council, a job he was very glad to accept. All reassignments of personnel are a difficult, delicate matter, and on each occasion I had to brace myself inwardly in order to tackle it. A major renewal of personnel was needed throughout the province, especially in the key jobs. I proposed, for instance, that the chairman of the provincial executive committee (PEC),[2] Borisov, should be retired on a pension.

The part played by the PEC under his chairmanship had been clearly unsatisfactory. The Soviet had to become involved in the economy, in social and cultural affairs and in the housing policy, so that these functions might gradually be transferred from party to Soviet organisations, leaving the party free to concentrate more exclusively on strictly political matters. Borisov agreed with me and took his retirement. A strong, intelligent person was needed in that job. As I reviewed a list of leading figures known to me, I remembered the name of Anatoly Mekhrentsev, general manager of the ZIK[3] automobile factory; holder of the decoration 'Hero of Socialist Labour', a master's degree and a state prize, he was already a man of marked distinction. I also knew of his outstanding human qualities, his erudition, his rapid grasp of a situation and his ability not to get bogged down in detail; in addition to all this, he was still comparatively young. I offered him the post. He began by refusing it, then promised to think it over – while I put some pressure on him! In the end, he took the job. Gradually he gathered momentum and in time, I consider, he became the best PEC chairman of all the provinces in our republic.

Thus I gradually built up my new staff, a strong and creative team and a high-powered *obkom* bureau.[4] We drafted programmes for all the main areas of responsibility, programmes that were serious, far-reaching and thoroughly well-worked out. Each programme was aired at the *obkom* bureau then adopted for implementation. Our bureau meetings were of two kinds – open and closed. At the closed sessions each member would put forward whatever demands he might have, including demands on me. I purposely set up this frank, business-like *modus operandi*, so that critical remarks aimed at me should become a normal part of standard procedure. Even though I did not always agree with the criticism, which could be damaging to my self-esteem, I tried to train myself to take it.

There began a period of furious activity and, as always in my life, I spared myself less than anyone. Gradually others, too, were drawn in to working at this pace; some would come close to it, some could keep up with it, including Mekhrentsev. Some could not maintain the pace and took on less work, but I made no special demands on them; the chief thing was that they should do their utmost and produce results. Although there were constant arguments and discussions, these were always business-like and constructive. It became a tradition to meet, together with our wives, to celebrate public holidays and this kind of human contact in our homes also had a good effect on our work. In view of the fact that our province contained forty-five towns (regional and rural centres) and sixty-three smaller townships, I promised myself that I would visit every one of them no less frequently than once every two years. I kept that promise and my visits, what's more, were not just excursions but were taken up with serious work. I would meet local party activists, professional people, workers, collective farmers, ordinary country folk and more besides. Strange as it may seem, by the way, one of these traditional annual journeys always fell on my birthday.

I have always shunned an excessive display of congratulations on my birthday. Obviously it was no use trying to hide at home or in the party offices – I would have been found there anyway – but I would go to some distant region and meet people on farms, in the fields, in fact anywhere where I couldn't be found. I don't like the traditional way of spending birthdays, when you sit down at a table and people tell you to your face how wonderful you are. It makes me feel uncomfortable. But by getting far away from town, by helping people, by taking this or that decision on the spot, I would get much more satisfaction because I had spent the day doing something useful, and thus had given myself a birthday present.

In his book *Tomorrow – Into Battle Again*, written after his victory over Alexander Korchnoi, the chess champion Anatoly Karpov directed a gentle but justified reproach at Sverdlovsk province when he noted that even such a large region as ours had no chess club. I telephoned Karpov and suggested that we agree on a date when he might come – and that by then there would be a Sverdlovsk chess club. We made the arrangement and the work began. An old house was vacated and fully renovated, and to it was added a spacious hall with adjoining rooms; the result was a decent enough chess club. I sent a telegram to Karpov, saying that I was expecting him on a certain date. When he arrived, he was not alone, but brought with him Sevastianov, the cosmonaut, who was also president of the national chess federation. In front of a large gathering of people, I told Anatoly Karpov that he should cut the ribbon, as he had initiated the project, and the ceremony continued in the hall designed for chess contests. Beforehand, I had told our local chess players that they should inscribe a large sheet of cartridge paper with the quotation from his book, word for word, in which he had said that there was no chess club in Sverdlovsk. When he had made his speech, this large sheet of paper was handed to him with the suggestion that he tear it into little pieces, and, what's more, that he should promise to make a correction in the next edition of his book, so that this shameful stain should no longer disgrace our province. To the delight of all those present, Karpov tore the sheet into pieces.

I did not give up my personal sporting activities following my appointment. Naturally I didn't join a particular team, but instead organised a volley-ball team from the staff members of the committee. Very soon it became hard to imagine life in the Sverdlovsk provincial committee without volley-ball. We played twice a week – at half past seven till ten or eleven at night on Wednesdays and Sundays. Whole families took part; the contests were highly temperamental – in fact I would say there was more excitement and enthusiasm than actual playing. Even so, it was fun and useful for relaxation. I did stop taking part in other forms of sport though, except, of course, for my daily physical exercises.

From the very beginning of my work in this job, I would organise meetings of various categories of workers. It might be school headmasters and teachers; or 1,000 workers in the health service; perhaps 1,500 students; or 40 leaders of the 'Young Pioneers' youth organisation; or industrial foremen; or factory managers; district party secretaries; young party workers – or, by contrast, those with long service and a lot of experience; the chairmen of district Soviet executive committees; writers and artists; social scientists; academics; and so on. In the [Brezhnev] 'era of stagnation', such meetings were the exception rather than the rule; at the time it was the usual practice not to answer difficult-sounding questions and if meetings or conferences were held at all, they were in honour of a great leader, a marshal of the Soviet Union, a much decorated hero, and so forth.

During that period Brezhnev did not concern himself with the country at all – or rather, let's say, he concerned himself with it less and less. The secretaries of the central committee followed his example, so that in practice we found ourselves working completely autonomously. We did receive occasional instructions, but they were pure eyewash, issued merely for the record. Whenever one went to Moscow to get a decision on a matter which we did not have the right to decide for ourselves – on a major construction project, for instance, or matters concerning food supplies, or about funds – one would naturally go straight to the man in the central committee responsible for our province (in our case this was a sector chief by the name of Pavel Simonov) and that would be all that was necessary. Simonov was, incidentally, the perfect man for the job; while adopting an attitude of non-interference in our party organisation, he was at the same time thoroughly well informed about our affairs, always knew what was happening and what our problems were. He would ring up now and again, sometimes to tick us off in a half-joking tone, and altogether we enjoyed an excellent working relationship.

At the very start of my spell as first secretary, he gave me an excellent and very memorable lesson. There was an exhibition of propaganda posters in the town; I went to the opening and our group was photographed as we entered the hall. This photograph was then published in our local party newspaper, the *Urals Worker*. The next day I received a phone call from Simonov and he began to teach me a lesson. He certainly knew how to do it; he never raised his voice, but was thoroughly sarcastic at my expense. 'Oh,' he said, 'how good you look in that photograph, really very good indeed. You're so photogenic, aren't you, and now the whole province will know how good you look in a photograph,' on and on in that vein. He would really get under one's skin, yet without ever being actually rude or nasty. Altogether he taught me a good lesson on that occasion and I have remembered it ever since. After that, my picture never appeared in a local newspaper again.

But people like him are the exception in the central committee. As a rule, I only ever went there for form's sake. A couple of times, perhaps, I would call to see Razumov, chiefly to make sure that he wasn't cooking up anything unpleasant to throw at me. I only ever visited the other central committee secretaries out of a sense of politeness. Real, substantive problems had to be solved in the Council of Ministers. I developed quite decent relations with the various ministers, and with Tikhonov, the then prime minister. I knew Nikolai Ryzhkov [the present prime minister] from his time at Sverdlovsk; we had got to know each other when he was managing director of Uralmash [Urals Machinery Trust]. Then he was transferred to the ministry, after that to Gosplan [state planning commission] and the central committee. When Ryzhkov was appointed chairman of the Council of Ministers, I tried not to abuse our long-standing acquaintance.

In contrast to Ryzhkov's conscientious efficiency, I will give another example of the way the country was run in those days. We needed to get a top-level decision on the construction of a Metro transportation system (Sverdlovsk was, after all, a city of 1,200,000 inhabitants), and for this we needed permission from the Polit-bureau. I therefore decided to go to Brezhnev. I phoned him and he agreed to see me. Knowing the style of work that was current at the time, I prepared a note, in his name, to which he only had to add his signature in approval. I went in and we talked for literally five or six minutes. (It was a Thursday, usually the last day of Brezhnev's working week; as a rule on Friday he would be driven out to his enormous *dacha* at Zavidovo, where he would spend Friday, Saturday and Sunday. On Thursdays, for that reason, he was in a hurry to finish all his work.)

The incident was typical and revealing. In the last phase of his life, Brezhnev, in my opinion, had no idea what he was doing, signing or saying. All the power was in the hands of his entourage. He was incapable of drafting a resolution himself. He said to me, 'Just dictate what I should write.' So of course I dictated it to him, 'Instruction by the Politbureau to prepare a draft decree authorising the construction of a Metro in Sverdlovsk.' He wrote what I had said, signed it and gave me the piece of paper. Knowing, however, that even with Brezhnev's signature on them, some documents might be misplaced or disappear altogether, I told him, 'No, you should call your aide.' He summoned an assistant, and I then said to Brezhnev, 'Give him instructions that he must first of all enter the document in the registry, and, second, take the necessary official steps to ensure that your instructions to distribute it to Politbureau members are carried out.' He then did all this; the aide collected the papers, Brezhnev and I said goodbye to each other. He had signed the document, authorising the construction of the Sverdlovsk Metro, without giving any thought to the meaning of what I was dictating. Granted, as a result of that signature, a good deed was done and soon Sverdlovsk received permission to build a Metro. But how many of the rogues and cheats, indeed plain criminals, who surrounded him, had exploited Brezhnev for their own dishonest purposes? How many resolutions or decrees did he calmly, unthinkingly sign, which brought riches to a few and misfortune and suffering to many?

No one – neither friend nor relative, neither close nor distant acquaintance – ever attempted to approach me, as first secretary of a provincial committee, with a request for help in any kind of personal matter. We are now well aware of the scale reached by favouritism and corruption in the Brezhnev era, and the extent to which this caused the whole system of government to rot from within. The word of a first secretary is law and no one would dare not to carry out his order or request, so much so that unscrupulous party officials and their henchmen abused their power unchecked.

Knowing my character, nobody ever approached me to ask favours. It is even hard to imagine how I would have reacted to any such request.

It is true that the power of a first secretary within his bailiwick is practically unlimited. And the sense of power is intoxicating. But when you try to use it for the public good, it turns out that even that power is insufficient; it cannot, for instance, ensure that everyone in the province is decently fed and housed – although it is sufficient to enable a first secretary to use it corruptly: to ensure that someone is fixed up with a good job; that someone else is allotted a nice flat; and to hand out similar favours to one's immediate colleagues. So it has been in the past, and so, indeed, it continues to be that a few dozen people live in the ideal conditions predicted as universal when we have reached the stage of 'full communism', while the population as a whole lives in conditions that are barely tolerable.

In those days, generally speaking, a provincial first secretary of the party was a god, a tsar – master of his province – and on virtually any issue, the first secretary's opinion was decisive. I used that power, but only in the name of the people, never for myself. I made the wheels of the economic machinery turn faster. I was listened to and obeyed, and thanks to that, it seems to me, every enterprise functioned better.

An area in which I never interfered was that of the law, the activities of the state prosecution service and the courts, though I once had to come to the rescue of the manager of a ball-bearing factory who had been indicted for over-expenditure on materials at his factory. I intervened on his behalf and requested that his case be carefully investigated. On a purely human level I felt sorry for this young manager, especially as I had held managerial jobs in industry myself and knew all about the multifarious instructions which tie such people hand and foot. He was a good lad who was trying to do his best and it would have been a shame to lose him. There was no self-interest in what he had done; in part he had been let down by others and in part he himself was to blame, but even so he had done nothing criminal and the manager in question remained a free man.

When the twenty-sixth party congress was due to be held, I made serious preparations for attending it. I wanted, of course, to deal a blow to the appalling state of stagnation in which the country found itself. I made a fighting speech on those lines, which stood out in contrast to the general chorus of adulation for Brezhnev, but as I said at the twenty-seventh party congress, I obviously lacked not only sufficient experience but also, more importantly, enough political courage to take a decisive stand against our rotten system of rule by the party bureaucracy. Furthermore, I still did not know the members of the central committee well enough to be able to exert a significant influence on affairs, although I could see that the holders of power at the centre were simply failing in their job.

I must say that we greeted Gorbachov's appointment in 1978 as secretary of the central committee for agriculture with enthusiasm, and we thought that at last Soviet agriculture really might get moving. This did not happen. Clearly he failed to grasp the essentials of the problem, and his attempts to improve matters with hasty measures did not produce any decisive changes for the better in agriculture.

Gorbachov and I first met when we were both working as first secretaries, he at Stavropol and I at Sverdlovsk. Our first encounter was by telephone. Quite often we needed to extend each other a helping hand: metal and timber from the Urals, food products from Stavropol. As a rule he never gave us anything over and above the limits imposed by Gosplan, but he did help us to build up our stocks of poultry and meat.

When he was elected as a secretary of the central committee, I went up to him, shook him by the hand and congratulated him with heartfelt sincerity. Later I went to see him on more than one occasion because agriculture was fraught with problems in Sverdlovsk province, being in a zone whose climatic and geological features have always made farming difficult. Although I devoted a lot of time to agriculture – probably about half my working hours – nevertheless, the climatic instability of the region never allowed us to be sure of reaching a predictable level of output, even though there was a definite increase in agricultural production during my ten years in office.

Whenever I entered Gorbachov's office, we would embrace warmly. We had a good relationship. And I think that when he first came to work at the central committee he was different from his present self; more open, sincere and frank. He very much wanted to improve matters in agriculture; he worked hard at it and kept in contact with the outlying republics and provinces.

One incident occurred which may have marked the beginning of a certain cooling in my relationship with Gorbachov. It happened when a commission of inspection came to Sverdlovsk from the central committee (there were a lot of them at the time) to check on the state of affairs in the countryside. Understandably enough, alongside the positive factors the commission also found not a few shortcomings, which undoubtedly existed; but in their final report, there were some obvious distortions of fact. The secretariat of the central committee issued a brief resolution based on the report, and issued it, what's more, without first asking for my comments. We were simply sent the resolution, shortly followed by a visit by Kapustyan, Gorbachov's deputy at the agriculture section of the central committee. Our leading party officials were assembled, and Kapustyan made a speech echoing the tone of the resolution issued by the secretariat of the central committee, then I spoke. While broadly agreeing with the conclusions drawn by the commission, I nevertheless said that there were certain points in the resolution which I could not accept, and I enumerated them. It was unheard of to challenge a document of this nature and there was an awkward silence. Kapustyan spoke again, to which I replied even more sharply. The upshot was that after a while I was summoned to Moscow.

That commission caused me a lot of worry. I tossed and turned at night, wondering whether I was doing right or wrong to stick to my own point of view. Kapustyan and Razumov, deputy director of the personnel department of the central committee, had prepared a memorandum officially notifying the members of the central committee that Comrade Yeltsin had not made a sufficiently objective appraisal of the shortcomings in his province; had contested certain conclusions drawn by the commission; and had objected to various points made in the secretariat's resolution, thereby infringing party discipline. There was more besides.

Before reaching Moscow I had learned that this memorandum existed, so that when I arrived at the central committee I was not surprised to learn that Kapitonov was waiting to see me. In a somewhat apologetic tone he began, 'Boris Nikolayevich, there is a memorandum to the central committee from two departments and I've been asked, well, not exactly to discuss it with you, but to make sure that you're aware of its contents.' And he handed me the memo. I read it, and immediately repeated what I had said at the plenum of the provincial committee – that I disagreed with several of the conclusions drawn by the authors of the memo. Kapitonov did not extend the conversation to discuss any other matters, and on that we parted.

On the same visit I also went to see Gorbachov. He greeted me as though nothing had happened; we talked, and only as I was leaving did he say, 'Have you read that memorandum?', with a hint of disapproval at what I had done. I said, 'Yes, I have.' Gorbachov replied, curtly and firmly, 'You should draw the necessary conclusions!' I said, 'Conclusions must indeed be drawn from the resolution, and that is being done, but I am not obliged to draw any conclusions from the subjective, inaccurate statements made in the memorandum.' – 'No,' said Gorbachov, 'you're wrong. You should take note of that memo all the same.' The matter ended there.

Then, as always Gorbachov addressed me as *ty*.[5] I have never yet met anyone whom he addresses as *vy*, the polite, more formal second-person plural form of 'you' in Russian equivalent to the French *vous*. He uses the familiar *ty*, for instance, to all the older, senior Politbureau members such as Gromyko, Vladimir Shcherbitsky and Vitaly Vorotnikov. This may be a lack of culture or a mere habit – it is hard to say which it is – but whenever he addressed me as *ty* I immediately felt a sense of unease; inwardly I objected to this form of address, although I never mentioned it to him.

On many occasions in the past when my frankness might have got me into trouble, I was saved by the fact that my speeches did not reach the ears of the top leadership. Pavel Simonov, the central committee's watch-dog over our province, picked up everything and would quietly consign it to the archives. In one of my frank conversations with Fidel Castro (he and I developed a good, trusting relationship) he said to me, 'You're wrong to be always reproaching yourself and lacerating yourself – it's simply that the situation is not yet ready for action. The central authority is so strong that it's armour-plated and can withstand anything.'

I also got along well with the members of the military council of the Urals military district. I would frequently visit army and air-force units, where I met both officers and men and attended training exercises; I was usually accompanied by members of the party bureau, who would sometimes drive tanks and learn about aircraft. We helped the military in getting their camps and barracks rebuilt; this was necessary because in some of the military bases conditions were terrible. The ministry of defence seems to regard soldiers as its vassals who are supposed to keep their mouths shut. At one of the meetings held at a particular division, I asked for the first time why there was no criticism about conditions from the ranks, why the soldiers never spoke up; had they nothing to say? The reaction to this was perplexity; naturally, my question filtered up to the top echelon, but they swallowed it. I continued to pursue this line, and gradually – although the matter was taken up through the Komsomol and party network [rather than through strictly military channels] – a certain genuine movement began to make itself felt. The Komsomol members pulled themselves together and eventually at party meetings and on other encounters with the military, critical remarks aimed at senior officers began to be heard. I regarded this process as essential.

I also developed reasonably good relations with the provincial directorate of the KGB. The head of the directorate, General Kornilov, used to take part in sessions of the party bureau as a candidate member. I frequently visited his department, asked for information about the work of the KGB, studied the way it functioned and acquainted myself with every one of its branches. I knew, of course, that there were certain matters which he kept secret from me. Even so, I got to know the KGB's system pretty thoroughly. Precisely for that reason my speech at the summer 1989 session of the Supreme Soviet, when Vladimir Kryuchkov was confirmed [as head of the KGB][6] was not fortuitous; I did, after all, know a lot about this organisation, which is normally closed to all outsiders.

This knowledge was helpful when a tragic outbreak of anthrax occurred in our region.[7] The deputy chairman of the KGB, V.V. Pirozhkov, came to Sverdlovsk to investigate and elucidate the circumstances of the case. This occurred during the early years of my tenure as first secretary. The three of us – Pirozhkov, Kornilov and myself – were seated in my office, calmly discussing the general situation, and Kornilov remarked, in passing, that the local KGB directorate was collaborating closely with the provincial committee of the party. Suddenly Pirozhkov barked out, 'General Kornilov – stand to attention!' Kornilov leapt to his feet and stood rigidly to attention. I was puzzled by all this. Then, rapping out every phrase Pirozhkov said to Kornilov, 'Now get this into your head, General! In all your work, whatever it may be, you are not supposed to "collaborate closely" with the party organisation: you are obliged to operate under its direction, and in no other way.'

I must say that in all my ten years as first secretary, the KGB never found even one spy, however hard they may have tried. Kornilov was very depressed about this, because it implied that he and his men were not doing their job properly. 'In a region like this, you might think there'd be at least one spy – but there's not a single one', he would complain wistfully.

We were also hit by some real emergencies, such as the accident at the Bieloyarsk nuclear power station, which took place between the night of 31 December 1978 and the morning of 1 January 1979, when the temperature was $-57°C$. Throughout the province, several major accidents occurred more or less simultaneously; at Bieloyarsk some metal structures in the generator hall collapsed and as they fell they struck a spark, some oil caught alight and a fire broke out. The firemen displayed tremendous courage and heroism. For several hours we deployed all our fire-fighting crews from Sverdlovsk; they could only work in gas-masks, because burning plastic was giving off thick acrid smoke which made breathing otherwise impossible. Above all, the fire had to be prevented from reaching the reactor hall. Hundreds of buses were held on standby to evacuate the population from the adjacent village, but the firemen, together with other specialists, nevertheless succeeded in winning this real battle and saved the power station. More importantly, they saved lives. Otherwise the consequences might have been utterly catastrophic; the province is thick with defence installations.

During the war, 437 factories were evacuated here from the areas occupied by the Germans. Machine tools were set up and put to work, literally on the foundations, without walls and roofs, in order to start immediately producing munitions for the front. The workers were housed in dug-outs and huts. For this reason, our region contained almost more hutted accommodation than anywhere else in the country.

I have already described my feelings about these wooden huts. Having spent nearly ten years of my life living in one of them, the memories of those appalling shacks, inhabited by anything between ten and twenty families, depress me even today. People should not have to live in such conditions in the twentieth century; yet when I was put in charge of Sverdlovsk province, several dozen families were still accommodated in huts. Soon a Politbureau resolution was passed ordering the huts to be demolished throughout the country within ten years. It was obvious to me that people would not tolerate such a long wait; we had to put an end to the matter much sooner, once and for all.

I asked for the necessary calculations to be made. It turned out that we would have to build about two million square metres of living-space in order to rehouse all the people living in huts. Two million was an impossible figure. The entire province built only two million square metres of accommodation in a year, and the waiting-list for housing included disabled people, large families and war veterans, as well as many categories of lower priority.

This was one of the many occasions in the life of an office-holder when I had to make a difficult decision, when it was a choice between the not very good and the downright bad. Which was the most important – either to get people out of the huts and to freeze all the housing waiting-lists for a year, or to continue to subject people to the torments of living in inhuman conditions, while housing all the others waiting in the queue?

We decided to freeze the housing waiting-list, which meant that nobody, except those living in huts, would be rehoused for a year. The others had to understand that the time had come to help the people who were living in the worst conditions of all. And indeed, broadly speaking, people did understand this, although I had to make a round of visits to explain and describe the situation and explain some more. Even so, the managers of many enterprises sent up howls of protest since in the Soviet Union, industrial and equivalent organisations are responsible for housing their employees. Every large factory has a construction department responsible for building housing as well as industrial structures. Our policy was a serious blow to them. We were exploiting their industrial strength and their capacity for housing construction while giving them nothing in return. Arguments based on moral considerations left them cold. But I understood their attitude; as an erstwhile industrial manager myself, I knew very well just how important decent housing was for the morale of a work-force, how eagerly it was awaited. And now the accommodation originally earmarked for their workers had to be given to someone else. It was a hard one to swallow.

In order to save the situation, in desperation I made a trip to Moscow. I saw Kirilenko and explained the matter to him, saying that if he received any complaints and curses directed at me because of our housing policy, he should be patient for a year and put the complaints on file: we simply had to get rid of those wooden huts. He agreed to this. Then I went to see Kosygin.[8] I again described the situation to him and explained that I wasn't asking for any favours: we required neither extra building materials nor industrial capacity, all we needed was moral support. Kosygin accepted my arguments; we agreed jointly to present the case to a session of the full Council of Ministers and to ask the ministers responsible for every branch of industry to disregard any complaints coming from managers in Sverdlovsk province.

And it happened as we had foreseen. The managers complained and protested, wrote letters attacking me, while we demolished one hut after another. We launched attacks on all the areas of hutted accommodation in turn and dismantled them. Within a year all the former hut-dwellers had moved into new, decently furnished flats. Later, the provincial executive committee compensated most of the enterprises which had suffered a loss of their housing allocations for that year.

Nowadays, in the era of *glasnost*, there has been much talk about the Ipatiev house in Sverdlovsk [the city was formerly known as Ekaterinburg], in the cellars of which the ex-tsar Nicholas II and his family were executed by a firing-squad in 1918. A return to the sources of our distorted and falsified history is a natural process. The country wants to know the truth about its past, including the terrible and unpalatable truths. The tragedy of the Romanov family is precisely such an episode that has not been dwelt upon [by Soviet historians].

It was during my tenure of office as first secretary of the Sverdlovsk provincial committee that the Ipatiev house was destroyed. I will describe how it happened.

People have always come to look at the Ipatiev house, although it was in no way greatly different from the other old houses in the neighbourhood. It had been converted for occupation by a number of small offices, but the terrible tragedy that occurred there in 1918 drew people to that place; they would peer through the windows or simply stand and stare in silence at the old house.

As we know, the Romanov family was executed as a result of a decision by the Urals regional committee of the party. I went to the provincial archives and read the documents of the time. Until quite recently, the facts of this crime were hardly known to anyone. There existed a falsified version, written in the spirit of [Stalin's] *Short Course in the History of the Bolshevik Party*, so it can easily be imagined how eagerly I read through the documents dated 1918. It is only very recently that certain detailed documentary accounts of the last days of the Romanov family have been published in the Soviet press, so that when I examined the archives I was one of the very few people to have had access to the secrets surrounding the execution of the tsar and his family. It made painful reading.

One of the dates connected with the life of the last Russian tsar was approaching. The results of new research were published in Western newspapers and journals, and some of this material was broadcast in Russian by Western radio stations. This stimulated interest in the Ipatiev house, and people even came to look at it from other cities. I treated this quite calmly, since it was obvious that the interest was caused neither by monarchist sentiments nor by any urge to resurrect a new tsar. The motives in this case were quite different – curiosity, compassion and a tribute to memory, which are normal human emotions.

Information about the large number of pilgrims visiting the Ipatiev house, however, found its way through certain channels to Moscow. I don't know what machinery this set in motion, what our ideologues were afraid of, or even what conferences and meetings were held, but I soon received a letter from Moscow marked 'secret'. Reading it, I couldn't believe my eyes: it was a decree of the Politbureau, adopted in closed session, ordering the demolition of the Ipatiev house in Sverdlovsk. Since the order was a secret one, this meant that the provincial committee of the party had to assume all responsibility for this senseless decision.

At the very first discussion of the matter in the party bureau I met a sharp reaction from my colleagues to this order from Moscow. It was impossible, however, to disobey a secret decree of the Politbureau, and in a few days' time the necessary machinery was driven up to the Ipatiev house in the middle of the night, and by next morning nothing was left of the building. Then the site was covered with asphalt.

That was yet another sad episode of the Brezhnev's 'era of stagnation'. I can well imagine that sooner or later we will be ashamed of this piece of barbarism. Ashamed we may be; but we can never rectify it.

Incidentally, it will be interesting to know when the central committee will decide to publish all the decrees of the Politbureau, both secret and open. In my view, that time has already come. Much would then be revealed and much that has been hitherto inexplicable would be explained.

I have never had any particular wish to enumerate the successes and achievements of my time as first secretary. I didn't even do this after Ligachov's speech at the nineteenth party conference, in which he insisted, 'Boris, you were wrong,' and declared that I had made a mess of my job at Sverdlovsk. Everyone, in my view, realised that this was a lie and I considered it simply beneath my dignity to argue with him and to prove the contrary.

Yet I did gain satisfaction from the fact that the food supply was improved and that we built the Sverdlovsk-Serov highway. Incidentally, I still cannot understand how we managed to accomplish that huge project – huge in both the effort that it cost us and in its significance for Sverdlovsk province.

The territory of the province is roughly in the shape of an upturned heart: from north to south the distance is 625 miles and from west to east it is 312 miles. There was no highway link between the cluster of large industrial towns in the north and Sverdlovsk and Nizhny Tagil in the centre. The north of the region is rich: there is bauxite, iron ore and precious metals, there are metal-working industries, there are the coal-mines at Karpinsk and Tura. To travel by rail from Karpinsk, Serov, Severo-Uralsk, Krasnoturinsk and so on to Sverdlovsk used to take days. People were almost cut off from normal life. The idea of linking these northern towns with the centre by a highway had long since taken shape, but the task was extremely difficult – the highway would have to cross swamps, ravines, mountains and several rivers. The distance is 220 miles. Due to the complexity of the region's topography, the cost per mile amounted to 1,600,000 roubles. So we had to find, somewhere, 350 million roubles in order to scrape together the funds for materials, wages, equipment – in fact we didn't know where to start. Meanwhile the need for the highway was growing more and more acute every year.

We asked the central planning authorities to allocate the funds to us. Their refusal came back very quickly. We called a meeting of all district and city first secretaries, chairmen of city and district executive committees and other leading figures in the province, to consult them in an attempt to find a solution. Could we raise the funds by pooling all our resources? The discussions lasted a long time and we finally decided that we had to build the road by our own efforts. We agreed to divide it into sections, allotting the responsibility for each section to particular towns; within the towns, individual enterprises and organisations would form mixed teams of construction workers, drivers of excavators, bulldozers and other machinery, and these teams would build their own section of the highway.

This whole cumbersome operation could only be made effective if given a clearly defined system of organising the labour-force as well as discipline and constant supervision exercised at the highest level. The special headquarters that was set up kept permanent watch on the progress of the work; we would drive up to the sections or fly by helicopter to the places which could not be reached by any other means. Building the road was tough going – nothing but swamps, peat bogs and sheer cliffs. I felt that nature was doing everything possible to stop us. Even so, the road was built solidly and conscientiously to high standards, with a multi-layered surface that was designed to last for many a year.

When we were about a year away from completing the road, we named the month, day and even the hour at which the route would be opened. We arranged to hire a fleet of buses, fill them with the leading party and Soviet officials of the regions through which the highway passed, and to set off along it in convoy. Anyone whose allotted section of road was not ready in time would have to get out. Since then this creation of all the people of Sverdlovsk province, the Sverdlovsk-Serov highway, has appeared on the map. It was our joint, shared victory and therefore especially dear to us.

People will no doubt say to me that to make senior city officials get out of the bus for all to see is not very . . . indeed, it is typical of the notorious 'command' system of running the economy by administrative fiat. That can't be helped, I'm afraid; in that particular instance it worked.

I was brought up in the system; everything was steeped in the methods of the 'command' system and I, too, acted accordingly. Whether I was chairing a meeting, running my office, or delivering a report to a plenum – everything that one did was expressed in terms of pressure, threats and coercion. At the time these methods did produce some results, especially if the boss in question was sufficiently strong-willed. Gradually, though, one became more and more aware that what had seemed to be reliable and correct instructions issued by the party bureau turned out, on checking, not to have been done at all; that more and more often when party officials or industrial managers gave their word that a thing would be done, it was not done. The system was clearly beginning to fail.

Towards the end of my decade in office, it seemed we had stretched ourselves to the utmost, that we had tried every possible method and every conceivable way of getting things done. It became more difficult to find any new approaches, even though we continued to hold a special gathering of the bureau at the beginning of each January, in order to explore new working methods which needed to be introduced into the party and, indeed, into every other organisation in the province. Yet I nevertheless felt – although I never admitted it to anyone – that my satisfaction in the job was beginning to diminish. Our stock of ideas and methods had been exhausted. Whatever the cause may have been, I caught myself giving way to a feeling of weariness, of being up a blind alley.

Yet the affairs of the province, as before, were not going badly.

4

Chronicle of the Election Campaign

22 February 1989

The pre-election adoption meeting for the Moscow city no. 1 constituency came to an end at about three o'clock in the morning. Three hours later I was sitting in an aeroplane bound for Sverdlovsk, flying back to my home town. I had given instructions to trusted people to send telegrams to all the other constituencies in which I had been nominated, thanking them and announcing my decision to stand elsewhere, although I did not name the constituency. I was flying to Sverdlovsk, though, because I simply could not just tell my own people by telegram that I was declining their nomination.

My plan to stay in Moscow and not to stand in constituencies where I had a practically 100 per cent chance of being elected was described by many – both opponents and supporters – as a big mistake, a crazy idea, sheer effrontery, overweening self-confidence, and so on in that vein. In fact, I had no answer to make to all those comments. I was, indeed, running a very great risk of not being elected. I might be depriving myself of what was, effectively, my only remaining chance of returning from political exile and back to public life. Having with great difficulty overcome the obstacles placed in my way, I had suddenly created a new obstacle for myself. No wonder it seemed strange.

Even so, I had to go for the Moscow no. 1 constituency, the most important one in the country. I was motivated neither by megalomania nor conceit. I had to prove both to myself and to those who supported me that a new time had come; that we were now able to decide our own fate; that we could now, despite all the pressure from the leadership, the *apparat* and official ideology, go to the polling booth and make a real choice.

Had I withdrawn my candidacy in Moscow to stand at Sverdlovsk instead, my election campaign would have virtually ended there. I would only have had to wait for polling day, 26 March, in order to wake up the next morning and check the size of my majority. The overwhelming proportion of people in Sverdlovsk would undoubtedly have voted for me.

I estimated my chances in Moscow as being about fifty-fifty, and my election campaign here is like an extension of the speech I made at the October 1987 plenum of the central committee. The difference is that there I was alone, with the entire upper echelon of the infuriated party bureaucracy ranged against me, whereas now the situation is quite different: my opponents are the same bunch as before – only this time I am not on my own. The multimillion population of Moscow is on my side – and not only of Moscow. Everyone else in the country equally detests the self-righteousness, hypocrisy, mendacity, condescending smugness and conceit with which the entire apparatus of government is riddled.

I reached Sverdlovsk early in the morning. Although I hadn't slept for a moment, the fact of being back in my home town caused all the fatigue, all the strain of the last few days to vanish in a flash. From the airport I went straight to a series of meetings with the people of Sverdlovsk. The first one lasted three hours. Then came a short break, giving me just enough time to embrace old friends, and then I went to another hall – the palace of culture of a big factory – with an audience of 1,500, who handed up about 500 written comments and questions. And on every other slip of paper the message was the same, 'Boris Nikolayevich, give up the Moscow constituency, they'll make mincemeat of you – you can't trust Muscovites.'

The meeting lasted until one o'clock in the morning. I explained to them as best I could the reasons why I must at least have a stab at Moscow. I think they understood me. They also said that if I were not elected in Moscow on 26 March, I needn't worry; they would vote for *every* candidate on the Sverdlovsk list on polling day, which would invalidate the vote; I might have a chance of standing in the second ballot that would inevitably ensue. And they obviously meant it, adding that on polling day anyone who possibly could would get a certificate removing their name from the electoral register, fly to Moscow and vote for me there as 'temporary residents', a procedure now possible under the new electoral law.

I had practically no time to sit and talk with any of my friends. Sad though it was, I had to leave. I was living at a crazy tempo then. It's not normal. There should always be time to spare for one's friends, but there is none. I went to see my mother. Lord, what she has had to endure in these last months! I embraced her quickly and left.

———

'Tell us – was it always your ambition to come to Moscow, or did it just happen?'*

'How did you find a flat in Moscow?'*

On 3 April 1985, we were sitting in the offices of the Sverdlovsk provincial committee, engaged in a fierce discussion of the problems connected with the spring sowing season. The situation was one of emergency; very little snow had fallen, resulting in a serious lack of moisture in the soil. All the specialists expressed the view that we should wait a little before starting to sow. We accepted that decision, but even so we also decided to visit all the regions of the province and consult the experts on the spot. That evening I drove around the food shops. In theory I knew the situation exactly, but I wanted to see what it was like with my own eyes one more time. Food supplies seemed to have improved; there were several sorts of poultry on sale, as well as cheese, eggs and sausage, but even so the total picture was less than satisfactory.

I never imagined that later that same evening my thoughts would be several hundred miles away. A call from Moscow came through

* (From questions handed up from the floor at meetings during the election campaign.)

71

on my car phone – 'Comrade Dolgikh, Politbureau member and secretary of the central committee would like to speak to you.' Vladimir Dolgikh said hello, for politeness' sake asked how things were going, then said that the Politbureau had instructed him to offer me a job in Moscow, to be put in charge of the central committee section responsible for the construction industry. After thinking for literally a couple of seconds, I declined the offer.

In my mind I was thinking about all the things that Dolgikh had not said: that I had been born in these parts; that I lived here; that I had studied and worked here. I liked the job, and although the changes I had brought about were small, they were real. But the chief consideration was the contacts I had built up with people – strong, enduring, worthwhile, the kind that take a long time to create. And since I was above all accustomed to working closely with people, it struck me as impossible to have to start afresh, leaving a host of unfinished matters here.

There was also another reason for my refusal of which I wasn't fully aware at the time, but which clearly had lodged somewhere in my subconscious – namely that for someone who was a member of the central committee, and with nine and a half years' service as first secretary of a provincial committee, to be made section head of the construction department of the central committee was somehow not very logical. As I have mentioned, Sverdlovsk province is the third largest in the country for industrial production, and the first secretary of a province – possessing unique experience and knowledge – should be transferred to a post where he would be used to greater effect. Traditionally, this has always been the case: Kirilenko and Ryabov, both former provincial first secretaries, had been promoted to be secretaries of the central committee – and I was being offered the [considerably more junior] job of a section head. Although Dolgikh put forward some fairly weighty arguments, I still declined and with that our conversation ended.

I continued, of course, to reflect on my future career practically all that night, knowing that Dolgikh's phone call would not be the last I should hear of it. And so it was. Next day I was rung up by Ligachov. Already aware of my earlier conversation with Dolgikh, he was more pressing. Nevertheless, I maintained my refusal, saying that I needed to stay where I was; that ours was an enormous, unique region of almost five million inhabitants, with many problems that were still unsolved, and therefore I could not leave. Then

Ligachov used an irrefutable argument, talking of party discipline, a Politbureau decision and so on, and that I, as a Communist Party member, was obliged to accept the proposal and move to Moscow. There was nothing for it; I could only say, 'Well, all right, I'll go.' And so, on 12 April 1985, I started work in Moscow.

I was extremely sad to leave Sverdlovsk, where I had very many good friends and comrades. There, too, was my Alma Mater, the Urals Polytechnic Institute; there I had been through the hard school of working in industry; there I had switched from industrial to party work – in fact, my whole life had been bound up with the place. I had married there, my two daughters lived there and now there was a granddaughter, too. On top of it all, I was fifty-four years old – no small consideration, at least when it was a question of changing both my whole way of life and starting on a very different kind of job.

In our country, attitudes to the 'Moscow syndrome' are something unique. They manifest themselves, first, in a dislike of Muscovites – but which is nevertheless combined with a passionate desire to move to Moscow and become a Muscovite oneself. The reasons for these conflicting attitudes are understandable; they are not inherent in people, but they derive from the strained socio-economic conditions that have arisen in the USSR, also from our age-old passion for creating Potemkin villages. Moscow, which is visited by so many foreigners, must at least be the one place which has to look outwardly attractive; where the food supply has to be tolerable; where there are goods to be had of whose very existence the provinces have long since forgotten. As a result, provincials flock to Moscow, stand in queues for hours at a time to buy imported shoes or sausages – and to seethe with envy at the Muscovites who are so lucky because they have everything. And the Muscovites, in their turn, curse the invading hordes from out of town because they pack the shops and make it impossible to buy goods. People in the provinces will do anything to send their grown-up offspring to Moscow, on any condition, no matter what humiliations and discomfort they may have to endure. A new word has even been coined, which until very recently was not to be found in any dictionary – *limitchik*. These are young men and women who live just beyond the Moscow city limits (hence the name), and who commute daily into the city, where they do mostly unskilled, menial work, which after a few years will make them eligible to be given a

Moscow residence-permit and thus become legal residents of the city.

I honestly admit that I, too, used to have a prejudiced attitude to Muscovites. Naturally, when I was living in Sverdlovsk and often had to make trips to Moscow on official business, I never had much opportunity to meet them socially; I chiefly came into contact with other politicians and officials at republic and national level, but even these contacts tended to leave a nasty taste in my mouth. No one made any attempt to hide their attitudes of snobbery and arrogance towards provincials, and my emotional reaction was to assume that all Muscovites behaved like that.

Furthermore, I had never had any ambition or even wish to work in Moscow. More than once I had turned down offers of jobs in Moscow, even including the post of minister. I have always loved Sverdlovsk; I still love it; I have never regarded it as 'provincial' and I don't think those feelings diminish me in any way.

Still, I was in Moscow. I was shown a flat, and because I was feeling depressed I didn't care what sort of place it was, I accepted what I was offered – in a block near the Belorussian station, on Second Tverskaya-Yamskaya Street. It was a noisy, dirty part of town. The leaders of our party usually live in the outer suburb of Kuntsevo, where it is quiet, clean and comfortable.

I plunged into the job at a furious tempo, and the section started to come to life. Not everyone, of course, could keep up that style of work, but that was natural. I would come home every evening around midnight or twelve-thirty, and by eight o'clock next morning I was at work again. I did not demand that others should work at that pace, but some colleagues, especially my deputies, did their best to keep up.

I never felt any kind of holy awe when I crossed the threshold of the central committee building on Moscow's Staraya Square and started work there; but there is no denying that the building is, in its way, the citadel of power in the USSR, the place where the might of the party's *apparat* is concentrated. It is from there that proposals, orders and appointments are issued; thence, too, comes a stream of grandiose but unrealisable programmes; relentlessly up-beat slogans; dubious schemes; and straight crimes. Decisions have been taken here in minutes, which later have shaken the whole world, such as, for example, the decision to send Soviet troops into Afghanistan.

I started work without giving a thought to such things. The section had to be got moving. I was well acquainted with the problems of the construction industry; I was, as it were, a manager in disguise, and therefore I knew all about the chief difficulties and problems of that branch of the economy.

It had been my fortune in life that until then I had practically never had to work as a subordinate, had never been anyone's deputy. I had been a section manager, but never an assistant manager; managing director but never the deputy managing director of a trust. Never having been a 'number two', I was consequently used to taking decisions without shifting the ultimate responsibility on to someone else. In the central committee, however, the structure of subordination, of a strict party hierarchy, has been taken to the point of absurdity – everything is hedged around with precautionary reservations, every proposal is issued *per pro* some superior figure. Working within such a rigidly bureaucratic framework was obviously a severe ordeal for someone of my free-wheeling and self-confident temperament. The construction section was subordinate to Dolgikh, one of the secretaries of the central committee, and he was the first person to come into conflict with my independent style of work.

I recall a meeting, chaired by Dolgikh, of the heads of those sections for which he was responsible; it was my first attendance at a gathering of this kind. Dolgikh made a speech; I noticed that everyone else had come provided with thick notepads and they were all scribbling away, trying to record every word. I listened, doing no more than note down the main points in single-word headings. Dolgikh, who was evidently accustomed to see practically every word of his written down, kept glancing at me with obvious displeasure and an eloquent expression which implied, 'What is this?! I am uttering pearls of wisdom – and you are not writing them down!' Admittedly he said nothing at the time, but on the next occasion he made a point of asking me, 'Have you any questions? Perhaps there is something you haven't remembered? If so, ask me.' – 'No,' I replied, 'I've remembered everything.' He was aware, I must admit, that my current position was temporary and that my status might be abruptly changed. In fact, I never had any conflicts or problems in my relations with him.

There was a very great deal of work to be done. Now, of course, I do not regret having worked in that section. I got to know the state of affairs in the country as a whole, and kept in touch with the republics and several of the biggest provinces. The job also meant having dealings with Gorbachov, who by now had become general secretary, but only on the telephone. I must honestly admit to being amazed that he made no move to meet me and talk to me. First, we did, after all, have a good personal relationship and, second, Gorbachov knew very well that, like me, he had also moved up to the central committee from the position of a regional first secretary – and from a region, what's more, which in economic potential was considerably inferior to the Sverdlovsk region – but *he* had been promoted to the rank of secretary of the central committee. I think Gorbachov knew that this was on my mind, but neither of us gave any sign of it.

After a while my wife joined me in Moscow, together with my daughter, her husband and my little granddaughter. My younger daughter was already living in Moscow. Between them they made the flat habitable while I worked. The moment has come to digress from my career in industry and party work and to say something about the people who are closest to me, particularly as I am describing my move to Moscow. My family consists of my wife, my two daughters and their husbands, a grandson and two granddaughters. They did not find it easy here: an unfamiliar city, a new tempo of life, new relationships. In such circumstances, the head of the family usually helps the others to find their feet, but I had neither the energy nor the time to keep track of how things were going at home; I was totally absorbed in my work, with the result that, if anything, I saw more of my family in Sverdlovsk than in Moscow. But to begin at the beginning – which means going back to my happy days at the polytechnic in the 1950s.

In the whirlpool of student life, a group of us formed a gang of our own – six boys and six girls. We lived close to each other, in two large rooms of a student hostel, and we would meet nearly every evening. Inevitably boys and girls fell in love with each other, and I, too, was attracted to some of the girls. Gradually, in that large, friendly student family I began to pay more and more attention to one girl in particular – Naya Girina. She had been born in Orenburg province, and was officially named Anastasia, but her parents and everyone else called her Naya, and the name has stuck, so much so that she is not used to being called by her given name. When she was a very young girl this did not bother her, but when she started work and people began addressing her in the formal manner by her first name and patronymic, she found herself so unused to it that she found it difficult to accept. Perhaps she ought to have accustomed herself to it, but instead she went to the register office and had her named changed to Naya. I preferred the name Anastasia, and for a long time afterwards I didn't call her by her name but simply, *devushka*, meaning girl.

She has always been modest, charming and essentially gentle. These characteristics are a very necessary contrast to my fairly extrovert nature. Our feelings for each other gradually grew, but we gave no sign of it; even when I kissed her it was on the cheek, as I did with all the other girls, and it did not reach the stage of any passionate declarations. Thus our platonic relationship lasted for a long time, although inwardly I realised that I had fallen for her, fallen hard, in fact, and there was no getting away from it. I remember the first time we admitted that we loved each other – it was in our second year, on the upstairs gallery that formed the entrance foyer to the Institute's assembly hall. And we kissed behind the pillars, this time not on the cheek but for real.

Then, in our final year at the polytechnic, I went away for a few months to play in volley-ball matches, and when I returned I plunged furiously into work on my dissertation. Having passed the final exams, I again went away on tour with the team, without even bothering to find out where I had been assigned to for my first job. On coming back home, I found that I was to stay in Sverdlovsk and she was being sent to Orenburg. Usually young couples are only assigned to the same town when they actually have a marriage certificate. All that we had, however, was our mutual admission that we loved each other; so we decided to test our love and to see how strong and how deep it was.

We agreed that she would go to Orenburg and I would stay in Sverdlovsk, but that after exactly one year we would meet on neutral ground – not in Orenburg and not in Sverdlovsk, but in Kuibyshev. There, we agreed, we would know for certain whether our feelings for each other had cooled in the meantime or whether they had, on the contrary, grown even warmer, firmer and stronger. And so it was.

I have already described how much strain I was under in that year – the year in which I would put myself through the process of learning the twelve basic manual trades in the construction industry, while still continuing to play in the city volley-ball team. And, by coincidence, exactly a year later the regional volley-ball tournament was taking place in Kuibyshev. Naya and I spoke on the telephone. She was very excited, so much so, in fact, that I hardly recognised her voice. I was in a high state of excitement, too, but my mood was more elated. We arranged to meet at a certain time in the town's main square.

The hotel in which our team was staying during the tournament was on that square. Sure enough, as I came out of the hotel, I saw her in the square. My heart was ready to burst with a flood of emotions; I looked at her, and I knew at once: we would spend the rest of our lives together. For the whole evening and all that night we walked around the town together, talking about everything under the sun. We recalled our student days and everything that had happened over the past year. I just wanted to go on listening and listening to this person I loved, to go on looking at her day and night, without saying anything – because we understood each other, just like that, without words.

The whole of my subsequent life has proved that we were brought together by fate. It was one of those one-in-a-thousand choices. Naya took me and loved me as I am – obstinate and prickly – and naturally she has not had an easy time with me. As for myself, I need hardly say that I have always loved her – gentle, tender and kind as she is – and will love her all my life.

Back in Sverdlovsk, at the hostel where I was living, we got together a bunch of lads and girls, our friends from the polytechnic. We told them that we had decided to get married, having first called in at the register office in Verkh-Isetsk. In those days you did not have to give advance notice of your intention to marry; you just turned up with your witnesses, the registrar conducted the ceremony, you signed the book and went home. During my time at the polytechnic, especially in the last year or two, when there were a lot of marriages, I was one of the chief organisers of so-called 'Komsomol weddings': noisy, cheerful occasions, with lots of ingenious, impromptu entertainment. Thus I was, in a way, present at the start of many families. Now all my friends got together and decided to get their own back and they arranged a splendid 'Komsomol wedding' for us.

Our friends arrived there from all over the country, since many of them were already working in other towns. It was a really magnificent wedding reception with about 150 guests. The boys invented countless amusing turns, especially my friends Yura Serdyukov, Seryozha Palgov and Misha Karasik. They did everything to ensure that we would remember that wedding for the rest of our lives. They composed an ode to us, presented us with a hilarious home-made newspaper, comic posters, and other delightfully funny surprises. Unfortunately those splendid presents have not survived; they were all mislaid with time, which was a great pity.

The wedding reception lasted all night. But that was not to be the end of it: my relatives demanded a second wedding reception. There had not been room for everyone at the first, where the guests had largely been young people. Then we went, after this, to Orenburg, where Naya's family demanded yet a third reception. She comes from a real peasant family, where old traditions were still observed. It was held in their home and about thirty people took part. Naya's parents owned their own small private house, complete with garden in the town. After the reception we were taken next door to spend the night with neighbours. Scarcely had we woken up next morning, when we heard people outside shouting, 'Show us the sheet!' According to ancient custom, on the morning after the wedding-night, the couple must hang their sheet out of the window, where it can be seen from the street. This, however, was our third 'wedding', so we had to go out on to the porch and give a frank account of ourselves to a crowd of guests who had gathered there.

Then we went back to Sverdlovsk, where Naya started working at the Institute of Waterways; she continued to work there for more than twenty-nine years, becoming chief engineer of a large project, in charge of a group of other specialists. Being conscientious and hard-working, her colleagues greatly respected her, and she found her professional life a great deal easier than I did – or at least so it seemed to me.

Slightly less than a year later I drove my wife to the maternity clinic. I, of course, wanted a son, but our first child was a baby girl. I was nevertheless delighted and we called her Lena. My friends and I gathered outside the clinic and threw flowers through the window. Then we went back to the hostel and marked the occasion with a dinner. A little over two years later I took Naya to the maternity home again. Although I am not superstitious, I observed all the customs ordained by people who know about these things – which included putting an axe and a man's peaked cap under the pillow. Friends of mine who are experts in such matters assured me that now my wife was certain to have a boy. None of these well tried devices worked, however, and we had another daughter – Tanya. She was a very gentle, smiling baby; she takes after her mother, I think, while Lena, our elder daughter, is more like me.

I must confess that I don't remember too many details of their childhood, such as when they first started to walk and talk, or the rare moments when I tried to help in bringing them up. The reason is that I was working almost round the clock, and we would only all meet on Sunday afternoons, when we had a big family lunch together. When my daughters grew a little older, we would arrange family parties in a restaurant, which they loved. The Great Urals restaurant was never very full in the daytime, and there we would order lunch – always finishing with ice-cream, a matter of particular importance for Lena and Tanya.

My girls have always treated me in a special way, affectionately and tenderly; they have always, it seems, wanted to please me. Both did well at school, always getting '5's, the top mark; I had told them at the start, when they first went to school, that a '4' was not a mark worth getting. Both worked hard, and generally speaking their upbringing caused no particular worries. There were, of course, the usual domestic problems from which everyone suffers; sometimes there was a lack of this, that or the other; there were sleepless nights when one of them was ill – but then that is ordinary, normal life.

Ever since our marriage, my wife and I have always spent our holidays together. Once, I remember, I went alone to Kislovodsk, a spa in the North Caucasus; we felt the girls were still too young to take with us, so Naya stayed at home with them. But after only five days I sent her a telegram, 'Come at once. Can't stand it.' Somehow Naya arranged for someone to look after the girls and she flew south to join me. We rented a private flat and once more we spent all our time together; from the time our daughters were six and eight, however, all four of us would spend our holidays camping in a forest by the edge of a lake. For me, those were our best and most memorable holidays.

When the children were older, we took a steamer trip down the Kama and Volga rivers, stopping at Gelendzhika, where we set up a whole tent-village. To this day I remember those holidays we spent in the wild, like savages: there was nothing but laughter from morning till night; we spent our whole time inventing funny games and quizzes and playing practical jokes. That was a real holiday, when one could relax psychologically – quite unlike the holidays I have now, when from almost the first day of my leave I can't stop thinking about work, work, work all the time. Nowadays people say that I seldom smile; perhaps it is true, although I am by nature an optimist.

When the girls were at school, I never once went to the parent-teacher meetings or parents' get-togethers. After school, Lena went to the Urals Polytechnic, where she followed in her father's footsteps by graduating from the faculty of civil engineering. She is now working at an exhibition of construction technology and methods. My younger daughter, however, was interested in mathematics and cybernetics, and when she left school she decided to go to Moscow University to study in the faculty of mathematical computation and cybernetics. I did not try to dissuade Tanya from going to Moscow, although my wife didn't like the idea at all. She would weep, convinced that Tanya would find living alone in Moscow very difficult. Even so, despite her gentle nature, our daughter proved to be very insistent; she had her way. I used to go to Moscow fairly often on business, thus we still saw a lot of each other. After graduation she stayed in Moscow for her first job. She now works with very powerful computers, with responsibility for programming and solving large, complex problems. So she has got the kind of job she wanted, and I think she is satisfied with it.

Lena met and married Valera Okulov, an aircraft navigator based in Sverdlovsk. Tanya's husband's name is Lyosha Dyachenko. Both my sons-in-law are good lads, and although they never call me father, I nevertheless regard my daughters' husbands as my children too. We are all together now, one big family, living in Moscow. The relationships between both young couples are excellent, based on kindness and mutual respect; I think they are sincerely to be envied. Lena was the first to give me a grand-daughter, Katya; then Tanya had a boy – Boris. As is possible under Soviet law Boris retains my surname – Yeltsin. I am very grateful to my children for this gesture; now there are two Boris Yeltsins in the world, the younger being my grandson. Lena has since had another baby daughter, Mashenka, who is a sweet, placid, happy child. Katya is different: lively, restless and bright. Young Boris is very energetic; he took up sport at an early age and began playing tennis at the age of seven. Now he plays in the Dynamo sports club and is also learning judo.

We share a flat with Tanya and her family. My older daughter and her family live separately, but being not far away they often come to see us, and sometimes we dine together. The fact is that I always get home late and can only see them all on Sundays. For me it is a real occasion when our whole big family gathers together. They are all concerned about me and very attentive, especially since I am always being bothered by my work. I am constantly having a fight with someone, often have sleepless nights and, as always, I sleep very little. I sense their distress and their sympathy for my problems; without that support, I doubt if I could have survived life's most difficult moments.

At the plenum in June 1985 I was elected secretary of the central committee responsible for the construction industry. To be honest, I felt no particular emotion at this; I considered it to be a natural progression and that this was a real job which measured up to my abilities and experience. And I was to see how the uppermost echelon of government lives in our country.

As a section chief I had been allowed a small weekend *dacha* in the country (one shared between two families), but now as the head of a department of the central committee, I was offered the *dacha* which Gorbachov had vacated; he had moved into a new one built specially for him.

I made plans for trips to various republics and provinces – to the provinces of Moscow and Leningrad, to the Far East, to Turkmenia, to Armenia, Tyumen province in Siberia and to other parts of the country. I also made another trip, to visit Tashkent for a plenum of the central committee of the Communist Party of Uzbekistan. A lot of people in the city had got to hear of my arrival, and consequently they very soon gathered outside my hotel, demanding to be allowed to come in and talk to me. The authorities, of course, began to chase them away, but I said that over the next two days I would see anyone who asked for an interview with me. And I asked my bodyguard to see to it that all those wishing to talk to me really were let in.

The first person to call on me was a member of the KGB, who told me about the appalling level of bribery that flourished in Uzbekistan. He said that after Sharaf Rashidov had been dismissed for gross corruption from his post as first secretary of the Uzbek Communist Party, nothing had really changed; Usmankhodzhaev, the new secretary, was taking quite as many bribes as his predecessor. This KGB official brought with him documents containing serious evidence against Usmankhodzhaev. He asked for my help. Only Moscow could do what was necessary, he said; here, on the spot, the least attempt to take any sort of action met the resistance of a corrupt *apparat*. I promised to read the documents carefully, and if what they revealed really was serious, I would report on the matter at the very top. He was followed by an endless stream of visitors, who kept on coming for two successive days. I listened to what seemed totally improbable but in actual fact entirely real stories of bribery in the highest echelon of the Uzbek Communist Party.

From all these stories there emerged a coherent system of corruption among a range of officials from top to bottom, in which an honest person needed real courage not to get caught up in the chain of bribery. It was precisely such honest people, in the main, who had come to see me. Nowadays these matters are reasonably well known, but at the time the picture that was revealed shocked me. I resolved to tell Gorbachov about it all as soon as I returned to Moscow.

As I travelled around the country, another event occurred which was symptomatic. I asked to pay the bill for the food and drink I had consumed in the hotel, and to my amazement, I was told it had already been paid. I asked the senior man in my bodyguard to explain to my hospitable hosts that I was not in the mood for jokes and that they must give me a proper bill. He came back looking depressed after a clearly embarrassing talk with the hotel staff, saying that there would be no bill because my food and drink had been paid for from a special fund held by the central committee of that republic. He had checked out this information and it was correct. Unable to restrain myself, almost shouting, I demanded to have my bill.

On the flight back to Moscow I carefully studied all the documents given to me by the KGB official and went to see Gorbachov. I gave him a detailed account of everything that I had found out, and ended by saying that firm action should be taken immediately, and above all that the accusations against Usmankhodzhaev must be investigated. Suddenly Gorbachov lost his temper, saying that I knew nothing about these matters, that Usmankhodzhaev was an honest communist, and that because he had been obliged to wage a campaign against Rashidov's reign of corruption the old mafia was trying to compromise him with false denunciations and slanderous rumours. I countered by repeating that I was only just back from Tashkent, and that Usmankhodzhaev had simply taken over Rashidov's system and was lining his pockets by utilising a machinery of corruption which he didn't even create himself. Gorbachov replied that I had been fooled, and that anyway Ligachov himself had personally vouched for Usmankhodzhaev. I had no answer to that; the fact that he had been given a clean bill by the no. 2 man in the whole party – as Ligachov then was – was a serious matter. Before leaving, I simply asked Gorbachov to take another close look at this serious matter. After my resignation from the Politbureau and the central committee, Usmankhodzhaev was sacked from his job, arrested, tried and convicted.

But I have run on too far and too fast. Those events were to happen later. Meanwhile I had been working as a secretary of the central committee for several months and was trying to draw up a realistic programme which might help the construction industry to get out of a crisis. I did not suspect that my fate was already decided. The telephone rang in my office. I was required to go at once to the Politbureau.

5

Chronicle of the Election Campaign

6 March 1989

As I watched my enemies make one mistake after another in their fight against me, I used to wonder what I would do if I were put in charge of a campaign to scupper Yeltsin as an election candidate for a people's deputy. Certainly I know very well what stupid errors I would not make. To start with I would remove the shroud of secrecy and mystery from the name of Yeltsin; he should be treated as just another ordinary candidate, like Ivanov or Petrov. I would immediately allow – no, I would force – every newspaper and magazine to interview him at least twice; in a month everyone would be bored to death with him. And, of course, I would make sure that he was often seen on television, on every suitable – and unsuitable – programme, such as *Countryside News*, *I Serve the Soviet Union* (a programme for the armed forces), *Viewpoint*, *Time* (news and comment on current affairs) and *Musical Roundabout*, until before long the electorate would be absolutely fed up with hearing his thoughts and ideas. Then I might have a hope of sabotaging the election chances of the undesirable Yeltsin.

In reality, everything has been done to give my name a martyr's halo, which gets brighter every day. The official press has kept silent about me, and the only interviews with me to be heard are those broadcast by Western radio stations. Every new move made against me only makes the Moscow voters more and more indignant; and since there have been a lot of such moves, the upshot is that my enemies have been doing everything possible to ensure that Yeltsin is elected deputy for the Moscow city no. 1 constituency.

Many people have asked me, almost seriously, whether in fact Lev Zaikov, my successor as first secretary of the Moscow city committee of the party, was not perhaps my secret supporter or the eleventh member of my team of ten campaign aides. At all events, everyone advises me that when polling is over and I have been elected, I must be sure to telephone Zaikov and thank him for the 'enormous help and support' that he has given me during the election campaign. Total ignorance of the laws of human behaviour and a complete inability to gauge people's reactions have invariably led my enemies to achieve the exact opposite of what they intended.

Western correspondents have often asked me whether I have worked out any particular tactics in my election campaign, whether I have any secrets, as it were, which might secure my hoped-for victory at the polls. Simple-minded though it may sound, I have had only one tactical weapon in the campaign – common sense. In practice, this meant never doing or saying anything which in any way might insult or denigrate my opponent, Brakov; at walkabouts and at meetings only ever to tell the truth, however uncomfortable or detrimental it might be for me; to be utterly frank; and, most important of all, always to sense people's thoughts and feelings.

Almost every day I held meetings with huge groups of people, and during the last month before polling day I even attended two such meetings daily. This was exhausting, but filled me with an inner charge of confidence that all would be well. And the main aim was not even that I should win; that was my personal objective. I was beginning to feel sure that with people like these, who had such a genuine hunger to see that justice and good should be done, we were bound, in spite of everything, to haul ourselves out of the midden in which we found ourselves.

Organised meetings I liked much less, especially with an audience of several thousand. There were occasions when up to a hundred thousand people gathered in Moscow's Luzhniki stadium and in those conditions you can't make out individual faces, you can't even see people's eyes. Nevertheless, I admit that such meetings are probably one of the hardest and most important schools for a politician. There, with words alone, one has to seize the attention of a vast mass of people; one false remark and you can be driven from the rostrum. Personally I regret that Gorbachov does not take part in such big meetings. He would find it more than useful. Accustomed as he is to talking to specially prepared, selected people, brought in by the bus-load to represent the toiling masses, the experience of holding those meetings at Luzhniki would be a most valuable lesson for him. Perhaps one of these days he will actually do it.

Mass meetings are a very dangerous weapon in political battle. People don't restrain their emotions and they don't use parliamentary language. Consequently, a speech made at such a meeting must be precisely worded and all the more carefully weighed up in advance. It is hard for me to be exact, but I have probably taken part in as many as twenty large meetings, each one attended by several thousand people. Complex feelings are aroused when a huge mass of people catch sight of you and start rhythmically chanting, 'Yeltsin! Yeltsin!' Men, women, young, old – to be honest, though, I feel no pleasure or elation at such moments. It is necessary to go up to the rostrum as quickly as possible, to take the microphone and to start to speak, in order to calm the wave of excitement and euphoria. When people start listening, then the atmosphere changes. I regard such enthusiasm with a certain inner caution, because we all know only too well how easily people can be thrilled, and then can equally easily lose faith in you. For that reason it is better not to fall prey to any false illusions. After meetings I would often get into arguments with my trusted supporters, who considered that the louder people chanted my name the greater the success of the meeting. That is nonsense.

But my campaign helpers and supporters are another story altogether. I shall always be grateful to them for their selfless support, their sincerity, devotion and loyalty. Many people asserted that I was making a terrible mistake by choosing as my campaign aides people who were not professionals – not politicians, not experts, but plain, intelligent, decent human beings. I knew none of them before the election campaign started; they either rang up or came to see me, saying that they wanted to be my campaign assistants. I was grateful for this, but warned them that it would be extremely tough going. They knew this, of course, and many were dedicated enough to have taken unpaid leave to help in my campaign. And they worked, without exaggeration, literally night and day. In charge of my campaign helpers was Lev Yevgenievich Sukhanov, a dedicated man, who took on the enormous task of co-ordinating my election campaign. They are wonderful people and I cannot thank them enough.

———

'What were the shortcomings in your work as first secretary of the Moscow city committee? Was authoritarianism one of them?'*

'Is it true that at your first meeting with the people of Moscow you received letters from party mafiosi and their wives, promising to "rip the feeble sails of *perestroika* into shreds?"'*

On 22 December 1985, I was summoned to the Politbureau. I did not know what the topic of conversation would be, but when I saw that the room contained no central-committee secretaries and only members of the Politbureau, I realised that the subject of this meeting was myself. Gorbachov began by saying that the Politbureau had discussed the matter and had decided that I, Yeltsin, should take over as head of the Moscow city committee of the Communist Party – an organisation of almost 1,200,000 party members and a city with nine million inhabitants. This was totally unexpected. I stood up and began expressing my doubts as to whether I was the right man for the job. First of all, I was a civil engineer by profession and had spent considerable time working in the construction industry. I still had a number of plans and some as yet unfinished projects for getting the industry out of the blind alley in which it found itself. I felt that I would be more useful if I continued my work as a secretary of the central committee. Furthermore, I knew very little of the people in the Moscow party organisation, and I would find the job very difficult.

Gorbachov and the other Politbureau members started to try and

* (From questions handed up from the floor at meetings during the election campaign.)

88

persuade me that my appointment was very necessary; that Viktor Grishin, the incumbent, had to be replaced; that the Moscow party organisation was in a state of decrepitude; that its working style and methods were such that not only did it not set an example but it was also, in fact, trailing behind the other party organisations in the country. Grishin, they declared, gave no thought to people and their pressing needs; he had let the work slide, being only concerned with outward show and putting on spectacular public events – noisy, carefully rehearsed and organised, the sort of events where everyone read their lines from sheets of paper. All in all, a rescue operation on the Moscow party organisation had to be mounted.

The discussion in the Politbureau turned out to be a difficult one, even embarrassing. Again I was told that there was such a thing as party discipline; that they considered I would be more useful to the party in Moscow. Finally, after forcing myself to admit that the Moscow party organisation certainly could not be left in its present state, and while still suggesting the names of other people who might be given the job, I accepted the appointment.

Since then, I have often wondered why Gorbachov came to choose me as his candidate for the job. Evidently he took account of my ten-years' experience at Sverdlovsk in leading one of the largest party organisations in the country, as well as my stint in industry. Furthermore, he knew my character and no doubt felt certain I would be able to clear away the old debris, to fight the mafia, and that I was tough enough to carry out a wholesale clean-up of the personnel. All this had been decided in advance. At that time I suppose I really was the most suitable candidate for the purposes that he had in mind. I agreed to accept the post, but with misgivings – not because I was afraid of the difficulties ahead, but because I fully realised that I was being used as the means of levering Grishin out of the job. Grishin was a man of no great intellect, and he lacked any kind of moral sense or decency. Instead, he was a mixture of bombast and servility; he knew, at any time, exactly what needed to be done in order to curry favour with the leadership. A man with an extremely high opinion of himself, he was laying plans to get himself eventually made general secretary, and was trying to do everything possible to prepare to take power. But, thank god, he was prevented from doing this. He had corrupted many people in the leadership of the Moscow city committee, although fortunately not the whole Moscow party organisation.

Authoritarianism exerted by someone lacking in intelligence is a terrible thing. Its effect was felt in all public affairs, on the people's standard of living, and on Moscow's outward appearance. Life in the capital was worse than it had been several decades ago: dirt, endless queues, overcrowded public transport.

On 24 December Gorbachov spoke at a plenum of the Moscow city committee. Grishin was dismissed – as usual, he 'retired at his own request as he was of pensionable age', the classic, stereotypical phrase for putting an unwanted politician out to grass. He proposed my candidacy as his successor, which, as far as I remember, surprised no one and evoked no questions. Literally in one sentence I expressed my gratitude for the party's confidence in me, adding that I promised them nothing but hard and difficult work ahead. The plenum then took its otherwise uneventful course.

A conference of the Moscow party organisation, to hear reports and elect new officials, was set for the following February, and I suspected that the main battle would take place then. Grishin's 'old guard' would try and reverse the course of events, and not only in Moscow. I had to concentrate on preparing for that conference. As part of the work on my report, I met dozens of people, visited enterprises all over the capital in order to analyse their problems, and in consultation with specialists I tried to find the best way out of what was a state of crisis. My report to the conference lasted two hours, and when I had finished Gorbachov said, 'You have brought in a strong and welcome gush of fresh air,' although he spoke without an approving smile and with an impassive expression on his face.

We had to start practically from zero. The first thing was to change the staff of the city committee's bureau, since it was full of Grishin's placemen. Grishin had long since become an empty, inflated bladder. He had never had any authority, and now that *perestroika* was gathering momentum his presence in the Polit-bureau simply compromised the party's highest decision-making body. Gorbachov had never acted very decisively, and in Grishin's case, too, he had procrastinated; the man should have been sacked earlier. When I started tackling the mess in Moscow, which he and his people had allowed to pile up, Grishin outwardly raised no objections. I was told that he was indignant over some of the things I did, but that was only talk; he never made any specific moves to cause me trouble.

With my parents, Klavdia Vasilievna and Nikolai Ignatievich

With my parents and brother, 1939

With my sister, 1952

Students relaxing

Provincials in Moscow, early 1950s

As coach of the polytechnic women's volley-ball team

1 May celebrations, 1960, with daughter Lena

Central-committee party secretary on construction site, 1985

First secretary potato picking in Sverdlovsk province

ЬI С САХАРОВЫ

Campaigning for Sakharov, spring 1989

A new hobby: tennis

With Naya, Tanya and little Boris, autumn 1989

The two Boris Yeltsins

Tanya embraces her beloved father

Campaigning, pre-election, 1989

I thank Alexei Kazannik for ceding his Supreme Soviet seat to me

Some fans go to
extreme lengths:
an icon in honour
of Boris Yeltsin

Making a
point while
Lenin looks on

Attempts were made to incriminate him in various shady deals, but the officials of the law-enforcement agencies were unable to discover any compromising evidence against him. I was told that it had obviously been destroyed. I do not rule out that possibility, because we couldn't even find the documents attesting to his entry into the party, and these, of all things, must have existed. Altogether, there was a mass of rumours about Grishin, but they were never confirmed. When I took over the job, his safes were empty. There may have been some evidence against him at KGB headquarters, but I just don't know.

I had guessed he would try and obstruct me, especially in the matter of personnel changes, and indeed he did try to do this, by recommending his man as chairman of the executive committee of the Moscow Soviet, which he engineered through other people. Every time a key post came up for replacement, I always wondered whether one of Grishin's men would be eased into the job, and I took certain steps to exclude any possibility of this happening. In my view, the permanent staff of the city committee, especially people who had worked for a long time under Grishin, should be replaced. These *apparatchiki* were infected with all the vices of the Brezhnev era: toadyism, servility and boot-licking. These attitudes had become thoroughly ingrained; there could be no question of trying to re-educate them and they simply had to be dismissed and replaced. And this I did.

My assistants (inherited from Grishin) I sacked at once, while the staff of the bureau and the *apparat* of the city committee were replaced slowly but surely. I began looking for people to replace them. Vasily Zakharov was recommended to me at the central committee as second secretary; he had recently been working in the science department of the central committee, and before that as a secretary of the Leningrad committee of the party.

The incumbent chairman of the executive committee of the Moscow Soviet was Promyslov, a man notorious not only to Muscovites. A not-unfounded joke about him used to circulate, 'Promyslov made a short stop-over in Moscow, while flying from Washington to Tokyo.' He came to see me on the day after my election and while still standing in the doorway he began to tell me how impossible it had been to work under Grishin, followed by a lot more unflattering remarks about him. Then, without drawing breath, he went on to say how glad he was that I was now first secretary. Finally he announced that he had miraculously got his second wind; he was full of energy which would undoubtedly last for at least another five years. I had to stop him and inform him that the news I had for him was rather different. I said fairly harshly that he was to be retired – but decently, 'at his own request'. He tried to make a few more flattering remarks to me, but I asked him to bring me his resignation at noon the next day and as he went out I urged him not to be late. He did not come at noon the next day, so I phoned him and mentioned that he had obviously paid no attention to my phrasing: I had proposed that he be retired 'decently', but there were, of course, other ways of doing it. He understood, and twenty minutes later he brought me his letter of resignation.

Over the next two days, four groups of people proposed four candidates for the post of chairman of the Moscow Soviet. Each group, I realised, was pushing its own man. Everyone knows what an important figure the chairman of the city soviet is – he is the mayor of the city, and much depends on him and I decided to use an unconventional method of selection. I went to the ZIL automobile factory, where I stayed from 8 a.m. till 2 a.m. the following morning. I walked round the workshops, met workers, specialists, active party members, designers and section foremen. But that was only one aspect of my visit. I also made the acquaintance of Valery Saikin, the general manager. As I toured the factory with him, I tried not to miss the slightest detail: how he talked to the workers, to the secretary of the party committee, to me. After a few days, I came to the conclusion that he would make a good chairman of the city soviet; not immediately, of course, as he would need help and support while he worked himself into this new and very different job. I discussed my idea by telephone with Gorbachov. He approved of it and although Saikin did not accept at once, he eventually agreed to take on the post, after giving it some thought. I continued my shake-up of the city committee by replacing all of the secretaries.

I then made a visit to the editorial offices of the newspaper *Moskovskaya Pravda* (*Moscow Pravda*), where I met the entire staff, and talked frankly with them for more than four hours. The newspaper had just acquired a new editor-in-chief, Mikhail Poltoranin, who had previously worked on *Pravda*. This honest and talented journalist had immediately changed the atmosphere of the paper. Articles were published which alarmed and frightened many people.

I remember, for instance, a feature entitled 'Carriages at the Door', which concerned the misuse of their official cars by party and government functionaries; it created a big rumpus in Moscow at the time. The articles were not only hard hitting; I would say they were very daring for those days. Poltoranin was summoned to the central committee, and before going there he telephoned to ask me what I thought of the article. I said I thought it was perfectly acceptable.

An equally stormy reaction was produced by the publication in the *Moskovsky Komsomoletz* (*Moscow Komsomol*) of articles on drug-addiction, prostitution and organised crime – subjects about which nothing had ever been written before. In general the Moscow city newspapers had stopped being discreet and obedient, which I welcomed. When people tried to persuade me that it was a bad thing to be so critical and to expose Moscow's problems – because it was the capital and the country's 'shop-window' – I responded by asking whether or not these negative phenomena existed. On being assured that they did, I suggested that by concealing these sore points we were not healing them but merely covering them up with sweet-smelling cream so that they wouldn't be visible. Any such social evils must be brought out into the open, however painful this may be.

I also had several meetings with the production staffs of Moscow's television. They had just moved into new offices and a new editor of news and current affairs had also been appointed. A number of interesting programmes began to be shown, in particular, and most importantly, *Moscow and the Muscovites* and *Good Evening, Moscow*. Moscow's television has livened up considerably as a result.

As might be expected, the new-style Moscow press and television very soon produced a strongly negative reaction to their output. I have already mentioned how Poltoranin was summoned to the central committee; this happened more than once. One day he was kept waiting for several hours outside the office of some highly placed bureaucrat, which was disgraceful. I defended him in every way I could. People kept complaining to Gorbachov, and one day, during a session of the Politbureau, he said to me, 'He's done it again, your Poltoranin!' To which I replied, 'Our Poltoranin runs a good newspaper, its circulation is going up all the time. You'd do better to keep an eye on Yuri Afanasiev.' (The editor of *Pravda*, which is the official and principal national newspaper of the central committee of the Communist Party.) At that time it had already become obvious that subscriptions to *Pravda* were falling off, despite the fact that every member of the Communist Party was obliged to take out a subscription to *Pravda*. When I was eventually dismissed from my job as first secretary of the Moscow party organisation in 1988, it soon became obvious that Poltoranin would not last much longer in his job, and indeed he was very soon given the sack.

But all that happened much later. Meanwhile, we continued fighting on Moscow's behalf. In 1985 absolutely everything was in a state of neglect. The city had fallen behind in attaining practically all the targets that had been set in 1972 in the general plan for the development of Moscow. As a result of workers migrating to the city from all over the country (so that about 700,000 people had been drawn into the capital), it turned out that by 1986 the actual population of Moscow exceeded the projected figure by 1,100,000. If to that one added short-term visitors numbering some three million a month in summer and two million a month in winter, and for which no provision had been made in the city's public services, then the result was the lamentable picture which we could all see with our own eyes: more queues and dirt, with the Metro and surface transport all overcrowded. The city's entire existence was literally at the outer limits of its physical capacity and the situation in Moscow's cultural life was equally bad. The number of theatre seats per thousand inhabitants was actually less than it was in 1917.

At the start of my period of office in Moscow, at least during my first year, the secretaries of the central committee and the members of the Politbureau did try to help, especially since Gorbachov was constantly urging them to do so. It was then, in fact, that I conceived the idea of organising fairs. I did not want them to be just one-off events, but was concerned that they should be a permanent feature of the city and thus provide a constant source of enjoyment both for Muscovites and visitors. Stalls and amusement-stands were set up on empty sites and contracts were signed directly with other cities and republics to supply fruit and vegetables. The fairs began. Not all of them were a success, but in many districts they became really pleasant places for family outings. This was all the more important because Moscow clearly lacked adequate public holidays and places of simple, cheap entertainment. The fairs have lived on to this day and Moscow people have grown used to them. They regard them, I think, as their own creation and could now hardly imagine life in Moscow without them.

I also introduced several traditions into Moscow which were customary in Sverdlovsk, one of which was for me to meet the city's inhabitants. One of the first of these was an encounter with the people who conveyed information and propaganda to the public on behalf of the party. About two thousand people were gathered in the great hall of the House of Political Education. First I made a speech, then offered to answer questions which people might like to put to me – any questions, even the most hostile. Fortunately there were not many of the latter, but there were a few, such as this one, 'You, Yeltsin, have started to tackle the Moscow mafia. We've been through this before – Khrushchev wanted to pack us all off to the labour-camps and we all know what became of that. If you go on like this, someone else will have your job in two years' time.' The funny thing is that this prediction was fulfilled: exactly two years later I was dismissed from the post of first secretary of the Moscow city committee of the party and from the Politbureau. Although I don't think the mafia had anything to do with that; it was a pure coincidence.

Nevertheless, there were a few instances of the mafia at work and I began receiving a mass of letters denouncing bribery and corruption in the retail trade and in the police. They were investigated, but the investigators couldn't – or wouldn't – uncover the system itself. The investigative departments of the ministry of internal affairs (responsible for the police) and the Moscow division of the KGB were brought in to help, as were the newly appointed heads of the trading network and the organisation responsible for Moscow's restaurants. We began replacing management personnel, but we still couldn't penetrate the closed circle. Yet more and more facts accumulated; people saw things and wrote to us about them, but mainly anonymously. I shall mention the cases that I encountered personally. One after another came the complaints about a particular chain of butcher's shops, involving the inflation of the number of slaughtered animals, in order to give the slaughterhouse workers more pay; in addition there was widespread bribery and theft. And it was all happening under the protection of the first secretary of a certain district. As a result the matter came up for discussion in the bureau of the city committee.

I discovered that a butcher's shop had received a delivery of veal, so I went and stood in the queue (it was still in the first few months of my spell in office and not many people knew my face). When it came to my turn at the counter I asked for a kilo of veal. The shop assistant replied that there was beef, but no veal, while I countered that this was not true and asked to see the manager. One or two people in the queue realised who I was and started kicking up a row. I insisted on being taken through to the back of the shop, and there in a room was the veal, which was being passed out through a back window to a van waiting outside. There was an almighty fuss and the management was sacked.

A second incident arose in a factory canteen when I asked why there were no carrots and was told that none had been delivered. Together with the factory management, I checked out the story. The carrots had been delivered, but they had been spirited away to an unknown destination on the same day. All this was told to us by the porters who unloaded the supplies and there were no documents that might have proved something; it was all very efficiently covered up.

And there was corruption again, this time in the manageress's office of a grocery store where mystery surrounded a large quantity of packages containing various delicacies. When I queried their allocation, I was told that they were outside orders awaiting delivery. I was greeted with silence when I asked if anyone could place an order. Then we began to question the manageress. She was forced to admit that the orders were distributed, on hierarchical lines, to officials of the district executive committee of the soviet, the ministry of foreign affairs, the district committee of the party and municipal offices. They were all different in contents, weight and quality. On examining the city's total balance-sheet for a series of grocery and delicatessen foods, I discovered an anomaly. Judging by the official statistics of consumption, several tonnes more of each item were brought into the city than were eaten, even after accounting for natural wastage.

No one, as a rule, ever reveals the workings of the system. But I did have a stroke of luck. By now many people knew that I often went into shops, markets and distribution depots; they knew what I was looking for, but were clearly afraid to come forward. Then one day as I was walking out of a shop, a young girl caught me up in the street. She said that she had something of the greatest importance to tell me. There and then I named a date and a time when she could come and see me in my office at the city committee. To this day I cannot recall her story of bribes and backhanders without a feeling of indignation. She had only just been drawn into the system and was unable to tolerate it. It was all amazingly well thought out. Each salesperson was 'obliged' to overcharge the customer and hand a certain sum each day to the supervisor, who kept part of it for himself and gave a part to the general manager of the store. Thereafter the money was shared out among the management, from top to bottom, and if you had to go to the distribution depot, the staff there also required payment of backhanders according to an agreed scale. Every employee knew two or three people in the chain. In the wholesale trade there was another, and much bigger, scale of kickbacks that had to be paid.

I did all I could to ensure that the girl was not recognised and victimised. She was extremely frightened and begged to be protected. After a while she was transferred to another shop. I then called together a circle of close colleagues and we decided to carry out a programme of dismissal and replacement: we would not just sack individual culprits but the managerial staff of whole sectors of the retail trade, of whole stores, whole departments, and whole sections of the work-force at distribution depots. We would replace them with young, 'uninfected' staff. In a period of just over a year, about 800 people were tried and convicted of criminal offences. But that was only part of the mafia. We were never able to get our hands on the really big operators in the 'black economy', which represents up to 15 per cent of the gross turnover of goods in the country's retail network, neither could we touch the top end of the mafia, with its links to politicians. We did not have enough time. My period of two years came to an end. In retrospect, my impression is that the Moscow city committee has lost much of its zeal for tackling this problem.

No one had the least doubt that we were faced with a lot of extremely hard work. Of the thirty-three first secretaries of district committees, twenty-three had to be replaced. Not all of them left their jobs, because they couldn't cope with them; some were promoted. Others were obliged to vacate their posts after a frank and very tough talk, either with me or the bureau of the city committee or at a plenum of the district committee. Most of them agreed that they were unable to work in a new way. Some had to be persuaded of this. Altogether it was an unpleasant, painful process.

The replacements were not always well chosen or irreproachable. It transpired that we had made several unsatisfactory replacements of people who failed to improve the style of work and the state of affairs in their districts. This happened for various reasons: first, as I have already mentioned, because I didn't know the Moscow party personnel well enough, and second, because a faulty practice had developed of selecting people for jobs purely on the basis of the questionnaires they submitted and their previous appointments. Essentially, this means that one doesn't promote the man but his curriculum vitae and consequently mistakes were made. Subsequently I was criticised for dealing harshly with the first secretaries, by sacking them right, left and centre. A later analysis of the situation revealed, however, that during my period in office, just 60 per cent of the first secretaries of district committees in Moscow were sacked. Yet under Gorbachov some 66 per cent of the first secretaries of provincial committees were replaced, so Comrade Gorbachov and I might well argue over which of us overdid things on the personnel question.

But the whole point was that both for him and for me there was no alternative but to replace the officials who were putting the brakes on the process of *perestroika*. They were all people hopelessly tainted with the Brezhnevite philosophy of stagnation, who perceived the power they were given as nothing but a means of achieving personal prosperity and grandeur. They were nothing but tinpot lords of their little fiefs. How could it have been possible to allow them to keep their jobs? At least if one judges by the severity with which my personnel policy was subsequently criticised, apparently they should have been left in place.

The tragic case of the former first secretary of the Kiev district committee of the Moscow party made a very painful impression on me. Six months after leaving the district committee, he was working in the ministry of non-ferrous metals as deputy head of the personnel department where, as far as anyone could see, the job suited him perfectly well. Then, completely unexpectedly, after a telephone call, he committed suicide by throwing himself out of a seventh-storey window. Later, when I was out of favour and started being persecuted, someone tried to use this tragic incident for their own ends, claiming that this man had committed suicide because I had dismissed him from his post. A legend was concocted, according to which he had come out of a discussion in my office and then jumped out of the window. This was an absolute lie; but what amazed me most was the fact that people were even prepared to use a man's death as a trump card against me.

There is another episode from my hectic days in the post of first secretary, of which people were to remind me long afterwards. Some senior official of the ministry of internal affairs telephoned me and announced, in a voice close to panic, that *Pamyat* (Memory) was assembling in the centre of Moscow, complete with slogans on placards, and were voicing certain demands.

It was the first unsanctioned mass demonstration to be held in Moscow for more than half a century. About three or four hundred people – perhaps as many as five hundred – had gathered in October Square. They stood there for a long time and unfurled banners with slogans of an entirely proper kind: something about *perestroika*, Russia, freedom, the rottenness of the *apparat* – and one which read 'We demand to see Yeltsin or Gorbachov.' Valery Saikin had been to see them several times, but the demonstrators refused to disperse. Several hours passed. The crowd began to grow. Something had to be done.

Since until now only two public demonstrations have been allowed to be held – on 1 May and on 7 November, and despite the constitution, which actually guarantees the right of peaceful demonstration – there existed a tried and tested method of dealing with this kind of event. The police should have been called out to surround the demonstrators and demand that they disperse. And if they wouldn't disperse, the police would start to break up the meeting, twisting arms and arresting people. In any case the result would be to bring the affair to a satisfactory end.

I decided to act differently. I said I would go and meet them and since then my – to put it mildly – ill-wishers have accused me of being friendly with *Pamyat*. If the demonstrators had received a few cracks over the head with truncheons, that would have appeased my opponents. I instructed Saikin to tell their leaders – I believe the organisation was then headed by Vasiliev – that I agreed to meet them. I gave them a choice of three venues: the House of Soviets; the city committee of the party; or the House of Political Education. They chose the House of Soviets and went there on foot into the big hall, which can seat nearly a thousand people. When they had all sat down, I proposed that they should declare the objectives of their organisation, so that we might find out what they wanted.

Several people got up and spoke. Some of their ideas were sound, such as the need to preserve the Russian language; objections to the distortion of Russian history; and the need to preserve historic buildings. There were also some extremist remarks. When they had finished, I spoke, saying that if they were really concerned about the fate of *perestroika* and of the country in general and not about their own political ambitions, they should start by dealing with the extremists in their own ranks. I asked them to bring me their programme, the rules of the organisation, and said that if they were prepared to act within the framework of the constitution, then they should register themselves as an officially recognised 'social organisation' and start work. And that, effectively, was the extent of my dealings with *Pamyat*. Subsequently, they showed little interest in such things as the framework of the constitution and the rules of their organisation. A sizeable group broke away from the organisation. For my part, I never had anything further to do with *Pamyat*.

At that moment we were all working with an unusual degree of enthusiasm. The national leadership not only had confidence in me, but was also helping us, realising the importance of Moscow and how essential it was to bring order into the administration of the capital city. The heads of the Moscow section of the ministry of internal affairs, of the KGB, and their deputies were all replaced, as were several other heads of administrative departments.

I demanded that the heads of the appropriate departments of the ministry of internal affairs and of the KGB should regularly report to me on the situation and on any unusual occurrences in the city. At the same time I tried to help them by mobilising public opinion, party organisations, the soviets and industrial enterprises to assist the law-enforcement agencies in bringing order into the life of the city. We conducted regular raids throughout Moscow, by putting all the police forces of the city on a state of alert. District by district, they did the rounds of every courtyard, every cellar, every attic and every derelict building. These raids produced some good results. Apart from flushing out hotbeds of crime and dens of alcoholics, parasites, addicts and drug-pushers, they also had the effect – to the surprise of the police, I believe – of running to earth criminals who were wanted nationwide. The main thing was that the raids were not just put on for show or as part of some one-off campaign, but were kept up permanently. We altered their frequency, making sure that they were not regular or predictable, so that people who had anything to fear from the police were unable to adapt their movements to these 'purges' of the city.

As I have already mentioned, Moscow was positively bursting at the seams. I wanted to see with my own eyes, and not only from statistical reports, just how badly the transport system was being overloaded. I made a point of not only travelling by Metro and bus, particularly at rush-hours, but also I wanted to get a physical feel of how Muscovites travelled to work and back again.

I knew, for instance, that many of the workers at the Khrunichev factory lived out at Strogino, a newly built outer suburb. I went to Strogino at 6 a.m. where, along with the crowds of still-sleepy workers, I got on a bus, and then changed on to the Metro. Then there was a change on to another bus, and at precisely 7.15 a.m., the start of the working day, I reached the factory gates. This was only one episode; I made many such journeys, during which, many of these tired, tense, wound-up people told me a great deal about the way we, the leaders, had ruined the country. I resolved to change things for the better and certain measures were instituted. For instance the Moscow enterprises were put on a flexitime system, by which the starting times of their working day were staggered; we created new bus routes and made several other innovations.

The reaction of the Politbureau to these trips of mine by public transport was somewhat odd. They expressed no open disapproval, but echoes of their annoyance nevertheless reached me. When the right moment came to criticise me, all their pent-up feelings came pouring out. My journeys by Metro and bus were described as an attempt to gain cheap popularity. My chief aim had been to discover what was actually happening to the transport system, what needed to be done in order to ease the burden on ordinary people of travelling at rush-hours. As for this smear about 'cheap popularity', funnily enough, no one but myself seemed to want to earn it! This was strange, since it was apparently so easy to do: hop on a bus, and there's instant popularity for you! Somehow my detractors never felt the urge to try it, even those who had long since forgotten what popularity is. Of course, travelling everywhere in one's ZIL limousine is really much more convenient. Nobody treads on your toes, nobody pushes you from behind, nobody digs you in the ribs. You travel fast and without stopping, every traffic-light is at green, the policemen on point-duty salute you – it's all very pleasant. I must say, though, that this furious reaction to my journeys on Moscow's public transport was unexpected. In Sverdlovsk it was something quite normal; people somehow paid little attention to the first secretary of the provincial committee sitting in a tram. If that was how he travelled, it was because it was necessary. In Moscow, however, for some reason it became an event that aroused a storm of back-biting.

During my term in office a number of far-reaching decisions about Moscow were taken by the city committee of the party. We accepted, for instance, a Politbureau directive on the long-term development of the capital. This included the very important decision to stop recruiting workers from the *limitchiki*. This phenomenon was having a disastrous effect on Moscow. Enterprise managers, given the chance of recruiting cheap labour, used the *limitchiki* to fill the most unattractive, unskilled jobs. This bad practice retarded the modernisation of many factories, because it was so much easier to draw on the bottomless pool of labour from out of town than to update and re-equip with new, labour-saving and efficient plant.

The *limitchiki* were, in essence, the slaves of late twentieth-century, Soviet-style 'developed socialism', as they had practically no rights at all. They were bound, like serfs, to a factory or other enterprise by their temporary work-permit, by having to live in a hostel and by the cherished dream of acquiring a permanent residence-permit for Moscow. Their employers could do anything they liked with them – break the law, for example, or disregard the health and safety regulations – simply because they knew that the wretched *limitchiki* would never complain and never write letters to anyone in authority. If there was ever a hint of a complaint from them they had an unanswerable come-back, 'Any more of this, we'll deprive you of your temporary work-permit and you can go to hell.' Many of these wretched people drowned their feelings of humiliation and injustice in vodka. The districts where the *limitchiki*'s hostels were concentrated were some of the worst breeding grounds of crime. Incidentally, a few months after my dismissal, the right of various enterprises to issue temporary work-permits to people living outside the city limits was reinstated.

Another important step taken during that period was to carry out a survey to determine which enterprises should be removed from

Moscow. This concerned especially those factories and other plants which were polluting the city and which were making goods that were sent out of Moscow; these measures were an attempt to bring about a potential deindustrialisation of Moscow. Plans were also drawn up to improve the structure and utilisation of the centre of Moscow with the aim of removing many of the countless offices and devoting the centre entirely to shops, theatres, museums, restaurants and snack-bars.

Major actions were also undertaken to deal with shortcomings in the Moscow State Institute of International Relations, the ministry of foreign trade and the ministry of foreign affairs. When I received the reports of the commissions of inspection set up to investigate these august institutions, I was horrified: they were riddled with nepotism and malpractices of every kind. The state of affairs in these organisations was astounding. It reflected most precisely the essence of a society steeped in double standards of morality and blatant hypocrisy. In all the media, from every weapon in the arsenal of propaganda we hear nothing but hysterical torrents of abuse denouncing the decay of capitalism, the terrible ills of Western society and the horrors of their way of life. Yet at the same time the bosses of our party establishment were doing everything possible and impossible to get their beloved offspring into the schools and institutes which trained diplomats and other specialists whose jobs would take them abroad. They were prepared to tell any lies, invent any fairy stories about 'developed socialism', about the last death-throes of the West, just so long as they could be sent there on an official trip to enjoy a bit of capitalistic decay for a month or so, but preferably for a year or so. There they could buy tape-recorders on their daily foreign-currency allowance, sell them in second-hand shops on their return and make themselves a profit in roubles running to a row of noughts.

It was our aim to bring some proper order into these organisations, which for years had been immune to inspection and criticism. It was not too difficult with the ministry of foreign affairs; Eduard Shevardnadze was now the foreign minister and he quickly sorted out the pseudo-experts who had filled the country's principal department for the conduct of external policy. The clean-up of the Institute of International Relations and the ministry of foreign trade proceeded more slowly, but there, too, it was nevertheless put into effect, by replacing the senior party and administrative officials in those organisations. Gradually the situation improved.

Even for me, tough as I am, the pace of our work had reached the limit of my capacity. I was working from 7 a.m. till midnight, sometimes till one or two o'clock in the morning, with Saturday a full working day. On Sundays I spent half the day driving around the fairs that I had initiated or I wrote speeches and answered letters, among other tasks. Whenever I hear people say that if a boss works twenty hours out of twenty-four he is a bad organiser and doesn't know how to set up a sensible work-schedule, I simply don't take such remarks very seriously. Of course I could have left the office at 8 p.m. and gone home to my family. And that would have been regarded as a sensible way of organising my work-load. But if after work I go from the office to a shop, to see what is on the shelves; if I then go on to a factory to talk to the workers and see how the evening shift is organised; and if I then return home at midnight – is that a badly organised work schedule? No, that is only what lazy people say in self-justification. In those days I didn't know the meaning of free time.

There were times when I would drive home, my bodyguard would open the door, and I hadn't the strength to get out of the car. I would sit like that for five or ten minutes while I gathered my senses, as my wife stood in the porch looking anxiously at me. I was so worn out, I lacked even the strength to raise my hand. I naturally did not demand such a level of performance from others, but I still cannot abide those remarks about the boss who only works long hours because he doesn't know how to organise his working time.

Despite the obvious changes for the better and the surge of optimistic emotion that was galvanising the whole country, I sensed that we were beginning to run up against a brick wall; that this time round we couldn't get away with nothing but bright new phrases about *perestroika* and renewal. We needed concrete results and a few steps forward. But Gorbachov didn't want to take these steps. Most of all he was afraid of laying hands on the party's bureaucratic machine, that holy of holies of our system. In the speeches that I made at meetings with Moscow's citizens I clearly went further. All of my remarks were reported back to him and our relations began to deteriorate.

Gradually I began to sense tension in the air at Politbureau meetings, which was directed not only at me but at the issues which I raised. A certain alienation was making itself felt. The situation got noticeably worse after several clashes in the Politbureau between Ligachov and myself on the subject of perks and privileges enjoyed by party officials. I had some equally fierce arguments with him on the subject of a decree on measures to be taken on drunkenness and alcoholism, when he demanded the closure of a Moscow brewery and the curtailment of all sales of spirits, even of wine and beer.

His entire campaign against alcoholism was simply amazingly ill-conceived and ridiculous. Nothing was taken into account, neither the economic nor the social consequences. He simply plunged ahead without proper thought, and the situation got worse every day and every month. I mentioned this to Gorbachov more than once, but for some reason he adopted a wait-and-see attitude, although in my view it was quite clear that you could never conquer drunkenness, that centuries-old evil, by going at the problem with the tactics of a cavalry charge. The attacks on me grew more bitter. Solomentsev joined forces with Ligachov. Statistics from various Soviet republics were quoted at me: in the Ukraine, for example, the sales of wines and spirits had fallen by 46 per cent. I cautioned that we should be patient and assess the situation in a few months' time. Sure enough, people were soon beginning to drink anything that was liquid and contained alcohol, they started sniffing solvents and the number of illicit stills increased sharply.

Nobody was actually consuming less alcohol, but the income from the sale of spirits was not going to the state but was diverted into the black market, into the pockets of moonshiners. The number of cases of alcoholic poisoning rose catastrophically and included many that were fatal. The situation was becoming critical, yet all the time Ligachov was issuing cheerful reports on the success of his campaign. At that time he was the no. 2 man in the party, and was issuing orders to everybody right and left. It was quite impossible to convince him of anything; I could not reconcile myself to his obstinacy and dilettantism, but I got no support from anyone. The time had come to think seriously about what I should do next.

I still placed my hopes in Gorbachov, in the belief that he would realise the absurdity of a policy of half measures and marking time. I thought that his pragmatism and simply his natural intuition would be enough to tell him that the time had come to tackle the bureaucratic *apparat* head-on; that he could not succeed in pleasing both sides, the party establishment and the people, simultaneously. After all, you can't ride two horses at once. So, I requested an interview with him to have a serious talk, which lasted for two hours and twenty minutes. Recently, when I was sorting through my papers, I found a note listing the topics that we discussed at the meeting. I remembered that I had returned from it stimulated and excited and, as everything was still fresh in my memory, I had quickly noted it all down.

Effectively the last, or as they say in the theatre the third bell before curtain-up rang for me at the session of the Politbureau when we discussed the draft of Gorbachov's speech to be delivered on the seventieth anniversary of the October 1917 Revolution. The text was given out well in advance to us as members and candidate members of the Politbureau and central-committee secretaries to allow us to study it carefully.

The discussion itself was fairly brief, and went round the table in our seating order. Almost everyone felt obliged to say a few words. Basically the assessments were positive, except for a few comments on inessential points. But when it came to my turn, I firmly made about twenty separate comments, each one of which was serious and substantive. My questions concerned the party and its *apparat*; the attitudes to the past; the conception of the way the country would develop in the future, and much else besides.

Something unexpected then happened. Unable to restrain himself, Gorbachov broke off the session and stormed out of the room. For about thirty minutes, the entire membership of the Politbureau and the secretaries sat there in silence, neither knowing what to do nor how to react. When he reappeared, he started a tirade that had nothing to do with the substance of my comments, but was aimed at me personally. Evidently he was letting fly with all the thoughts, complaints and resentments that had been building up inside him over recent months. What is more, his choice of words was highly critical, almost hysterical. I wanted to leave the room in order to avoid listening to so many remarks that were close to being insults.

He said that everything in Moscow was going badly; that everyone was making a fuss over me; that a certain trait of my character was intolerable; that I never did anything but offer destructive criticism, such as the observations I had just been making to the Politbureau; that he had laboured long and hard over this draft, and that even though I knew this, I had nevertheless allowed myself the liberty of making all these negative comments. He went on talking for quite a long time. I naturally did not take note of the time but I think it was about forty minutes.

There can be no doubt that at that moment Gorbachov simply hated me. I can honestly say that I hadn't expected this. I knew that he would react to my remarks in some way or another – but that he should have done so in such terms, almost in market-porter's language, and practically without referring to the substance of anything I had said. Incidentally, a lot was subsequently changed in the text of his anniversary speech, and he did take account of some of my comments, though of course not all of them.

The others just sat tight, saying nothing and just hoping that no one would notice them. Nobody defended me, but nor did anyone attack me. It was an awkward situation. When he had finished, I got up and said that I would naturally take note of some of his remarks and consider whether they were justified, that those which were justified I would take to heart and apply them in my work, but that I did not accept the majority of his reproaches against me. I did not accept them because they were biased, and furthermore they had been expressed in unacceptable terms.

That was effectively the end of the session, and everyone departed in a downcast mood, myself most of all. But that was only the beginning. The beginning of the end. At subsequent sessions of the Politbureau he seemed to disregard me, although we met officially at least twice a week: on Thursdays at the Politbureau sessions and at some other event or conference. He even did his best to avoid shaking my hand, greeting me with a silent nod of the head, and never talking to me. I sensed that from that moment on he had decided to get me out of his hair. I was too obviously a misfit in his otherwise obedient team.

6

Chronicle of the Election Campaign

10 March 1989

I will never get used to it. Every time that I am slandered, every time someone purposely sets out to provoke me I am terribly disturbed and I suffer, although it is high time I learned to react calmly and dispassionately. But I can't! Recently several people phoned me to say that all the district committees of the party in Moscow had received an anonymous, methodical guide of ten typescript pages on how to discredit candidate Yeltsin. Very soon I was brought a copy. I forced myself to read it and was once more deeply upset. Not because the electors might desert me – I assumed that no normal, decent person would take any notice of an anonymous letter of this kind. What amazed me was the degree of poverty of thought, the evidence that our ideological *apparat* could stoop so low, could descend to such base, shameless behaviour.

I never did succeed in discovering the authorship of this pamphlet, but it must have come from a fairly highly placed source, because it was the obvious inspiration behind a number of immediate and active attempts to cause trouble for me. The district committee secretaries of the party summoned the active party members in their local enterprises and organisations to the district committee premises and read this libel to them aloud. I cannot resist quoting some of the particularly memorable passages:

'Paradoxical though it may seem he [Yeltsin], while favouring the most authoritarian methods in his handling of personnel matters, nevertheless has no qualms about joining the council of Memorial.[1] Are not his political sympathies spread too wide? Besides Memorial, whose other members include Solzhenitsyn, there is also *Pamyat*, with which he readily associated himself in 1987. Is this not flexibility of the sort which in practice amounts to a total lack of principle?'

'He is fighting hard to be elected as a people's deputy, on which he has effectively staked everything.'

'What motivates him? The interests of ordinary people? If so, why can he not defend those interests in his present ministerial capacity? It is more likely he is motivated by injured pride, ambition (which he has so far been unable to satisfy) and a lust for power. In that case why should the voters become pawns in his hands?'

'One has the impression that in standing for election as a deputy he is looking for an easy way back into a position of political influence.'

'He is not a politician, but a kind of political *limitchik*.'

The intention was that after reading this document party officials were to go back to their districts and open the eyes of the workers to what a nasty, not to say repulsive type this Yeltsin person was.

The plan failed. Of course the party ideologists certainly took the message to the grass roots; but what a reception they got there! Many, in fact, disobeyed orders and did not go to the rank-and-file membership, just to be on the safe side. Some were simply infuriated when this scandalous pamphlet was read out and demanded that these dirty tricks aimed at a duly adopted candidate should cease. In general, reactions differed. But the fact is that in the end this brain-child of the *apparat* had absolutely no effect whatsoever. My thanks are due to the newspaper *Moscow News*, which published an exposure of this operation.

Once, when I found time to sit down and count how many big and small booby traps had been set for me with the sole aim of preventing my election, even I was amazed: the total number of dirty tricks was enough to have torpedoed every member of the

Supreme Soviet. Meetings with workers' groups that were cancelled because no hall was available; the organised distribution of anonymous libels; falsification and deception. I had the lot, and in full measure.

Saddest of all was when the central committee of the CPSU joined in. This happened at a plenum, at which, incidentally the positively shameful nomination took place of the non-elective deputies from the CPSU in its capacity as a 'social organisation'. At the same time a special resolution about me was passed. Next day, all the newspapers published a decree on the setting-up of a commission, headed by the Politbureau member Vadim Medvedev, to investigate statements I had made at meetings with voters.

It all began with a speech by a worker named Tikhomirov, a member of the central committee and one of those classic figures, an obedient and dependable pseudo-activist of the working class, cherished and favoured by the system. There have been a lot of these pseudo-representatives of the workers in recent years. In the name of the working class they used to chant a chorus of approval of any action by the party or the government, however mistaken, risky and ill-conceived, starting with the invasion of Czechoslovakia, the expulsion of Solzhenitsyn, the persecution of Sakharov, and ending with noisy support for the war in Afghanistan. For purposes of this kind, the authorities could always mobilise the required number of puppet 'workers'.

So Tikhomirov spoke at the plenum, declaring that the central committee could no longer tolerate people like Yeltsin in its otherwise solid ranks; Yeltsin was making speeches at election meetings in which he was slandering the party and even daring to make critical remarks about the Politbureau; what's more, he was a bureaucrat himself, yet he continually attacked the bureaucracy in his speeches. 'Once,' Tikhomirov went on, 'I tried to see him in his office, but he kept me, a member of the central committee, waiting in the ante-room for forty minutes.'

This was the usual lie. He did indeed come to see me and did wait in the ante-room, but he came without warning, at a moment when I was holding a meeting with some of the senior technical staff of Gosstroi. But as soon as my secretary informed me that Tikhomirov was waiting to see me, I asked my visitors to take a break of ten minutes or so; I knew Tikhomirov and suspected he was out to make trouble. He and I had a talk, which revealed that the pretext of his visit was utterly trivial. I wondered at the time whether he had really come on his own initiative, or whether he had been put up to it. Then, when he got up to speak at the plenum, it was all made clear.

I spoke immediately after him and said that his speech was pure slander. Given the situation, Gorbachov should have handled the matter with a little more finesse and disregarded this clearly frivolous attack on me. But he was evidently in a hostile mood, and it is more than likely that this whole scene had been fixed in advance. It was he who proposed setting up a commission of inquiry.

The news of the commission caused an explosion among the public. I received letters and telegrams from all over the country, protesting at its creation. That decision of the plenum, I am honestly convinced, increased my vote at the election by several percentage points.

———

'Tell me, do our party leaders know that the country is short of the basic necessities: enough to eat, enough to wear, soap to wash with? Where do they live – in another world?'*

'Since *glasnost* has been permitted, we have, it seems, been told everything. Even the political secrets of the not-so-distant past have been revealed. So why is there nothing but silence about our present rulers? Why don't we know anything about our leaders – their incomes, their standards of living? Or is that a secret?'*

'Tell us what it felt like to live in the "establishment paradise". Is it true that the ease and plenty promised for the historical stage of "full communism" has long been the rule "up there"?'*

* (From questions handed up from the floor at meetings during the election campaign.)

Gorbachov's election as general secretary at the March 1985 plenum of the central committee has given rise to a large crop of rumours. One of these declares that the four Politbureau members who promoted Gorbachov's candidacy decided the fate of the country. Ligachov said this in so many words at the [June 1988] party conference; by doing so, in my opinion, he simply insulted Gorbachov and, indeed, everyone else who took part in the election of the general secretary. There was, of course, a fight. In particular, as I have already mentioned, Grishin's list of Politbureau members, who would support him, has been found, which he had drawn up when he was aiming to become the leader of the party. In it he did not include Gorbachov in his group of supporters; nor were many other Politbureau members included either.

In fact, on that occasion it was the plenum of the central committee which decided who was to be general secretary. Practically all the participants in that plenum, including many senior, experienced first secretaries, considered that Grishin's candidacy was unacceptable, that it would have meant the immediate end of both the party and the country. Within a short space of time he would have succeeded in causing the USSR's entire party organisation to shrivel up into nullity, just as he had done with the party structure in Moscow. This simply could not be allowed to happen. Furthermore, it was impossible to overlook the defects of Grishin's personality: his smugness, his blinkered self-assurance, his sense of his own infallibility and his thirst for power.

A large group of first secretaries concurred in the view that of all the Politbureau members, the man to be promoted to the post of general secretary had to be Gorbachov. He was the most energetic, the best educated and the most suitable from the point of view of age. We decided to put our weight behind him. We conferred with several Politbureau members, including Ligachov. Our position coincided with his, because he was as afraid of Grishin as we were. Once it had become clear that this was also the majority view, we decided that if any other candidate were to be put forward – Grishin, Romanov, or anyone else – we would oppose him *en bloc*. And defeat him.

Evidently the discussions within the Politbureau followed along these lines. Those Politbureau members who attended that session were aware of our firm intention, and Gromyko, too, supported this point of view. He it was who spoke at the plenum, proposing

Gorbachov as the Politbureau's candidate. Grishin and his supporters did not dare to risk making a move; they realised that their chances were slim (or rather, to be precise, zero), and therefore Gorbachov's candidacy was put forward without any complications or problems. That was in March 1985. On 23 April 1985, the famous 'April plenum' of the central committee of the CPSU took place, at which Gorbachov announced the basic points of his programme for the future – the programme of *perestroika*.

I believe that when Gorbachov first came to power there can have been few people in the country who realised what a heavy burden was awaiting him. Indeed, I doubt whether he himself fully understood quite how disastrous was the legacy he was inheriting. What he has achieved will, of course, go down in the history of mankind. I do not like high-sounding phrases; yet everything that Gorbachov has initiated deserves such praise. He could have gone on existing just as Brezhnev and Chernenko existed before him. I estimate that the country's natural resources and the people's patience would have lasted for the length of his lifetime, long enough for him to have lived out the well-fed and happy life of the leader of a totalitarian state. He could have draped himself with orders and medals, the people would have hymned him in verse and song, which is always enjoyable. Yet Gorbachov chose to go quite another way. He started by climbing a mountain whose summit is not even visible; it is somewhere up in the clouds and no one knows how the ascent will end: will we all be swept away by an avalanche, or will this Everest nevertheless be conquered?

I have sometimes wondered why he ever decided to launch the process of change. Was it because he is still relatively young, and he detests the lies and hypocrisy which have almost totally destroyed our society? Was it because he sensed that we still had a chance to make one last effort to break free of the past and become a civilised country? I still cannot find an answer to these questions. I would like to believe that one day he will tell us about the trials and tribulations which assailed him in April 1985.

The chief problem of his launching of *perestroika* was that he was practically alone, surrounded by the authors and impresarios of Brezhnev's 'era of stagnation', who were determined to ensure the indestructibility of the old order of things. After a while, it became easier for him, and then he himself began to lag behind events. But, at that all important initial moment of his reforming initiative, he operated with amazing finesse. In no way did he frighten the old mafia of the Party *apparat*, which retained its power for a long time and which, if necessary, might have eaten any general secretary alive without so much as a hiccup. One after another he neatly pensioned off the members of the old Brezhnev-Chernenko team, and very soon he had gathered around him his own men, with whose help he could take any decision that was necessary.

He was to have even greater successes abroad, although admittedly the circumstances there were rather more propitious for him; after Brezhnev, any leader of the Soviet Union who could even speak normally was regarded as a hero. Yet even so that was not all there was to it. Seen quite objectively, Gorbachov is popular abroad and whenever I see how well he is received in foreign countries, I cannot help but feel sorry for him, because he has to come back to a country that is so torn apart by problems and contradictions. Back home no one is going to shout at him in ecstasy: 'Misha!' Life here is too stern a business for that sort of thing.

But let us return to April 1985 when people had faith in Gorbachov as a politician who was a realist and they accepted his foreign policy based on 'new thinking'. Everyone realised that to go on living and working as we had done for many years was simply impossible. It would have been tantamount to national suicide. A big step had been taken in the right direction, although, of course, it was a revolution from above. Such revolutions inevitably turn against the bureaucratic *apparat*, if it is unable to keep the popular initiative within acceptable bounds. And that *apparat* started to resist *perestroika*, to slow it down and fight against it, with the result that it has effectively skidded to a halt. What is more, I'm afraid, it has turned out that the concept of *perestroika* was not properly thought through. To a large degree it appeared to be represented by nothing but a selection of new, fine-sounding slogans and appeals.

When I read Gorbachov's book *Perestroika and the New Thinking*, I thought I would find in it an answer to the question of how he sees our way forward, but somehow the book did not give me the impression of conceptual wholeness. It is neither clear how he sees the overall restructuring of our house, nor from which materials he proposes to rebuild it and from which set of drawings he is working. The main trouble with Gorbachov is that in this respect he has never worked out a systematic, long-term, strategic plan. There are only slogans. It is amazing to think that more than four years have passed since April 1985 when *perestroika* was proclaimed.

Somehow this period has everywhere been referred to as 'the beginning', 'the initial stage' and 'the first steps'. Yet, in actual fact, this is a long time. In the USA it is the length of a presidential term, and in those four years a president must do everything that he promised to do, in so far as he is able. If the country has not moved forward in that time, another president is elected to replace him. Under President Reagan, a number of improvements took place in many respects and he was re-elected. He turned out not to be such a simpleton as we had been led to believe – although, of course, several sore spots remained, which in eight years he was unable to cure. Nevertheless, the major improvements, especially in the American economy, were there for all to see. With us, on the other hand, the situation has grown so critical over the past four years that today we are even afraid of what tomorrow will bring. In particular, the state of the economy is catastrophic. There, Gorbachov's chief weakness – his fear of taking the decisive but difficult steps that are needed – has been fully revealed.

Let us not, however, run too far ahead. Let us go back a little in time. Having become a secretary of the central committee, and then a candidate member of the Politbureau in 1986, I was plunged into a completely new kind of life. I took part in all the sessions of the Politbureau and sometimes in the secretariat of the central committee. The Politbureau met every Thursday at 11 a.m., and would finish its sessions at varying times: at 4, 5, 7 or even at 8 p.m. In this respect the sessions were not at all like those which Brezhnev chaired, when the wording of various draft decrees was merely finalised and everything was dealt with in fifteen or twenty minutes. He would ask if there were any objections, which there never were, and then the Politbureau would disperse. At the time Brezhnev had only one passion – hunting, and he devoted himself to it till the very end.

Under Gorbachov it was all very different. The sessions usually began with the full members of the Politbureau gathering in one room. The candidate members, as the second category of Politbureau membership, and the central-committee secretaries as the third category, were drawn up in a row in the conference room itself to await the appearance of the general secretary. After him the other full members would file into the room in order of seniority.

Usually Gorbachov was immediately followed by Gromyko, then came Ligachov, Ryzhkov, and thereafter the others entered in alphabetical order. Like two ice-hockey teams they would pass along our rank, shaking hands with each one of us, sometimes saying a word or two in passing, or often simply in silence. Then we would all sit down on either side of the long table; each person's place was pre-ordained, while the chairman – Gorbachov – would take his seat at the head of the table, facing down the middle.

Amusingly enough, during the lunch-break we also sat down to eat in the same separate categories. This reminded me of my days in Sverdlovsk, where I had made a point of making our lunch the occasion for an informal exchange of views on general matters. During those thirty or forty minutes of lunch-time, the secretaries and members of the party bureau (we sometimes invited section chiefs as well) usually managed to reach decisions on a whole series of questions. Here on the summit of Olympus, the caste system was most scrupulously observed.

When the session was declared open, Gorbachov practically never asked whether anyone had any questions about the agenda. He might begin by recalling something he had seen in the past week, including things that he had noticed in Moscow. In my first year as first secretary of the Moscow party organisation he did not, as a rule, make such comments, but in my second year he would begin with increasing frequency by making remarks about matters in the capital: this or that was wrong, this or that seemed to be going badly in Moscow, thus putting me in a state of nervous tension.

Then would begin the discussion of some issue, for example the confirmation of a newly proposed minister. Sometimes Gorbachov had already spoken to the would-be minister, sometimes not, in which case the candidate would be summoned to the Politbureau. On arrival, he would go up to the rostrum to answer a few questions, usually of little significance, with the main aim being to hear the sound of his voice, rather than to learn anything about his views and attitudes. Generally speaking, the confirmation of a ministerial candidate lasted about six or seven minutes.

As a rule, the discussion of any issue assumed a prior knowledge of the matters on the agenda for that session. In my view, however, we were always given such material too late. Sometimes, it is true, we were notified a week in advance, but more often it was only a day or two beforehand, thus making it practically impossible for us to make a thorough study of matters which were of fundamental concern to the welfare of the country. We should have been given enough time to consult the experts and discuss the topic with people familiar with the particular issue. But we never had adequate time to do this – either on purpose or from sheer inefficiency. The questions raised by the secretariat of the central committee usually had to be dealt with as a matter of extreme urgency, so they were discussed in great haste, on a largely emotional basis and without enough factual knowledge. This arm-twisting method was especially favoured by Ligachov when he was running the central committee secretariat. *De jure* he was not the second man in the party, but *de facto* the man in charge of the central-committee secretariat is always regarded as such.

The secretariat meets every Tuesday. It has become a convention that the administration of the party is divided between these two bodies – the Politbureau and the central-committee secretariat. The secretariat deals alone with minor questions, whereas if the issue is a serious one it is dealt with at a joint session of the Politbureau and the secretariat. But despite the outward appearance of a democratic procedure, these are essentially internal discussions within the *apparat*. The *apparat* prepares the drafts, after which they are approved by the Politbureau, essentially by people who are out of touch with the real-life situation and unaware of the actual state of affairs. Certain matters are discussed in the presence of senior officials, mainly those who prepared the material from which the *apparat* wrote its draft. Thus the process is, in fact, a closed circle. I was well aware of this, having spent six months as a section chief within the *apparat* of the central committee, which enabled me to observe its workings from within.

The introductory remarks to any discussion were generally made at some length by Gorbachov, sometimes quoting letters or other documents in support of his ideas. As a rule, this prelude usually predetermined the outcome of the discussion of the project or decree that had been drafted by the *apparat*; the usual result being that in reality the *apparat* controlled everything passed by the Politbureau. More often than not, the Politbureau members' contribution to the debate on such issues was a mere formality. Recently Ryzhkov has tried to break with his practice by discussing the topics in advance at the Council of Ministers or with the relevant experts.

After the general secretary's remarks, comments were solicited around the table from left to right, to give all the members (they usually spoke for from two to five minutes, sometimes less) the chance to have their say, 'Yes, yes, very good . . . it will influence . . . improve . . . broaden . . . deepen *perestroika* . . . democratisation . . . acceleration . . . *glasnost* . . . alternatives . . . pluralism.' The members were beginning to get used to the new buzz-words and enjoyed repeating them.

At first the emptiness of our sessions was not so noticeable, but the longer I took part in them the clearer it became that what we were doing was often pointless. Gorbachov was growing more and more fond of the sound of his own voice. It was obvious that power was exerting its hold over him; he was losing touch with reality, possessed as he was by the illusion that *perestroika* was developing widely and in depth, that it would soon encompass the whole country and the broad mass of the people. In real life, however, it was not like that at all.

I cannot recall anyone at those meetings attempting even once to voice a serious disagreement, though there were times when I tried to do so. At first, of course, I chiefly listened, but, in time, whenever I had had a chance to study in advance the drafts presented to the Politbureau, I began to speak out, at first quietly, then more loudly and, finally, when I saw that an issue was being decided wrongly, I started objecting quite insistently. My arguments were mainly with Ligachov and Solomentsev. Gorbachov tended to stay neutral, although if the criticism were aimed at a topic on which he had done the preparatory work, he naturally could not let it pass without comment and felt obliged to rebut the criticism.

Here I would like to give a few words of description of my colleagues in the Politbureau with whom I worked during my membership of that body and no doubt I should begin with Andrei Gromyko. At that time he was a member of the Politbureau and chairman of the Supreme Soviet of the USSR, that is, the *ex officio* head of state. Gromyko's role was a strange one: he appeared to exist; he did things; met people and made speeches – yet in actual fact he seemed to be of no use to anyone. As chairman of the presidium of the Supreme Soviet of the USSR, protocol required him to preside over international gatherings and to receive official guests, but because the talks were mainly conducted by Gorbachov or on occasion by both of them, he was effectively excluded from the real business of politics, and was relegated – perhaps without fully realising it himself – to the status of a purely formal figure. Gromyko was an anachronism; he did not have a very good grip on what was happening around him, in particular the events which largely form the subject-matter of this and subsequent chapters. He almost always spoke at Politbureau meetings, and on practically every issue. His remarks were always lengthy, and when international affairs were being discussed he felt the need to reminisce in detail about the past – about the situation in America when he had been the Soviet ambassador to the USA; or about the days when he was the minister of foreign affairs. Sometimes these harmless but usually irrelevant and pointless reminiscences of an old man would last for up to half an hour, and it was obvious from Gorbachov's expression that he could barely keep his patience.

This once active man was living out the end of his life in an isolated and self-created world. When he would suddenly make announcements at the Politbureau meetings such as, 'Do you realise, comrades, that in a certain town there is no meat?', it would arouse great amusement. Everyone present had known that for a long time there had been no meat anywhere. Gromyko had his own, fairly elastic timetable; he would come to his office at 10 a.m. and leave at 6 p.m., and he did no work on Saturdays – he did not exert himself greatly, and indeed no one expected it of him. It was important that he should play his part properly and should not make a nuisance of himself. His relations with me were good. What is more, after my speech at the October 1987 plenum, when I was still a member of the Politbureau, he was, I think, the only one who continued to behave towards me as before: he would greet me and ask me how things were going, as though nothing had changed.

Nikolai Ryzhkov is chairman of the Council of Ministers of the USSR, but despite his high appointment, he has always stayed in the shadows. After the tragic events of the earthquake in Armenia, when in a situation of utter disaster he was obliged, literally with his own hands, to shake the rusty machinery of emergency aid into action; when he went without sleep for days on end, then I believe that our people became aware for the first time that we actually had a prime minister. Even so, it is my impression that Ryzhkov finds his job a hard one and especially now, when the country has to be dragged out of economic chaos, out of the abyss into which it has fallen. He is a good, I would say a diligent and hard-working executive, but he is no strategist. He is precisely the kind of figure who suits Gorbachov, who has always been ready to praise his prime minister.

Later, in my position as first deputy chairman of the state committee for construction (Gosstroi), I had to attend the sessions of the Council of Ministers. After being there a couple of times I realised how impossible it was for a normal, sensible person to endure such a disorganised, confused gathering of dunderheads. One minister complains about another, who vents his spleen on a third; they stand up to speak without proper preparation; they push each other away from the microphone, and naturally in such an atmosphere it is almost beyond the wit of man to reach any kind of collective decision. I therefore did not waste any more of my time there and stopped going to the sessions. One would like to believe that the meetings of the Council of Ministers are now conducted rather differently. The ministers have been subjected to a fairly serious purge by the Supreme Soviet, and furthermore the situation in the country is such that there is nowadays simply no time to spare for such chaotic behaviour and empty talk.

Mikhail Solomentsev is a Politbureau member and chairman of the party commission, which keeps a check on the personal affairs of all party office holders. Latterly he was behaving with an air of uncertainty, as though expecting something, and he rarely spoke. Admittedly, if the topic under discussion related to the decree on the anti-drunkenness campaign, he invariably supported Ligachov, and they found each other to be natural allies. When Solomentsev was removed, Ligachov was very depressed; there was no one left who would support that ludicrous decree. Fate brought me together with Solomentsev when he, as chairman of the party commission was instructed to demand an explanation from me about my statements to the Western press. But the conversation did not proceed along quite the lines that Solomentsev had wanted. I refused to confess to having done anything wrong, since I regarded myself as being absolutely in the right, and none of my critical remarks about members of the Politbureau or the tactics of *perestroika* violated either the Soviet constitution or the statute of the CPSU. Throughout this encounter, Solomentsev looked nervous and lacking in confidence. At times I even felt sorry for him: he had been given a task which he was incapable of carrying out.

At first Viktor Chebrikov, chairman of the KGB, hardly ever spoke, unless the debate concerned either the jamming of foreign radio stations or the number of people who should be allowed to go abroad. Quite soon he gave up his chairmanship of the KGB and became a secretary of the central committee. This sideways move on the political chess-board suited Gorbachov, and the obedient and devoted Kryuchkov was put in charge of the KGB. But, as before, all the law-enforcement agencies and the KGB remained in Chebrikov's hands. Above all, Chebrikov still had the psychology of a KGB man: he saw Western subversion and spies everywhere, he didn't want to let anyone go abroad and he wanted to treat everyone as a potential defector. Today's mild pluralism and *glasnost* are like a knife thrust to his heart, a blow at the system that has been functioning well and obediently for so many years.

It was Vladimir Dolgikh's misfortune that Viktor Grishin had included him in the list of his closest supporters; he was planning to make him a member of the Politbureau and chairman of the Council of Ministers. Those who had been listed in Grishin's team were virtually doomed, and indeed many of them very soon lost their jobs. But Dolgikh survived. He was, I think, one of the most professional and efficient secretaries of the central committee, but remained only a candidate member of the Politbureau until his retirement. While still very young – he was not yet fifty – he came from Krasnoyarsk to be a secretary of the central committee. Dolgikh was exceptional for his systematic approach to his work and his sober judgment: he never proposed a hasty, quick-fire solution to any problem, although his independence of thought always remained within the bounds of what was permissible.

When my candidacy for a central-committee secretaryship was being discussed in the Politbureau (naturally without my participation), everyone actively supported the proposal, knowing that I was, as it were, 'Gorbachov's man'. Only Dolgikh volunteered his own point of view, saying something to the effect that Yeltsin was sometimes over-emotional. Soon after I was duly elected a secretary of the central committee, somebody told me what Dolgikh had said about me. I went to see him, not to have a row but simply to hear his opinion of me at first hand; in any case, I felt it important to learn about my mistakes, now that I had started to work in the central committee. He calmly repeated what he had said at the Politbureau, adding that he regarded my appointment to the central-committee secretaryship as entirely correct, but that I must learn to restrain the emotional side of my nature. Strangely enough, this episode, although somewhat unpleasant for me, did not drive us apart but, on the contrary, has brought us closer together. A particularly warm and trusting human relationship grew up between us – a very rare commodity within the walls of the central-committee building. At Politbureau meetings he and I would sit side by side. We would often discuss the country's problems extremely frankly and would criticise the cavalier way in which they were handled: always hastily, always going off at half cock. When he spoke he did not like to criticise, but would simply express his own view, which was always clear, concise and judicious. I think he was a very useful member of the Politbureau, but quite soon he was pensioned off.

Anatoly Lukyanov was for a long time almost the most inconspicuous among the whole of the party's top echelon. He held the post of first deputy chairman of the Supreme Soviet of the USSR. When the legislature was reformed, with contested elections to the Congress of People's Deputies, the importance of his role in the Supreme Soviet was sharply increased. Immediately the ingrained bureaucratic nature of this highly placed *apparatchik* began to manifest itself in full measure – inflexibility, incapacity for independent thinking, narrow mental horizons. Unable to handle the unforeseen situations which frequently arise in the work of the Supreme Soviet, he often gets into a panic, starts to lose his temper and almost shouts at the members as he bangs his fist. Now, given the present make-up of the membership of the Supreme Soviet, a first deputy chairman of this kind is still just about suited to the job; but with genuinely free elections – which I am convinced will come – it will be hard for Lukyanov to remain in his post.

General Dmitry Yazov is the minister of defence. He is the classic bluff, honest soldier, both sincere and hard working. One might perhaps entrust him with the command of a military district or an equivalent headquarters, but he completely lacks the grounding for the post of minister of defence. Intellectually limited, he is completely unable to take criticism, and were it not for the literally fierce pressure that Gorbachov puts on the deputies, Yazov would never have been confirmed in that appointment. It is a mystery to me how anyone expects this 100-per-cent product of the old military machine to effect any positive changes in the armed forces, or to develop a new approach to solving the problems of national defence. A classic old-style Russian general, when he contemplates the country's civilian population he is obviously longing, in his heart of hearts, to conscript every single adult for permanent military service. I exaggerate, of course; but I personally prefer the American system, under which the secretary of defence can only ever be a civilian. Every professional soldier's brain is more or less set in the military mould. He is always seeing an external threat somewhere, and he never quite loses that deep-down urge to do a little fighting.

Vladimir Shcherbitsky, first secretary of the Ukrainian Communist Party. This man's membership of the Politbureau demonstrates to the full Gorbachov's indecisiveness and half-heartedness. I am almost entirely certain that by the time this book is published, Shcherbitsky will have been dismissed, probably in disgrace.[2] At present, however, in August 1989, he is still in place, albeit a totally discredited man. Gorbachov, however, is afraid to touch him, just as he previously refused to grasp the nettle and solve the problem of Geidar Aliev [former first secretary of the Communist Party of Azerbaijan] when it was clear to everyone that to keep this deeply corrupt man in the Politbureau any longer was simply impossible. I specially supplied Gorbachov with a folder of documents and spent almost an hour trying to persuade him to dismiss him. Although he did not listen to me at the time, in the end Aliev was retired with the award of a special private pension. But why did it take so long to deal with that crying scandal for which there could only be one solution?

Alexander Yakovlev, secretary of the central committee and member of the Politbureau is a most intelligent, sensible and far-seeing politician. It always gave me pleasure to hear his extremely precise comments and analysis of the topics under discussion by the Politbureau. Of course he was careful and never made a direct lunge at Ligachov, as I did; but they were undoubtedly poles apart, and Yakovlev's model of socialism was diametrically opposed to Ligachov's conception of it as a mixture of the barracks and the collective farm. Nevertheless they were obliged to find a *modus vivendi* with each other, and both echo Gorbachov in forcing themselves to utter the ritual phrases about the unity of the Politbureau.

Vadim Medvedev is secretary of the central committee and a member of the Politbureau. After Gorbachov had ordered the two chief opponents on matters of ideology – Ligachov and Yakovlev – back into their corners, by giving the former agriculture and the latter foreign policy, Medvedev became the country's chief ideologist. He manages his job with great difficulty, or, to be more precise, he doesn't manage it at all. His chief virtues, for which Gorbachov put him in that post, are obedience and a total lack of new ideas. As has become obvious, however, in today's stirring times these qualities are not enough to cope with that job. Nowadays, in the era of *glasnost* and *perestroika*, even to defend the status quo of the party bureaucracy and the command system of running the economy, a different, more flexible and subtle mind is needed. When I was still first secretary of the Sverdlovsk provincial committee of the party, I remember Medvedev came to speak at Sverdlovsk and after half an hour, without even having finished his speech, he was obliged to leave the rostrum in disgrace. Even in those days his clichés, his grossly sententious remarks and his stale vocabulary that reeked of hack journalism were unbearable. Today he deals with ideology to the best of his extremely modest ability, and the main party newspaper, *Pravda*, the mouthpiece of the conservative forces, is steadily losing circulation. More recently, Viktor Afanasiev was replaced as editor of *Pravda* by Ivan Frolov, a former aide and political consultant to Gorbachov, and that newspaper's fortunes have started to recover. But Medvedev is firmly in place and will remain there until he brings about a total collapse of the party's ideology.

Re-reading the above few lines about my former Politbureau colleagues has depressed me. This, after all, is the 'general staff' of *perestroika*. This is the brain of the party, the best minds in the country. But then, what else did I expect? All the members of the Politbureau are either career bureaucrats who have slowly clambered the ladder of the central committee's hierarchy, *apparatchiki* to the marrow of their bones, or they are former regional or provincial secretaries – such as Gorbachov and Ligachov – not forgetting, by the way, a certain Yeltsin, who also made his party career during Brezhnev's 'era of stagnation'.

I have always understood why many decent people continued to regard me with suspicion even after I had fallen into disfavour. It is because Yeltsin is still seen as a party functionary, a former first secretary of a provincial committee. It is impossible to attain that position, still less to be promoted to the central committee and remain decent, fair, courageous and independent minded. To make a career in the party (and this belief is universally held by Soviet people), a person must excel at adapting his personality and convictions to whatever is required by the powers that be at any given moment; he must be dogmatic; and he must learn to do or say one thing while thinking something else. It is no use trying to justify oneself and make excuses; the only thing a party official can do is to win people's confidence by hard work and by the way he uses his power on their behalf.

I sometimes wonder how I managed to land up among all these people. Why was it that a system, perfected over the years and specifically designed to select only people of a certain type, should have suddenly failed so badly as to choose Yeltsin? Admittedly I didn't last long among them, and I bolted like a caged animal when I could stand it no longer, but this had never happened over seven decades. Evidently, something in the mechanism had failed to work properly, something had broken down.

Every potential candidate for central-committee secretaryship or for membership of the Politbureau is carefully vetted. Everything about him is known: what he thinks, what he wants. There are no enigmas. Gorbachov knew about the peculiarities of my character and my independent views. No doubt, when planning how to deal with the future problems of *perestroika*, he thought it necessary to have someone in the Politbureau who would not behave obediently. But then his attitude to these things changed; he fell more and more into the grip of the processes of power, the urge to be in control, and he wanted to feel that power, every minute and permanently. He wanted only his orders to be carried out, only his opinion to be final, ultimate and correct. He very quickly became accustomed to this, and he had no more use for anyone who was likely to argue with him.

The yes-man attitude towards Gorbachov has filtered down from the top of the pyramid of party rule to the lower levels. The way the central-committee *apparat* works is a unique phenomenon. We often curse the ministries because they produce nothing yet are always sitting on the backs of the enterprises they control; even so, their function can be considered as contributing, even if indirectly, to any success achieved by their particular sector of the national economy. But the central committee really does produce absolutely nothing at all, except paper. And the success of what it does is gauged by those mountains of utterly useless information sheets, reports, answers to projects, summaries, analyses, projects and plans. Nowadays the *apparat* is as good – or as bad – as are the Politbureau and the central committee themselves. It does not exist to analyse the situation, to work out the party's strategy or tactics. It functions to provide an ideologically-based service to the uppermost echelon of the party. In the recent past, for instance, Brezhnev coined the phrase 'developed socialism' as a description of the current phase in the evolution of Soviet society, whereupon the whole huge machine of the central committee started churning out myths about it: how well we were living under 'developed socialism'; how it was progressing and would progress; something about its stages and the path it was taking.

Initially, Gorbachov had his own perception of *perestroika*, a more cautious version than his subsequent view, and the central-committee juggernaut obediently manufactured explanations for this relatively restrained conception of the country's future development. In time, Gorbachov was compelled to move 'leftward' under the pressure of circumstances, and the central-committee *apparat* obediently announced the different, but also uniquely correct path that was being mapped out by the general secretary, all of this being done on the principle of 'anything you say, sir'.

Everyone remembers the tragic story of how, when Gorbachov visited the VAZ (*Volzhsky Avtomobilny Zavod* – Volga Automobile Factory) at Togliatti, he announced that in the near future the USSR would manufacture the best car in the world. The press and television, as usual, picked this up and turned it into a slogan urging people on to ever greater achievements. The engineers and technicians, however, were overcome with shame and horror on learning about this. To make such a claim was to reveal a total lack of understanding of the country in which we lived. A car is not just pieces of metal attached to an engine; it is a highly complex chain of interaction between design, engineering and manufacture; it involves roads, servicing facilities and spare parts. Take out only one link in that chain, and the whole project collapses and it becomes irrelevant, whether or not your car is mediocre, better or worse than others. But no, he had to say, 'We will produce the best car in the world!' And the point is that it wasn't even Gorbachov himself who thought it up; someone prompted him. If the statement had been his own, it would have been possible to qualify or explain it, in order to avoid disgrace. But no, with the aid of the party's highly efficient propaganda machine, it has always been our practice to pass off even the most rank nonsense as the pinnacle of human sagacity, ingenuity and wisdom.

A party *apparat*, run by full-time salaried officials, is of course necessary, but not one of such overblown proportions. It needs a drastic reduction in size. It should be staffed by the best brains in the party, in order to analyse any situation and determine clear paths for future development. This is particularly important when one takes into account the role that the party plays in our society. Has a single source of conflict ever been foreseen and predicted, has a single crisis ever been instantly and correctly resolved? For example, the new laws on state enterprises and co-operatives; Nagorno-Karabakh and the quarrel between Armenia and Azerbaijain; and the urge for independence in the Baltic republics. Any such acute problem starts by quickly reaching a stage of apparent insolubility; then an apparently *ad hoc*, and invariably wrong solution is applied.

Think of all the words that were uttered about the mendacity of bourgeois propaganda in concocting the story about the secret protocols to the Molotov-Ribbentrop pact! How many times did Gorbachov have to say that it was all a pack of lies? Yet it was obvious to any sensible person that it was pointless to go on denying what everybody had long known to be true. Then, after a while, we admit that secret protocols do exist, but how much respect and credibility have we lost for behaving with such wooden-headed obstinacy?

These are just some examples of the way the central committee works, issuing orders and instructions to the country. But I will repeat: the *apparat* as such is not at fault; it is simply that the party leadership needs it to stay as it is, obsequious, obedient and unchanging. An intelligent, independent-minded official of the central committee is a combination of words so paradoxical that one's tongue cannot even utter them. Obsequiousness and obedience are rewarded in turn by privilege: special hospitals; special sanatoria; the excellent central-committee canteen; the equally excellent service for home delivery of groceries and other goods; the Kremlin-line closed telephone system; the free transportation. The higher one climbs up the professional ladder, the more there are comforts that surround one, and the harder and more painful it is to lose them. One becomes therefore all the more obedient and dependable. It has all been most carefully devised: a section chief does not have a personal car, but he has the right to order one from the central-committee car pool for himself and his immediate staff. The deputy head of a department already has his personal Volga car, while the head has another and better Volga, fitted with a car-phone.

But if you have climbed your way to the top of the establishment pyramid, then it's 'full communism'! And it turns out that there was no need of the world revolution, maximum labour productivity and universal harmony in order to have reached that ultimate, blissful state as prophesied by Karl Marx. It is perfectly possible to attain it in one particular country – for one particular group of people. In using the expression 'communism', I am not exaggerating; it is not simply a metaphor for an over-bright communist future: 'From each according to his abilities, to each according to his needs.' And so it is for those at the top of the party pyramid. I have already mentioned their abilities, which, alas are not outstanding – but their needs! Their needs are so great that so far it has only been possible to create real communism for a couple of dozen people. Communism is created for them by the ninth directorate of the KGB.

This all-powerful directorate can do anything. The life of a party leader is lived beneath its unsleeping, all seeing eye and it satisfies their every whim, starting with a *dacha* behind a high green fence encircling spacious grounds alongside the Moscow river, with a garden, tennis courts and games pitches, a bodyguard under every window and an alarm network. Even at my level as a candidate member of the Politbureau, my domestic staff consisted of three cooks, three waitresses, a housemaid, and a gardener with his own team of under-gardeners. My wife, my family and I, long accustomed to doing everything with our own hands, simply didn't know what to do with ourselves. And, surprisingly, all this luxury was incapable of producing either comfort or convenience. What warmth can there be in a marble-lined house?

It was almost impossible to meet or contact anybody in the ordinary, normal way. If you wanted to go to the cinema, the theatre, a museum, indeed any public place, a whole squad of heavies was sent there in advance; they would check and cordon off the whole place, and only then could you go yourself. But the *dacha* had its own cinema, and every Friday, Saturday and Sunday a projectionist would arrive, complete with a selection of films.

As for medical treatment, the medicines and equipment are all imported, all of them the last word in scientific research and technology. The wards in the 'Kremlin hospital' are huge suites, again surrounded by luxury: porcelain, crystal, carpets and chandeliers.

Afraid of taking responsibility, an individual doctor never makes a decision and diagnoses and treatments are invariably agreed upon by a group of between five and ten doctors, sometimes including the most highly qualified specialists. Yet in Sverdlovsk I was looked after by one general practitioner, Tamara Kurushina, who knew me inside and out, always made a precise diagnosis in any situation, and prescribed the treatment herself, whether it was for a headache, a cold or just general debility. I regarded those faceless groups of consultants with great suspicion and since I reverted to going to the usual district polyclinic, my head stopped aching and I have begun to feel much better all round. I haven't been to see a doctor for several months. It may be coincidence, but it is also symbolic. When you are a member of the Politbureau, your own personal physician is obliged to examine you every day, but a lack of professional and personal freedom hangs over him like a sword of Damocles.

'The Kremlin ration', a special allocation of normally unobtainable products, is paid for by the uppermost echelon at half its cost price, and consists of the highest-quality foods. In Moscow, a total of some 40,000 people enjoy the privilege of receiving these special rations, in various categories of quantity and quality. There are whole sections of GUM [*Gosudarstvenny Universalny Magazin* – the huge state department store which faces the Kremlin across Red Square] closed to the public and specially reserved for the topmost élite, while for the officials a rung or two lower down on the ladder there are other special shops and so on down the scale, all of them graded by rank. All are called 'special': special workshops, special dry-cleaners, special polyclinics, special hospitals, special houses, special services. What a cynical use of the word special! A specialist is supposed to be someone who has a particular training or talent. There was a time when a highly skilled craftsman really was a special-ist. Nowadays in our country the word 'special' has a specific meaning, of which we are all too well aware. It is applied to the excellent food products that are prepared in special kitchens and are subjected to special medical tests; to the medicines packed in several layers of wrapping-paper and guaranteed safe by the signatures of several doctors (only medicines certified in this way can be given to the Kremlin élite). How many of such special people are there, one wonders, pampered by the system even in what seems like the most insignificant details?

When they want to go on holiday, for example, they can choose virtually any place in the warm south. There is bound to be a special *dacha* there. For the rest of the year these *dachi* are empty. There are other chances to go on leave, too, because in addition to the summer break there is also a two-week winter holiday. There are also excellent sports facilities, for 'special' use only, on the Lenin Hills, for instance – indoor and outdoor tennis courts, a large swimming-pool and a sauna. Then there are trips in one's personal aeroplane. It may be an IL–62 or a TU–134, and in it is a central-committee secretary, a candidate member or a full member of the Politbureau, alone, except for a few men of his bodyguard and the cabin crew.

The joke is that none of this belongs to those who enjoy these privileges. All these marvellous things – *dachi*, rations, a stretch of seaside fenced off from everyone else – belong to the system. And just as the system has given them, so it can take them away. It is an idea of pure genius. There is a man – Ivanov, say, or Petrov – who climbs his way up the career ladder, and the system gives him first one class of special privileges, then as he rises higher, another class, and the higher he goes the more special delights are handed out to him. Soon Ivanov begins to think he is an important person. He eats what ordinary mortals only dream of, he takes his holidays in places where the *hoi polloi* are not even allowed to come near the surrounding fence. And stupid Ivanov doesn't realise that it is not he who is being thus favoured but the position that he occupies. And if he suddenly were to stop faithfully serving the system and standing up for it, Petrov or someone else would instantly be put into Ivanov's place. Within this system nothing belongs to the individual. Stalin cunningly brought this machinery to such a state of perfection that even the wives of his immediate colleagues did not belong to them; they, too, belonged to the system. And the system could take those wives away and imprison them, just as Stalin imprisoned the wives of Kalinin and Molotov, and neither man dared to utter so much as a squeak of protest.

Nowadays, of course, times have changed, but the essence of the system remains the same. As before, a wide selection of perks is handed out to the position that a person occupies, but each 'gift' – from a soft armchair with its numbered metal tag up to the bottle of normally unavailable medicine certified 'safe' by the fourth directorate of the KGB – bears the stamp of the system. This is so that the individual (who, as before, is no more than a little cog in the machine) should never forget to whom all this really belongs.

I will now describe how this system of privileges works using some examples from my own experience. Every central-committee secretary, member or candidate member of the Politbureau has attached to him an officer in charge of his bodyguard; this man is his aide-de-camp and organises his life for him. My bodyguard commander, a most attentive man, was called Yuri Fyodorovich. One of his chief duties was to see to the fulfilment of any wish that might be expressed by his – I almost said, lord and master – for whose safety and comfort he was responsible. Do you want a new suit? Certainly, and precisely at the appointed hour comes a discreet knock on the door of your office; in comes a tailor who takes your measurements; next day he returns for a fitting and very soon you have an elegant new suit. Do you need a present for your wife for 8 March [the date celebrated in the USSR as International Women's Day]. No problem: you are brought a catalogue with a choice of gifts which would satisfy even the most sophisticated female taste – and all you have to do is choose! On the whole, the attitude to families is considerate. There is a Volga for their use, with drivers working in shifts and bearing prestigious 'Kremlin' number-plates, for either taking your wife to work or bringing her home, or taking the children to and from the *dacha*. The big ZIL, of course, is reserved for the father of the family.

This essentially cynical system will sometimes exhibit an equally cynical lapse where the immediate family members of the head of the clan are concerned. When, for instance, the chief bodyguard was instructing my wife and children that they must not feed me fruit and vegetables bought in the market, because they might be poisoned, my daughter asked timidly whether they – she and my wife – might eat market-bought produce? She was told that they could, but I must not. In other words, you can go ahead and be poisoned, but he is sacred.

Muscovites usually stop and watch whenever a government ZIL flashes past with a hissing of tyres at great speed. They do not stop out of any great respect for the occupant of the car, but because it is a really impressive sight. Even before the ZIL has driven out of your gateway, the traffic-police posts all along your route have been informed. The lights are green all the way, the car races along without a stop, and you drive quickly and pleasantly. Senior party leaders have obviously forgotten that there are such things as traffic jams and traffic-lights at red.

Politbureau members are also escorted all the way by another car, a Volga. When I received a number of threatening letters, I was also allotted a Volga to accompany me. I demanded that it be removed, but was told that matters concerning my personal security were outside my competence. Thus for a while it became impossible to kill me. I was surrounded by guards. Fortunately, these extra guards were soon withdrawn. The ZIL, however, was alongside me round the clock. Wherever I might be, the car, with its radio, was always near. If I drove out of town to spend the night at the *dacha*, the driver was put up in a special lodge, so as to be ready to drive away at any moment. And the *dacha* is a story in itself.

Before it was allotted to me, it had been occupied by Gorbachov, who had moved into another one that had been built specially for him. When I drove up to the *dacha* for the first time, I was met at the door by the commander of the bodyguard, who introduced me to the domestic staff – the cooks, the maids, the rest of the body-guard and the gardener. Then began the inspection of the house. Even from the outside I had been overwhelmed by the size of the place. I went into a hall measuring about thirty by fifteen feet with an enormous fireplace, marble panelling, a parquet floor, large carpets, chandeliers and luxurious furniture. We went on, passing through first one room, then a second, a third and a fourth, in each one of which was a television set. Also on the ground floor was an enormous veranda with a glass roof and a small cinema that was also a billiard-room. I lost count of the number of bathrooms and lavatories. There was a dining-room with an incredible thirty-foot long table, behind it a kitchen big enough to feed an army, with a refrigerator that was a separate underground room. We went up the steps of a broad staircase to the first floor. Again a vast landing with an open fireplace and a door into the solarium, furnished with rocking-chairs and *chaises-longues*. After that came the study, the bedrooms, two more rooms intended for I know not what, more lavatories and bathrooms. And everywhere there was crystal, antique and modern chandeliers, oak, parquet floors *ad infinitum*.

When we had finished the tour of inspection, the commander of the bodyguard, beaming with delight, asked me what I thought of it. I mumbled something inarticulate, while my wife and daughters were too overcome and depressed to reply. Chiefly we were shattered by the senselessness of it all. I will not even bother to discuss such notions as social justice, the stratification of society and the huge difference in standards of living; all of that goes without saying. But what was the point of the whole thing? Why was it thought necessary to give material expression in such an absurd degree to the fantasies of property, pleasure and megalomania harboured by the party élite? No one, not even the most outstanding public figures of the contemporary world, could possibly find a use for so many rooms, lavatories and television sets all at the same time. And who pays for all this? The ninth directorate of the KGB. It would be interesting to know, by the way, how all this expenditure is accounted for and under which heading of the KGB's budget. Combating spies? Subversion of foreigners by bribery? Or perhaps under a more romantic heading such as satellite intelligence in space?

There is also a wide choice of places at which to spend one's holidays: Pitsunda and Gagry, on the Georgian coast of the Black Sea; the Crimea; the Valdai Hills, a beautiful region midway between Moscow and Leningrad. The senior office of one's bodyguard was given, if I'm not mistaken, about r.4,000 – just for out of pocket expenses. In other words, there was no need to spend any money on the holiday. These summer *dachi* are as luxurious as the year-round residences. One is driven to the beach by car, even though the distance is no more than a couple of hundred yards. I used to walk, of course, as part of my attempt to get a little exercise. I also organised two volley-ball teams. My daughter and I, my assistant and my driver played against the guards; they were young, strong and fit lads, but even so we often won. In short, I tried my best to introduce something human, competitive and energetic into that oasis of artificial communist perfection.

It may be a somewhat controversial opinion of mine, but I do believe that *perestroika* would not have ground to a halt, even with the tactical mistakes that have been made, if only Gorbachov had been able to get rid of his inhibitions over the question of the leadership's perquisites, if he himself had renounced all those completely useless but pleasant, customary privileges. If he had not had built for himself a new house on the Lenin Hills and a new *dacha* outside Moscow, had not had his *dacha* at Pitsunda rebuilt and then an ultra-modern one built at Theodosia in the Crimea. And then, to cap it all, at the Congress of People's Deputies he announces with pathos that he has no personal *dacha*. Didn't he realise how hypocritical that sounded? Everything might then have happened differently, because people's faith in his slogans and appeals would not have been lost. Without faith even the best and most enlightened changes to our society will be impossible to accomplish. And when people know about the blatant social inequality that persists and they see that their leader is doing nothing to correct the party leadership's shameless appropriation of luxuries paid for from the public purse, then the last droplets of the faith they may have had will evaporate.

Why has Gorbachov been unable to do this? I believe the fault lies in his basic cast of character. He likes to live well, in comfort and luxury. In this he is helped by his wife. She, unfortunately, is unaware how keenly and jealously millions of Soviet people follow her appearances in the media. She wants to be on view, to play a noticeable part in the life of the country. No doubt in a rich, prosperous, contented society that would be accepted as natural and normal – only not in our country, at least not at this time.

Gorbachov, too, is at fault, in that he does not sense people's reactions. But, then, how can he sense them when he has no direct, reciprocal contact with the people? His meetings with workers in public are nothing but a masquerade: a few people stand talking to Gorbachov, while all around them is a solid ring of bodyguards. Those people chosen to play the part of 'the people' have been carefully vetted and selected, and are brought to the spot in special buses. And it is always a monologue. If somebody says something to him which does not fit into his picture, he doesn't hear it, because he is too busy putting across what he wants to say.

And what about his wife's ZIL? What about Gorbachov's proposal to raise the salary of Politbureau members? Things like that cannot be kept secret; people will always find out somehow. My daughter, at her place of work, is given one small cake of soap per month, which is barely enough for her. When my wife has to spend two or three hours a day queuing in shops and cannot buy the most elementary things with which to feed her family, even she, a calm, balanced woman, begins to get irritated, nervous and distressed.

Of course, our 'establishment' cannot run away and hide; the moment will come when they will have to give up their *dachi* and answer to the people for having hung on to their privileges tooth and nail. Even now some of them are starting to pay the price for their former 'establishment' status: the massive defeat at the polls suffered by party and government officials who stood for election is the first warning bell for them. They are now being forced to take steps to satisfy the demands of the electorate. But they make such concessions reluctantly and grudgingly; they so much don't want to relinquish their privileges that every possible contrivance, including lies and sheer deception, is being deployed; they will, in fact, do anything to slow down the process of reform.

Ryzhkov announced recently that the issue of special rations would cease and that the special grocery shop on Granovsky Street had been closed. It was indeed closed, but the Kremlin rations continued to be given out as before, only now they are made available by telephone through the 'social orders' departments of other stores. So everything, in fact, was unchanged. The party bigwigs and permanent officials of the Soviets; ministers; academicians; newspaper editors-in-chief and other high-ups simply sent their drivers, who piled the shopping-bags, bulging with good things, into the boots of huge black cars and took them home to their bosses.

As I write in late 1989, I still do not know the outcome of the commission that was set up to investigate the matter of 'undeserved privileges and perquisites'. The second Congress of People's Deputies did not debate the topic either. I suspect though, that there will be no more of this shamelessness. We will give up (and I hope, for ever) the system of rationing minor luxuries to a bureaucratic caste and adopt the civilised method, where the only yardstick of all material values will be the honestly earned rouble. I greatly hope this will be so.

When people say behind my back that I refused all such privileges as *dachi*, special rations and special hospitals for the sake of cheap popularity, to play up to the feelings of the mob which wants everything to be levelled down and demands equal misery for all, I pay no attention to these remarks and I am not offended. I know who are saying these things and why they say them. But there are quite different people – my friends and allies – who also, when a specific situation arises, ask why, for instance, do I have to refuse the special medical services provided by the fourth directorate of the KGB? How, they ask, can one get the necessary medications nowadays (at that moment I happened to have a cold) – they are simply not to be found: neither antibiotics, simple pain-killers, nor vitamin C tablets?

The following instance occurred quite recently. In the summer of 1989, when the Congress of People's Deputies was in session, I was writing this book in bursts, sometimes at night after a sitting of the Congress, or on Sundays – in other words, I lacked the time for proper, normal work on it. In August the Congress rose for the recess, and I decided to devote all my time to the manuscript. In my study, of course, this was impossible; there were a million problems, even at home I could not escape the ceaseless telephone calls and I decided to rent a *dacha* for a few weeks in the countryside outside Moscow, where no one could find me. It then transpired that it was impossible to rent a *dacha* in August; it has to be done in early spring. We began a feverish search, not even for a *dacha* but for a little shack where I could lock myself away. The holiday was short, every hour counted. It was then that I was subjected to a hail of reproaches; it serves you right, you and your sermons about social justice: you shouldn't have refused to have a state-owned *dacha*; you've got nowhere to work, you should have written your book – *then* you could have refused as many *dachi* as you like. In the end we did find a little cottage. Its chief advantage was that it was a very long way from Moscow – nearly 125 miles, in fact. The surrounding countryside was wonderful – the birds, the forest, mushrooms galore. All other conveniences, however, were also out of doors. Such were the splendid natural surroundings in which this book was born.

But I digress. To return to the question of privileges. Naturally everyone wants to eat delicious, healthy food; everyone wants the doctors to be kind and attentive; and everyone would like a holiday on a lovely beach. And naturally, when I refused to accept all these things, my family immediately encountered numerous problems, exactly the same problems, in fact, which confront millions of Soviet families. Altogether, we are longing to live in the way that the rest of the civilised world lives. And that is why I shall never understand why Gorbachov proudly announced to the Congress that he did not own a private *dacha*. What is there to be proud of in that fact? It is a disgrace that he doesn't own one. The general secretary ought to have a private *dacha*, built with his own money that he earned by the sweat of his brow, just like a workman, a writer, an engineer or a teacher. But a state *dacha* on loan suits him better. And as long as no one can build or buy their own *dacha*, as long as we continue to live in such relative poverty, I refuse to eat caviare followed by sturgeon; I will not race through the streets in a car that can disregard traffic-lights and other cars; I cannot swallow excellent imported medicines, knowing that my neighbour's wife can't get an aspirin for her child. Because to do so is shameful and writing about all this evokes a host of thoughts about our country; about the way we have chosen to go; about the reasons for our low standard of living; about the perpetual shortages; about spiritual values; about morality and about the future.

Many people are concerned about a big question: where are we going? Are we building the right house, the kind that we need and in which we may not necessarily prosper but at least lead a tolerable existence? At the moment our society is trying as hard as it can to give old notions a thorough shaking-up and to find, at last, the right way to go. So far we have strayed and got thoroughly lost. But the ways back to the high ground are blocked with lies and every kind of dogmatic rubbish, and we all have to work hard in order not to get lost in the debris of the past.

If one is to believe the textbooks, we built socialism long ago, but then for some reason we began to build annexes and outhouses to it until at last we had built it 'fully and finally' [in the words of Khrushchev]. But to the ideologists even this was not enough; they then announced, not without the help of Leonid Brezhnev, the emergence of something called 'developed socialism'. Now they are racking their brains over what to call the next stage. After all, they must call it something; we seem unable to manage without these labels. The Soviet way of life, if we again believe our theoreticians, is characterised by no less than twenty-six specific features. Soon, no doubt, there will prove to be at least as many varieties of socialism.

If one puts the theory and the practice of socialism side by side and compares them with an unprejudiced eye, it becomes clear that of all its classic component elements, the only one to have been put into effect is the socialisation of property, and even that has been done very crudely. The other elements of socialism are either completely missing from our society or have been so heavily retouched as to be unrecognisable.

To have an idea of where we are going, we need to know where we've come from. In the 1920s Stalin successfully blocked off the democratic route and began to steer us forcibly along the road of the authoritarian state, of 'socialism' administered by a vast bureaucracy. Democracy was nipped in the bud, and a voiceless, stifled population could do nothing but create a caricature of a socialist society. The people, deprived of free speech, were unable to reach any agreement among themselves. Countless intimidating gestures were used, accompanied by a total lack of political dialogue between the party and the people. A political dictatorship was imposed, backed by terror.

A quite different prospect was offered to us by the promised democratisation of society, in which individual interest and individual responsibility would be paramount, to which should be added a withdrawal of state subsidies from industry that was genuine and not merely a cover-up for hidden subsidies. But alas it has not happened: subsequent economic policy has been devised exclusively on the basis of 'public interest'. Beneath this umbrella, all the most unsuitable and inefficient methods of economic management have remained in place, which have been successfully manipulated by Soviet bureaucrats, who interpret the 'public interest' as meaning their own narrow, self-serving aims – but which in practice has nothing to do with the interests of the worker or the peasant.

Much is being written about the 'renewal' of Soviet socialism; but that is, to put it mildly, a poor way of defending socialism, because it is only possible to renew something which already exists in time and space. If a house has been built, you can refurbish it, add on to it, extend it and reconstruct it. But what if it doesn't exist at all? My view is this: we are still only building socialism. We need an intellectually honest, truly scientific theory which would be capable of generalising, and, without grinding any axes, assessing and drawing conclusions from our experience of the past seventy years. Dogmatic concepts of socialism will not disappear overnight; they will continue to feed on the inertia of past years.

The absolute insistence on the primacy of economic factors (to the detriment of the social and political dimensions) has affected the general strategy of *perestroika*. Economic reforms were not complemented soon enough by a simultaneous restructuring of political institutions (indeed, it would have been better if political reforms had *preceded* economic change). *Perestroika* should have begun with the party and its *apparat*. The party's role in society and its principal functions should have been clearly defined. As this was not done, the result was that for a time we were trying to restructure the economy while still in thrall to dogmas and traditions inherited from a dead past, while lacking a comprehensive package of new legislation on poverty, on land, on co-operatives, on renting, on the tax system and on a new system of price formation.

Today, in accelerating the political reforms, we are trying to make up for lost time. Even the little that has been done had led to a healthy and noticeable politicisation of public opinion. The people have begun to take an active part in politics. 'People power' in politics, which began with 'people's diplomacy', has enlarged the arsenal of its means, forms and methods. Public opinion was literally galvanised by the [miner's] strikes in 1989 and the formation of strike committees. The national press has been supplemented by the publications put out by the unofficial organisations – funds for this or that, initiative groups and so on. In several republics and regions National Fronts have been formed and are in action, many of them almost regarded as being new political parties. I am in favour of the creation of National Fronts, but only on condition that their programmes and actions do not run counter to accepted human values. In the Baltic republics the National Fronts have raised questions which the party has always refused to face: I refer to the problems of ethnic independence.

Perestroika has stirred people up, has awakened their constructive energies and summoned them to a creative approach to social problems. These emerging forms of popular political expression must occupy a suitable place in society. They should serve as a rallying-point for everyone who is alarmed about the fate of the country. If dissidents are excluded from the struggle for *perestroika*, it will dilute and weaken the forms of popular self-expression. Dissidents should be paid thirteen months' salary for a year, otherwise our mindless unanimity will bring us to an even more hopeless state of stagnation. It is especially important to encourage unorthodox thinking when the situation is critical: at such moments every new word, every fresh thought is more precious than gold. Indeed, how can people be deprived of the right of thinking their own thoughts?

7

Chronicle of the Election Campaign

12 March 1989

The television debates have just finished. We are learning the methods of present-day electioneering from the civilised countries, and now we even have such a thing as televised debates between candidates. It's not easy. The camera inhibits you and tends to make you behave not quite naturally, in addition to which you are keenly aware that it is a live broadcast. It was also my first appearance on Moscow television since my dismissal from the post of first secretary of the Moscow city committee of the party. This, too, laid a weight on my shoulders. I wanted people to see that I was in good form and had been able to survive the events of the past eighteen months with dignity.

If one is to treat electioneering seriously, one must learn how to behave on television. It is a special means of contact with the electorate, which has nothing in common with the traditional ways of meeting voters. There you face live people; you feel the breathing of the audience, the reaction to your every word and gesture: you feel all this physically, as energy is transmitted from the people to you and back from you to them. But in a television studio your audience is the cold glass eye of the camera lens, which reflects nothing but light and your own image, and somehow you must imagine, out there beyond it, the existence of real people sitting at home, drinking tea, or listening with only half an ear.

But that is all theory. In reality, we arrived at the Moscow television studios in the suburb of Ostankino about half an hour before the start of the transmission. We sat and talked to the presenter, who told us how he would structure the programme, and explained briefly how a phone-in programme worked. A television debate required each candidate to answer several questions that would be put to them by viewers in the Moscow area. The presenter himself would select the questions that we were to answer.

The live transmission began. Yuri Brakov spoke, outlining his election platform, then I was given ten minutes to do the same. As I have already mentioned, I behaved and spoke in a more inhibited way than usual. But even so I managed to explain my political programme to the viewers.

It is, of course, not very pleasant when you suspect someone of something, but I must honestly say that the selection of questions surprised me. The questions given to Brakov to answer were ordinary and uncontroversial, mostly concerning strictly industrial topics about ZIL, about the future of the factory and the car industry in general. I, on the other hand, had to fend off a succession of personal attacks. Inwardly I grew very tense, but that may have been an advantage, because I started talking more emotionally and forcibly. It is understandable that in order to sharpen up the tone of the debate the presenter may select the questions as he thinks fit. Somehow, though, he managed to pass on to me questions from people who (some journalists later ascertained) didn't exist at all, or if they did exist, never actually phoned in with a question. Here, for instance, is one example: 'Why do you always play to the gallery, Boris Nikolayevich? Even your regular visits to the doctor are reported by journalists and newsreel cameramen.' Questioner: So-and-so, living at such-and-such an address.

Indeed, that very morning I had had an appointment at our local polyclinic, having long since declined the medical services of the fourth directorate of the KGB. Incidentally I remember that when I went to register at the clinic, the elderly lady who was taking down my particulars – age, address, place of work – almost dropped her pen when, in answer to her question, 'Occupation?', I replied, 'Minister.' Then she said, 'This is the first time in my life that I have ever registered a minister as a patient in a district polyclinic.'

When I had left home that morning, a camera crew had been

lying in wait for me. They took shots of me going into the clinic and coming out again. And that was all. The interesting fact was that all this had taken place at 8 a.m. that morning and it was a five-minute walk to the polyclinic; in other words, they would have had to follow my every step to have noticed that on this particular morning I had been filmed taking my regular walk to the polyclinic.

In the television debate my reply to that question was that personally I was bored to death with all the reporters, photographers, film and television cameramen, who never gave me any peace, but clearly the question as to why they were always hovering round me should be put to them. They hadn't been able to photograph me for such a long time and there had been no news of me, so perhaps that explained this sudden flurry of interest.

But that wasn't all. The next day, that same television crew, feeling that without wishing to they had somehow caused me unnecessary embarrassment, went to the address of the man who had asked that loaded question, found him and discovered that he had never even phoned the television station. Furthermore, he had never asked a question to be put to me and knew nothing whatever about that polyclinic or that I had any connection with it. He finished by asking the television crew to tell Yeltsin not to worry; he was going to vote for him anyway. The crew shot this whole interview on videotape and gave me the cassette as a present. My campaign assistants also checked several other addresses of people who had allegedly phoned in, and the picture was the same: either no one of that name lived at the address, or if they did, they had never sent in any questions to the programme.

———

The October 1987 plenum of the central committee of the CPSU, which later aroused such controversy, was a mysterious affair that was kept secret, but at which I asked to speak and was given the floor. Afterwards I often wondered whether I might have chosen a different approach; whether I really needed to have charged in as I did, guns blazing; to have caused the uproar which resulted in such a drastic change in my whole life. I had, after all, been aware that there was a good chance that I would not survive my imminent 'civil execution'. So why did I have to do it?

142

After a lapse of nearly two years, I can say with absolute conviction that the speech I made then was indeed necessary, that it was the logical outcome of all the events that had led up to it. Everyone had been wallowing in such triumph and euphoria about *perestroika* that they had been unwilling to see that it had produced no concrete results except for a few changes in the direction of *glasnost* and democratisation. Instead of a realistic and critical assessment of the situation as it had developed, the only reaction in the Politbureau was an ever louder chorus of praise for the general secretary. My conflict with Ligachov had also reached its logical culmination. In order to solve Moscow's most painful and difficult problems, I needed the help of the whole Politbureau: the capital city is such a complex, conglomerate entity, where virtually every strand of the country's political, economic and social fabric criss-cross and intertwine, that without our joint efforts the necessary moves would never be made. In fact, far from getting their help I had noticed that there was an active unwillingness in the Politbureau to help the city in tackling the problems that had built up. In those circumstances, how could I carry on? I could have done so, but I would have had to become a different person – to stop speaking my mind; not to notice that the country was sliding into an abyss while at the same time proclaiming proudly that the party organised and inspired, of course, by its general secretary was the architect of *perestroika*.

Who can have known how these hypocritical slogans infuriated me! First the party's bureaucratic *apparat*, hiding behind the party's façade, had ruined the country, and now that concealment was useless. Something had to be changed in that putrid system, and yet they were shouting, 'Don't touch the party, it's the architect of *perestroika*!' How could we not touch it, when it had been drummed into everyone from kindergarten onward that we were supposed to thank the party for all our achievements? In any case, its role as inspirer and organiser is written into Article 6 of the constitution of the USSR. So who was to blame for what had happened? Was it the Soviet people, that 'new historical entity' (this concept was one of Brezhnev's contributions to Marxist–Leninist theory)? Or was it still the institution that had been 'inspiring and organising' for the past seventy years? Every day and from all sides curses are being hurled at the party *apparatchiks* – yet we are sternly reminded that the authority of the party is unshakeable. We shall not allow you to touch the party with your dirty hands!

In the two years since the October 1987 plenum of the central committee, Soviet society has come a long way; people have grown aware of their role: not as little cog-wheels but as human individuals; a nationwide attack on the party bureaucrats has begun, forcing them into a feverish, terrified defence of their more than shaky position. But back then in 1987, when I realised that I had to speak out, the climate was very different and one was only allowed to criticise whatever did not cast aspersions on the reputations and achievements of those in high places. The general secretary had reverted to being equivalent to the 'tsar, father of his people' and to express the slightest doubt about his actions was an unthinkable act of sacrilege. One could express only awestruck admiration for the general secretary, or delight at being so fortunate as to be able to work alongside him; one was allowed to be mildly indignant at the fact that he was so modest, that he would never allow himself to be praised and so on *ad nauseam*.

When I mounted the rostrum at the October 1987 plenum of the central committee, I had no intention of my speech becoming some kind of step forward, of expanding the limits of *glasnost*, or of reducing the area that was beyond criticism. None of this entered my head. The important thing was to screw up my courage and say what I had to say. As I have already mentioned, I did not write out my speech, but had only jotted down a few headings on a small sheet of paper. Therefore I will now quote my speech from the transcript of it that was published in the second issue for 1988 of the *Bulletin of the Central Committee of the CPSU*:

YELTSIN: The reports, made today and on the seventieth anniversary celebrations, were discussed in draft form in the Politbureau, and in view of the fact that I, too, made some suggestions for insertion into the text and some of them were accepted, I therefore have no comments to make on that report today, and I fully endorse it.

I would like, however, to raise a number of issues that have been causing me some concern during my time as a member of the Politbureau. I entirely agree that at the present time some very great difficulties have arisen in the process of *perestroika*, and that this lays great responsibilities and great obligations upon all of us. I consider that above all we need to restructure the work of the party committees, indeed of the party as a whole, beginning with the secretariat of the central committee, a point which was made at the June plenum of the central committee. I cannot help remarking that although five months have passed since then, nothing has changed in the style of work of either the secretariat of the central committee or of Comrade Ligachov.

Despite the fact that Mikhail Sergeyevich [Gorbachov] said here today that bullying reprimands and dressings down of all kinds are impermissible at any level, they are still used. This form of coercion is used by party bosses in industrial enterprises and in other organisations of all kinds – but they are intolerable at any level, especially now, at a time when the party has to set out on a revolutionary course and act in a revolutionary way. There is no sign of any such revolutionary energy or party comradeliness in the central committee's attitude to grass-roots party committees and many individual party members.[1]

It seems to me that we must draw lessons from the past, that we really must fill in those blank spots in our history books and study them, as Mikhail Sergeyevich [Gorbachov] said today; and while drawing the conclusions that apply to the present day, we must above all draw conclusions for tomorrow. What must we do? How are we to put right what was done and make sure the same mistakes can never be made again? Because in the past our Leninist principles have simply been discredited, subsequently this has led to the fact that those Leninist principles have been largely banished from the standards of behaviour in our party.

I believe that despite what was said at the [party] congress about what *perestroika* [is to achieve] in two or three years – two years, or nearly two years, have already passed, and now we are again told that it needs a further two or three years. This greatly disorients people; it disorients the party and the population as a whole, since we, who are aware of the people's mood, can now sense the [tidal] wave-like nature of their attitudes to *perestroika*. At first there was a tremendous surge of enthusiasm. And it maintained a great intensity and a strong impetus up to and including the January 1987 plenum of the central committee of the CPSU. Then, after the June plenum of the central committee, people's faith began somehow to ebb, and that worries us very much indeed. This happened, of course, because those two years were largely spent in drafting all those documents, which did not reach the people. This meant that they became anxious, since during that time they were given nothing substantive.

It therefore seems to me that this time we must, perhaps, adopt a more cautious approach to announcing a realistic timetable for *perestroika* in the coming two years. We understand that this is all proving very, very difficult to implement, and even if we start now to introduce far-reaching (and it must be done) revolutionary changes in the work of the party – specifically the party, and the party committees – that cannot be done in two years. And after two years we may well find, I would say, that in the eyes of the people the party's authority as a whole has drastically fallen.

I must say that the repeated call [to the central committee] to issue fewer documents – while at the same time the quantity of documents issued constantly increases – is beginning to produce a certain attitude to all those decrees all over the country. At local level, there is a tendency, I would say, to treat them with scant attention and to disbelieve them. They go on pouring out, one after another. A call has gone out, for instance, to cut those research centres which are not doing anything useful. To take the example of Moscow: a year ago there were 1,041 research institutes, and after enormous efforts made by the state committee for scientific research, seven institutes were closed down. Yet somehow the number remaining totalled not 1,041, but 1,087, because during that year decrees were issued setting up new research centres in Moscow. That, of course, directly contradicted party policy and the decision of the party congress and the appeals that were made to us.

I have also been reflecting on another matter. It is not an easy one to discuss, but this is a plenum of the members of the central committee of the party, a most trustworthy and open-minded assembly, to which one can and must say everything that is in one's mind and in one's heart, as a communist should.

I must say that the lessons of the past seventy years are harsh lessons; there were victories, too, as Mikhail Sergeyevich has reminded us, but there were lessons to be learned as well. Harsh lessons, serious defeats. These defeats have accumulated gradually, thanks to the fact that there was a lack of decision-making by consensus; due to the fact that cliques were formed; due to the fact that the power of the party was put into a single pair of hands; due to the fact that he – one man – was totally immune from all criticism.

Personally I am very worried that there is still not a good atmosphere in the Politbureau, and that recently there has been a noticeable increase in what I can only call adulation of the general secretary by certain full members of the Politbureau. I regard this as impermissible, particularly now, when we are introducing properly democratic forms of relationship between each other, a truly comradely relationship. This tendency to adulation is absolutely unacceptable. To criticise to their face – yes, that is necessary – but not to develop a taste for adulation, which can gradually become the norm again, can become a 'cult of the personality'. We cannot permit this. It must not be allowed. I realise that this has not yet reached the point of a certain impermissible degree of falsity and distortion, but even so the first traces of such an attitude are there, and it seems to me that it must be prevented from going any further.

And finally . . . I am clearly out of place as a member of the Politbureau. For various reasons. Evidently there is my lack of experience, as well as other factors; perhaps it is simply the lack of a certain support from some quarters, especially from Comrade Ligachov which, I would stress, has led me to believe that I must put before you the question of my release from the duties and obligations of a candidate member of the Politbureau. I have already handed in my request to be allowed to resign. As far as my position as first secretary of the Moscow city committee of the party is concerned, that will, of course, be decided by a plenum of the city committee of the party.

Having said all that, I sat down. My heart was pounding, and seemed ready to burst out of my ribcage. I knew what would happen next. I would be slaughtered, in an organised, methodical manner, and the job would be done almost with pleasure and enjoyment.

Even now, when so much time has passed, a rusty nail is still lodged in my heart and I have not pulled it out. It protrudes and it bleeds. I still find this hard to explain. Did I really expect anything else from the then largely conservative membership of the central committee? Of course I didn't; I knew the impending scenario only too well. It had been prepared in advance and, as I now realise, it had nothing to do with my speech.

Gorbachov would, so to speak, set the tone, then one accuser

147

after another would come dashing up to the rostrum and would indict me for threatening party unity, for overweening ambition and for political intrigue. So many labels would be stuck on me there would be enough for an entire opposition party. There would even be too many central-committee members thirsting to demonstrate their zeal to encompass the moral destruction of a party colleague who had 'strayed from the fold', and the number of speakers would have to be restricted.

And so it was and I shall here again quote the stenographic transcript of the plenum:

GORBACHOV: Perhaps it might be better if I took over the chair.
LIGACHOV: Yes, please do, Mikhail Sergeyevich.
GORBACHOV: Comrade Yeltsin has, I think, made a serious speech. I didn't want to start a debate, but we must discuss what has been said.

I would like to sum up the salient points of his speech. First, Comrade Yeltsin said that we must galvanise the party machinery into action, and that this should begin with the central committee, specifically with the secretariat. In this connection, certain reproofs were directed at Comrade Ligachov.

Second, the question was raised of the pace of *perestroika*. It is stated that a period of two or three years was named as the time needed for putting *perestroika* into effect. The comment was made that this period was a mistaken choice; that this disorients people, leads to even greater confusion in society and in the party; that the situation was fraught with consequences which might ruin this policy.

Third, we are drawing lessons from the past, but, apparently, from Comrade Yeltsin's point of view, not thoroughly enough, because no mechanisms have been created in the party, at central committee and Politbureau level, which would prevent the recurrence of serious errors.

Finally, he raised the question of his continuing to work in his present capacity. Comrade Yeltsin considers that he cannot go on working as a member of the Politbureau, while in his opinion the question of his further tenure of the post of first secretary of the Moscow city committee will not be decided by the central committee but by the city committee.

This seems to be something new. Perhaps he is talking about

the Moscow party organisation splitting off from the party? Or has Comrade Yeltsin decided to put the question of his resignation from the Politbureau, while remaining first secretary of the Moscow city committee of the party? This sounds like a wish to fight the central committee. This is how I understand him, but of course I may be overstating his intention.

Unable to restrain myself, I could not help interrupting Gorbachov. With remarkable finesse, he had distorted and falsified what I had said. Now, it seemed, I was planning to lead the Moscow city committee into a fight against the central committee. A political case had been set up against me; the tone and the keynote had been given. Naturally I leaped to my feet then and there to protest, but it was too late.

GORBACHOV: Sit down, sit down, Boris Nikolayevich. You did not put the question of your resignation from the city committee to this plenum: you said it was the business of the city committee to decide it.

And I have, I think, covered all the points raised in your remarks, apart from your objection claiming that I have misunderstood you as to whether you are or are not asking the central committee to deal with the question of your work as first secretary of the city committee.

Have I summarised your speech correctly, Comrade Yeltsin?

Let us hear your opinions, comrades. The questions that have been raised are, I think, matters of principle. This is precisely the occasion, on the seventieth anniversary of the October Revolution, to discuss such matters, and they contain lessons for me, for the central committee and for Comrade Yeltsin. In fact, for all of us.

This question must be cleared up.

You, the members of the central committee know all about the work of the Politbureau; you can assess its policies, and you, more than anyone else, know what needs to be said. I invite you to speak, but I won't insist. If any member of the Politbureau wishes to have the floor, I will naturally call on him.

Comrades, will anyone who wishes to speak please raise their hand?

From then on the scenario was almost, although not quite, as I had expected. As I mentally assessed the situation, wondering what arguments would be put up to refute my remarks, wondering who would speak, I imagined that no really big guns would be wheeled up and that nobody whom I regarded as a friend would attack me. But when it started in earnest – when, eyes ablaze, people came up to the rostrum who had long worked beside me, who were my friends, with whom I was on excellent terms – I found it extremely hard to bear this kind of betrayal. I feel sure that these people are now ashamed to read the invective which they hurled at me on that occasion. But what's said is said and cannot be unsaid. As speech followed speech, the tone was largely demagogic, and they all added up to more or less the same message: Yeltsin is an expletive four-letter word. Words were repeated, epithets were repeated, labels were repeated. How I endured it, I don't know.

One of the first to speak was Ryabov, whose colleague I had been for so long in Sverdlovsk. Why did he have to do it? To prepare a path for himself upwards, if not into the future then perhaps for a better pension? And he, too, began to douse me with a bucketful of filth. It was most unpleasant. Then came Boris Konoplyov, first secretary of Perm province; Gennady Bogomyakov from Tyumen province in Siberia; and others, all people who had been my colleagues and with whom I had, I thought, eaten a peck of salt in my time. But each one was thinking of himself, each one reckoned this was an opportunity to earn himself a few plus points for good behaviour. Of the Politbureau members, I found Nikolai Ryzhkov's and Alexander Yakovlev's speeches particularly unexpected and hurtful; I had no idea they were capable of saying such things. It seemed to me that Gorbachov particularly wanted these two to speak, because I had always treated them with respect; consequently, I would find listening to them especially painful.

I already knew that after this, another long process would begin which I would have to endure, and that here, at the plenum, I would not be dismissed from candidate membership of the Politbureau. I would have to wait for the next plenum of the Moscow city committee, at which I would first be relieved of my post of first secretary, and then, at another plenum [of the central committee], I would be dismissed from the Politbureau. And so it was. At the end of this [October 1987] plenum the members voted on a brief resolution criticising my speech as 'politically erroneous' and proposing that the Moscow city committee should consider the question of my re-election. There was, of course, nothing remotely 'politically erroneous' in my speech, and anyone who later read the transcript of it was able to see that for themselves.

Incidentally, when the forthcoming publication of the *Bulletin of the Central Committee of the CPSU* was announced, which contained the transcript of the October 1987 plenum, I made no effort to read that text prior to publication. As I subscribe to it, I waited for my copy to be delivered to my home. I read my speech. I was mildly surprised, having been under the impression that my remarks had been altogether tougher and sharper, but evidently time was to blame for this misapprehension. Since then Soviet society has moved far forward and many fierce discussions have taken place, both at the [June 1988] nineteenth party conference and during the election campaign. At the time [October 1987], my speech was the first piece of criticism aimed at Gorbachov, the first attempt – not over the kitchen table but in a party forum – to discuss openly why *perestroika* was making no progress. It was, as it were, the first expression of the pluralism that had been declared to be so desirable. I did not, however, read the speeches made by the other so-called orators. I could not bring myself to do so. Reading them would have been almost like experiencing all over again that terrible sense of injustice, that feeling of betrayal and I just couldn't do it.

It was a difficult time; I took it all very badly. For a few days I kept going literally by will-power alone. I stood on top of Lenin's tomb [as a privileged spectator of the Revolution Day parade] on 7 November, certain that I was standing there for the last time. Most of all I was annoyed that I had not been able to complete much of what I had planned to do for Moscow, and that I would leave behind me more than enough urgent, pressing problems. I believe I had managed to give the Moscow party organisation a thorough shake-up, but there was still a lot that I had not been able to do. I felt guilty towards the city committee, towards Moscow's party members and towards the Muscovites themselves. On the other hand, however, given that the Politbureau's attitude was hardly likely to change and in order to spite me, my proposals for improving the life of the city were running up against a brick wall, I could not allow the Muscovites to become hostages to my situation. I really had to go.

An interesting episode took place on that 7 November. I was still a candidate member of the Politbureau, since the central-committee plenum which was to decide on my resignation had not yet taken place. On that day, which commemorates the October Revolution, the secretaries and first secretaries of the communist parties of the socialist countries assembled in Moscow. They arrived for a joint conference, apart from which, each of them had separate talks with Gorbachov. Without doubt they asked him questions about me and he, of course, told them the whole story. I can only guess at what he said, but naturally he regarded me as being entirely to blame. So on 7 November, I, along with the entire complement of the Politbureau and the central-committee secretaries, was walking solemnly towards Lenin's tomb, in the customary strict order: full members of the Politbureau in alphabetical order; candidate members in alphabetical order; central-committee secretaries in alphabetical order, with Gorbachov, of course, heading the procession. The leaders of the foreign communist parties greeted him, as usual, with a simple handshake and no more. Then, in turn, they would shake the rest of us by the hand. When I came up to Fidel Castro, he suddenly embraced me three times, in the Russian fashion, and said something in Spanish. I didn't understand it, but I could sense that it was said with comradely sympathy. I clasped his hand and thanked him. I was naturally in a depressed mood. A few paces further on, Wojciech Jaruzelski did the same thing and told me in Russian to stand firm. In a low voice I thanked him, too, for his sympathy and support. All this took place under the eyes of Gorbachov and all our other party leaders.

This, I think, only increased their suspicion of me. They avoided talking to me, lest anyone else should see them engaged in this strange activity. At that point, though, I think that a few Politbureau members, in their heart of hearts, supported me; perhaps not totally, but they were at least sympathetic. Some of them had sent me greetings cards with good wishes for the 7 November holiday. Gorbachov did not send one; but then I didn't send one to him, either. I only sent them to those who had sent one to me. There were, and still are, people in the Politbureau who understood my position, who to some degree appreciated the independence of my judgment and who inwardly supported my proposals; but they were few. On such occasions I was usually attached to one of the general secretaries or first secretaries of a foreign communist party, generally Fidel Castro. He and I always got on very well together. But this time I was left on my own. Naturally I felt extremely uncomfortable at the reception after the parade, and I tried to stay on the sidelines.

On 9 November I was taken to hospital with a severe bout of headaches and chest pains. Evidently my body had been unable to withstand the nervous strain and I had suffered a physical breakdown. I was at once pumped full of medicines, mostly tranquillisers, which relaxed my nerves and muscles. The doctors forbade me to get out of bed, constantly giving me drips and more injections. It was particularly bad at night, and between 3 and 5 a.m. I could scarcely bear the appalling pain of my headaches. My wife wanted to come and see me, but they would not admit her, saying that I was too sick to be disturbed.

Suddenly on the morning of 11 November the bell rang on my special Kremlin-line telephone, plugged into the so-called automatic telephone exchange no. 1. It was Gorbachov, and he spoke as if he were not calling me in hospital but at my *dacha*. In a calm voice he asked me to go round and see him for a short while and then, perhaps, to attend the plenum of the Moscow city committee together. I said I couldn't come because I was in bed and the doctors wouldn't even let me get up. He told me cheerfully, telling me not to worry, that the doctors would help me to do so.

I shall never be able to understand that. In the whole of my working life I have never heard of anyone, whether a worker or a manager, being dragged out of a hospital bed in order to be dismissed. It's unheard-of. My complaint is not that it is a crass violation of our labour laws, because the provisions of the code of labour law have never, it seems, applied to politicians. However much Gorbachov may have disliked me, to act like that was inhuman and immoral. I simply hadn't expected it of him. Why was he in such a hurry, I wondered? Was he afraid that I might change my mind? Or did he reckon that with me in this condition he could most easily make short work of me at the plenum of the Moscow city committee? Perhaps he actually wanted to finish me off physically? I could not understand such cruelty.

I began to pull myself together. The obedient doctors, who only a few hours ago had not only forbidden me to get up and move about, but still less to go outside, started to pump me full of sedatives. My head was spinning, my legs were crumpling under me,

I could hardly speak because my tongue wouldn't obey; when my wife saw me she begged, implored, demanded that I should not go. Scarcely able to shuffle my feet, I was almost like a robot; I understood practically nothing of what was happening around me, and in that state I got into a car and was driven to the offices of the central committee.

Worn out by the strain and worry caused by my illness, my wife could not restrain herself and had some extremely sharp words with Plekhanov, the head of the ninth directorate of the KGB. She told him that to discharge such a sick man was sadism; that whereas the KGB was supposed to be guarding me and taking care of me, they now might easily cause my death – and all because of their cowardice in being unable to stand up for me on grounds of simple humanity. He, of course, had nothing to say in reply; he was just another little cog-wheel in the system, which always functioned 'wonderfully' whatever the circumstances. If it was their job to guard Yeltsin, they would guard him; if orders came to fetch him when he was an incapable invalid, then they would fetch him. I believe that if they had been so ordered, they would have hauled me, dead, out of my grave and delivered me to a plenum or to anywhere else.

I was thus barely conscious when I appeared at the Politbureau. I was in the same condition when I arrived at the plenum of the Moscow city committee. All its members were already seated when the entire top brass of the party entered the hall, and took their seats on the presidium, like a row of waxwork dummies, while the full complement of this plenary meeting stared back at them, as frightened and mesmerised as a rabbit looking at a boa constrictor.

What do you call it, when a person is murdered with words? Because what followed was like a real murder. After all, I could have been dismissed in a sentence or two, then and there, at the plenum. But no; they had to enjoy the whole process of public betrayal, when comrades who had been working alongside me for two years, without the slightest sign of discord in the relations between us, suddenly began to say things which to this day my mind refuses to absorb. If I hadn't been so heavily doped, of course, I would have fought back, I would have refuted the lies and shown up the treachery – yes, the treachery! – of everyone who spoke. I blame the doctors, first, for allowing me to be dragged there at all, and second, for stuffing me so full of drugs that I could hardly take anything in. Although, perhaps, I should be grateful to them for

154

that; the fact that my perceptions were so blunted may have saved me from a fatal heart attack.

Afterwards I would often go back in my mind to that November plenum, in an attempt to understand what made those people go up to the rostrum, how they salved their conscience and flung themselves on me at the bidding of the chief huntsman: tally-ho! Yes, they were a pack of hounds. A pack ready to tear me in pieces. I don't think I can describe it in any other way. Their speeches contained little real argumentation, mostly consisting of either demagogy, conjecture, fantasy or plain lies. Some attacked me simply out of fear: we've been told to savage him so we'll do it, there's no getting out of it. Others suddenly revealed a really nasty streak in their nature: at last I can put the boot in – you were my boss and I couldn't say a word against you, but now! All of this, taken together, added up to something terrible, something inhuman.

So I was dismissed, ostensibly at my own request, but it was done with such a ranting, roaring and screaming that it has left a nasty taste in my mouth to this day. The entire proceedings of that plenum were published in *Moskovskaya Pravda*. One of the first things I did as first secretary of the city committee was to demand that this newspaper should start publishing reports of plenary meetings in full: the reports and speeches, without cuts. To this day the central committee has been unable to sanction this, because it is afraid to do so. Thus I was hoist with my own petard. I'm joking, of course; on the contrary, truth and frankness can never do harm. To unprejudiced people that publication in *Moskovskaya Pravda* was a severe blow; it plainly revealed the attitudes of fear, cowardice and bootlicking which prevailed in the upper echelons of the party.

Then I went back into hospital. I managed to haul myself out of it before the February 1988 plenum, although it was my fourth stroke. The plenum passed off calmly enough, and Gorbachov moved my dismissal from candidate membership of the Politbureau. He also cautiously floated the possibility that I might retire on a pension and my team of doctors at once advised me to think about it. At first, after talking to my wife, I told them to wait, that I would return to that topic after my discharge from hospital. Then I thought seriously about it, and decided that a pension was not for me. It meant certain death, as I would be incapable of retiring to my *dacha* to grow dill and radishes. I would go barking mad or die of boredom. I need to be among people, I need to work;

otherwise I am lost. I told the doctors that I would not take retirement.

After a little while Gorbachov again telephoned me in hospital and offered me the ministerial post of first deputy chairman of the state committee for construction (Gosstroi). As I have already explained, at that moment I didn't care what job I might do and I accepted it without a second's reflection. People have often asked me – and later I used to ask myself the same question – why Gorbachov didn't decide to get me out of the way once and for all. The removal of political opponents has always been successfully managed in the Soviet Union. I could easily have been pensioned off or sent as ambassador to some faraway country. Yet Gorbachov let me stay in Moscow, gave me a relatively highly placed job and, in effect, kept an inveterate opponent close by him.

It is my belief, therefore, that if Gorbachov didn't have a Yeltsin, he would have had to invent one. Despite the dislike of me that he has shown recently, he realises that he needs someone like me – prickly, sharp-tongued, the scourge of the over-bureaucratised party *apparat* – and for this reason he keeps me close at hand. In this real-life production, the parts have been well cast, as in a well-directed play. There is the conservative Ligachov, who plays the villain; there is Yeltsin, the bully-boy, the madcap radical; and the wise, omniscient hero is Gorbachov himself. That, evidently, is how he sees it.

I also think that he decided not to pension me off and not to send me as ambassador to Upper Volta because he was afraid of the power of public opinion. When I was dismissed, the central committee, *Pravda*, and indeed all the national newspapers and journals were flooded with letters protesting against those decisions of the central committee and the city committee. Willy-nilly, he had to take account of that.

I had now to haul myself up by my bootstraps out of the crisis in which I found myself. I looked around and there was no one there. A kind of void, a vacuum, had been created: a human vacuum. Life is strange. I had, I thought, been working in contact with people. I like company; I have always been drawn to people and I shun solitude. And when they betray you, one after another, then by dozens – people with whom you have worked, people you have trusted – you begin to feel a strange sense of being doomed. Is this, perhaps, a characteristic feature of the modern age? Perhaps people in Soviet society have grown so hard, after so many black decades, that all the goodness has been driven out of them? It was as though a circle had been traced round me which no one could enter for fear of contamination. As if I were a leper, especially for anyone who trembled for their career; for those who strove to please the mighty; for opportunists; but also, sad though it may be, for people who are quite normal but are also dogged by some fear.

Yes, many turned away from me. The majority of them were time-servers who had once seemed to be friends and comrades, but in reality were simply there for the ride as long as it was taking them in the right direction, for whom I was useful as a boss, as first secretary – and that's all. At plenary sessions of the central committee and other gatherings, when there was no avoiding me, our leaders would acknowledge me, nervously and cautiously, with a nod of the head, making it clear that although I was, of course, alive, I was only nominally alive. Politically I didn't exist; politically I was a corpse. And then another thing that made me vaguely depressed was the absence of telephone calls from people who had once been constantly phoning me and now had suddenly stopped calling. I often wondered how I would have behaved in their place. I am at least absolutely certain that I would not abandon someone when they are in trouble. It would be too glaring a violation of elementary human principles.

It is hard to describe the state I was in. A real battle with myself had started up within me. I would analyse every step I had taken, every word; I would analyse my principles, my view of the past, the present and the future; I would analyse my personal relationships with people and even with my family. I was engaged in a constant, obsessive process of analysis, day and night, night and day. I would sleep for three or four hours, and then the thoughts would come creeping back. In cases like this people often seek solace in God; others seek it in the bottle. Neither of these escape routes interested me. All that was left was faith in people, but of a very limited sort: only my true, devoted friends. None of my previous, often naïve faith remained. Mentally I summoned up the images of hundreds of people – friends, comrades, neighbours and colleagues. I reviewed my relationships with my wife, my children and my grandchildren. I reviewed and examined my beliefs. All that was left where my heart had been was a burnt-out cinder. Everything around me was burnt out, everything within me was burnt out.

It was a time of fierce struggle with myself. I knew that if I lost that fight my whole life was lost. The tension within me was thus extreme, and for that reason my strength was at a very low ebb. I was tormented by headaches almost every night. The emergency medical service would often come, I would be given an injection and for a time the pain would go, only to return. My family, of course, supported me in every way they could. For night after sleepless night my wife Naya, my daughters Lena and Tanya, would sit beside my bed and do all they could to help. Especially at the onset of those appalling bouts of headache, I felt like crawling up the wall and could hardly restrain myself from crying out aloud. It was like the tortures of hell. Often my patience simply snapped and I used to think my head was about to split open.

I had faith in a few doctors, for example Yuri Kuznetsov, Anatoly Grigoriev and one or two others, who told me that it would all pass, that it was the effect of overstrain, which only time could cure. Yet my brain never switched itself off. It was in working mode almost round the clock, day in, day out. My nerves would give way. My moods were inconsistent, and sometimes I vented my feelings on my family. When I calmed down again, I felt ashamed and embarrassed in front of the people who were closest to me. My family had to put up with a lot during that time – but they always forgave me.

My wife and daughters would try to calm and distract me, but I was aware of the efforts they were making and it only wound me up even more. Altogether I gave them a very hard time. And it is largely thanks to them that I managed to survive and pull out of that time of trial. Later, I heard people saying that I had been contemplating suicide; I don't know where those rumours came from. Admittedly, the state I was in was such that it might drive a person to that simple way out. But I am not like that; my character will not allow me to give in. No, I would never have taken that step.

Although I was living the life of an outcast, I was not quite on a desert island. I was on a peninsula, and my peninsula was joined to the mainland by a narrow path. It was a human path, a path of faithful devoted friends, many from Moscow, many from Sverdlovsk, indeed from all over the country. They were quite undisturbed that the authorities suspected them of being in contact with me.

I started going for walks around the streets. In the days when I had been working, I had completely forgotten what it was like, simply to go out and take a walk without bodyguards or aides, like any ordinary Muscovite. It was a wonderful feeling, perhaps the only pleasure that I experienced in the whole of that black time. Complete strangers would come up to me in the street, in shops, in the cinema, with a smile of greeting. This made things easier to bear for me, and at the same time it made me think: here were ordinary passers-by, whose behaviour was more decent and honourable than many of those who had once called themselves my friends.

The fact that I was a political outcast was made clear to me everywhere, and even though as first deputy chairman of Gosstroi I was holding a position of ministerial rank, constant attempts were made to represent me as a flawed person who was very much on the wane. In this atmosphere it was, of course, extremely difficult, if not impossible, to solve problems and get things done in my new job. Those eighteen months were, in fact, something of a nightmare, and to be honest the work didn't suit me either. Although I had, as usual, dived into it head first, I still felt an urge to be back in political life. The job didn't allow me to have enough contact with people.

The Western press continued to take an interest in me, and the sequel to any interview that I gave was invariably a scolding from the party, because I always tried to tell the truth. When I met Western journalists I had no wish to hide anything or to suppress any facts. For decades it had been drummed into us that the Western press only ever lied or deceived people, and did nothing but write slanderous filth about us. In reality, the correspondents of the serious Western press are more often than not distinguished by their competence, professionalism and strict observance of journalistic ethics. I'm not talking about the yellow press; unfortunately I have had occasion to encounter that too.

I took quite a philosophical attitude to the fact that the Soviet press ignored me; I knew that the journalists themselves were not responsible for this. Indeed, I saw how Soviet newspapermen would try to slip stories about me past their bosses, reports in which there was a brief paragraph or even just a mention of my name. But such stories were always censored out, and more than once the journalists got into serious disputes on this score. But there were other articles, too, that were unfair and malicious.

My relations with the intelligentsia were not easy either. Someone started circulating the myth, no doubt linked to the defects in my character, that I was a leader of the Stalinist type – which was, of course, absolutely untrue, if only because with all my instincts, with my whole being I detested what had happened during the Stalin years. I remember only too well when my father was taken away in the middle of the night, even though I was just six years old at the time. Yet at the same time it was the intelligentsia who refused to be manipulated by the *apparat* and extended the hand of sympathy to me. Irina Arkhipova, Yekaterina Shevelyova, Kyrill Lavrov and Mark Zakharov, together with many other writers and artists sent me greetings on national holidays, wrote to me, came to talk with me, invited me to the theatre and to concerts. I recall in particular a telegram, as funny and kind hearted as ever, sent to me by Eduard Uspensky, the children's writer [who created the TV cartoon characters of Cheburashka and Gena the Crocodile]. I greatly cherished all these messages.

Gradually and with great difficulty I overcame my own inner turmoil. Month by month I would feel a little better, albeit not all at once, but the process was taking place. I stopped being tormented by headaches, although I was still sleeping as badly as ever. The people who remained faithful through thick and thin, who suffered for me truly and sincerely, who would come to offer me their support at the worst moments, were the friends of my student days. I am eternally grateful to them. And they still feel sympathy for me, because it has so happened that I still seem to be engaged in a perpetual conflict of one kind or another.

Slowly, bit by bit, I began to settle down again. I became actively involved in the work of Gosstroi. To my own surprise I discovered that I had not lost my professional standards as a civil engineer, and that all the problems that fell within my competence were familiar to me. I had feared that I might have become out of date.

I neither met nor talked to Gorbachov. We only bumped into each other once, during a recess at a plenum of the central committee. He was walking up the aisle of the auditorium and I was standing on one side of it, so that he couldn't have gone past without noticing me. He stopped, turned towards me, took a pace forward and said 'hello'. I decided to keep to whatever tone he adopted, and replied similarly. The rest of the conversation had to be linked to what had happened literally a few days before.

Despite the fact that I was in disfavour and was, in effect, a political exile, I had been invited to the Higher Komsomol School for a meeting with the young people who studied there. They had had great difficulty in arranging this. The first to take the initiative had been Yuri Raptanov, secretary of the school's Komsomol committee, and he had been supported by nearly all the students, most of whom were mature, intelligent and energetic.

Raptanov first went to the rector of the school, who gestured dismissively on hearing that they were planning to invite Yeltsin. But Yuri was insistent, and approached the party committee, whose secretary was cast in a different mould, being more open minded and progressive. He proposed that the question should be discussed at the party committee's next meeting. It was there that it was decided to invite Yeltsin. When the rector saw that everyone was voting in favour of this proposal and realising that if he were to be the only one voting against it he would find his job extremely difficult in future, he too voted in favour. The students telephoned me and we agreed on a date and time for our meeting. Naturally everyone got to hear about this, in particular the central committee of the Komsomol, and I was told that Viktor Mironenko, the first secretary of the Komsomol central committee, went twice to the Higher Komsomol School to try and prevent the meeting from taking place. Even so, the students ignored him.

I knew in advance that the occasion would be fraught with risk, and this turned out to be the case. I began by making a speech, taking a general look at various political, economic and social problems, and describing the processes that were taking place within the party. My remarks immediately set the tone for keen and searching questions that were put to me, and my answers to them. It has always been my principle to answer the most awkward questions first. The questions handed up were tough and complicated to answer, sometimes offensive and difficult – in fact, all sorts. There were also questions of a personal nature, as well as others about Gorbachov and other Politbureau members and secretaries of the central committee. I answered all of them. I even answered questions about Gorbachov's failings, which at the time was almost unthinkable. The meeting lasted for about five hours and I remained standing at the rostrum for the whole of that time. The audience's reactions were boisterous, extracts from the speeches were published in the school's newspaper – in condensed form, but in terms which went well beyond the level of *glasnost* that was normal in the Soviet media at that time. Naturally the KGB tape-recorded the entire five hours.

So, during the recess at the central-committee plenum, when Gorbachov and I exchanged greetings, he asked me how I had found my meeting with the Komsomols, to which I replied that it had been very lively and interesting. He went on to say that he had heard that I had criticised them by saying that they gave inadequate attention to the Komsomol. I told him that he had been misinformed and that I didn't say 'inadequate attention', rather that they were treating the Komsomol 'badly'.

He stood there for a moment, evidently at a loss for an answer. We walked a few paces side by side. I said that he and I should meet, as problems were arising which ought to be cleared up. He agreed that probably we should. And that was all. With that our conversation ended, as I felt that the initiative should come from him. That was, I think, our only encounter in eighteen months; apart from that we neither met nor spoke to each other. Even so, I had the feeling that the ice was breaking up. My incarceration was coming to an end. New times were on the way, unpredictable and unfamiliar, in which I had to find a place for myself.

8

Chronicle of the Election Campaign

26 March 1989

Sunday. The last day. I sense that everyone at home is in a state of mild anxiety, expressed in a slightly excessive level of domestic bustle and fuss. This is somehow transmitted to me, although of course only my wife and children are able to detect this unusual state in me. At one point I looked out of the window and saw with horror that Western television crews were already waiting in the courtyard, right outside our front door. For several months past the close proximity of foreign journalists has become almost as familiar to me as the presence of my campaign helpers. As the election date grew closer, I had been unable to step out of doors alone, and it was impossible to hide from them. Of course I realised that they were only doing their job, but I must confess that it had been difficult to withstand such constant pressure. I realised, though, that today would see the peak of journalistic interest in me. For the first time my wife and children would see it, too, would feel what it is like, and it occurred to me that it would make a distressing impression on them.

We got ready and dressed up in our best – polling day is, after all, a national holiday – and went out of the front door. Immediately a horde of journalists flung themselves at us. There were practically none from the Soviet media; the crowd was largely made up of

163

Western correspondents. For some reason they wanted to film our family's progress from home to the Palace of Pioneers of Frunze district, where the polling station was located. I could not honestly see why they wanted to take these 'historic' shots, but they hovered around us all the way, filming us now from behind, now from in front.

At the polling station itself the scene was quite appalling. About a hundred people with cameras, flash bulbs and tape recorders surrounded me, pressing in, asking questions, interrupting and shouting in every language under the sun. As I forced my way through the crowd, I looked round to see how the members of my family were faring. They were holding their own, but clearly with a great effort. I went up to the first floor surrounded by this mass of people, and there my name was checked against the electoral register and I was handed a ballot-paper.

As I approached the ballot-box dozens of lenses were trained on me and suddenly I was overcome by a sense of the ridiculous. I recalled the thousands of similar photographs taken in the recent past, when our ageing leader, Brezhnev, had stood, frozen in a solemn pose at the ballot-box; he had clearly enjoyed both the event and the thought that tomorrow his photograph would be on the front page of every newspaper and magazine: 'Comrade Leonid Ilyich Brezhnev, general secretary of the central committee of the CPSU and chairman of the presidium of the Supreme Soviet of the USSR, at the polling station.'

So, when all those film, television and camera lenses were aimed at me, I couldn't help feeling how stupid it must seem to an onlooker. I muttered, 'This won't do. It's like a flashback to the Brezhnev era', quickly dropped my ballot-paper into the slot, and made a dash for the exit. I do not think anyone actually managed to photograph me at the solemn moment of casting my vote into the ballot-box; all the journalists then flung themselves after me, managing to destroy one of the voting-booths in the stampede. I felt truly sorry for the members of the electoral commission manning the polling station, who had been overwhelmed by this tornado, and I tried to get out on to the street as quickly as possible in order to draw the surging mass of journalists out of the building.

For about half an hour I could not force my way out of the solid, encircling ring, while I answered questions about the election; about my own chances of being elected; and about the past. Finally I struggled free, and together with my family we almost ran away from the pursuing journalists to the home of my elder daughter, who lived close by the polling station. We took refuge there, where we were able to get our breath back in peace and to reflect on the events of that day. For the day was a decisive one; it would decide the outcome of my pre-election battle – not against my opponent, but against the party *apparat*.

My selfless assistants were to be found at practically every polling station in the capital. Their first objective was to watch carefully for any dirty tricks or rigging of the electoral process (although I did not believe that anyone would stoop to that), and second, to pass on to me the outcome of the voting when the first results started coming in.

We had every reason to worry about the figures, to be concerned about practically every individual vote. We had heard of an unexpected decision taken by the authorities, according to which all the Soviet officials working abroad in twenty-nine different countries were to be registered as voters in the Moscow city no. 1 constituency. No doubt this was one final attempt to influence the result of the election. Everyone realised that the figures for these overseas votes would be dismal. It was most likely that in every Soviet embassy the officials and employees would vote obediently in line with the ambassador's preference. They were, after all, abroad. For that precise reason, therefore, the number of votes had to be overwhelmingly in my favour, to counteract any unfavourable weight of votes coming from Soviet citizens abroad.

When the journalists on watch outside my daughter's front door realised that it was pointless to wait for me any longer and dispersed, we emerged from our refuge and decided simply to take a walk around the city. There was something joyous about that walk around Moscow. Passers-by greeted us, smiled and wished me good luck. That evening I was told the preliminary results of the count. I was well in the lead in every polling district. There was now practically nothing that could prevent me from winning the seat.

———

'Boris Nikolayevich! People all over the country have a very good opinion of you. Even so, it is strange that you were chosen as a delegate to the June 1988 party conference from Karelia, of all places. Why didn't you go as a delegate from Moscow? Or from Sverdlovsk?'*

'Tell us why Gorbachov didn't support you at the party conference.'*

'Do you remember Chikiryov, and who he was defending when he pounded his chest?'*

'Don't you regret criticising Gorbachov's "cult of the personality" at the seventieth anniversary of the October Revolution, instead of at the nineteenth party conference? Didn't your sense of political timing let you down on that occasion?'*

Everyone in the leadership and the *apparat* prepared themselves earnestly for the nineteenth all-union party conference; the party, and indeed society as a whole, were expecting a lot to come of it. It is now possible to say that the conference did, of course, give a push to the development of Soviet society; it did not, however, become the historic turning-point in the life of the country that a party conference should be. Certain of its decisions were more conservative than was the mood of the country at the time. The proposal, for instance, to combine the functions of party and Soviet leaders, starting with the general secretary and ending with the secretaries of local party committees, struck people as a bolt from the blue. Even Stalin, it will be recalled, did not allow himself to combine these two duties. The population at large did not lend this proposal active support, but a majority of conference delegates obediently voted for the resolution to that effect.

The delegates to the conference were chosen more carefully than usual and were even elected according to special instructions drawn up by the central committee. An active part in organising these

* (From questions handed up from the floor at meetings during the election campaign.)

pseudo-elections was played by Razumov, the first deputy chief of the organisation branch of the central committee. Virtually all personnel matters were in his hands and consequently the results fully reflected his subjective sympathies, antipathies and favouritism.

At the time I was in exile, as it were, working in Gosstroi, and the party leadership naturally did not want me to return to political life. But I felt the desire and the strength to start another political career from scratch; in any case, my principles would not allow me to leave the political arena meekly, without putting up a fight. My speech at the October 1987 plenum of the central committee was still not publicly known and, somewhat naturally, an aura of mystery still shrouded the whole episode. Party organisations around the country were starting to propose me for election as a delegate to the party conference, so it became a primary objective of the *apparat* to prevent my election. I held ministerial rank, a fairly highly placed position, and there seemed no doubt that ministers would be elected as delegates to the conference. I noticed, however, that while ministers were being elected to the delegations from various regions, I was not among them. Total silence. There was, of course, a real chance of not being elected to attend the nineteenth party conference at all. At first I somehow did not realise how great a likelihood this was; but the *apparat* was hard at work, time was passing and it soon became clear that I was the only minister not to be elected as a delegate to the conference. It was then that I realised the seriousness of the situation.

I felt that I had to attend the party conference and speak there. But I had no idea what I should do if the party *apparat*, which was manipulating the delegate elections like a skilled conjuror, succeeded in isolating me. I could not pick up the telephone and make demands to Gorbachov or to any other Politbureau member, reminding them that I was a member of the central committee and was not being put forward as a delegate, that this was improper and dishonest.

I did not conceal – at least, not from myself – that the nineteenth party conference would, first of all, give me the opportunity to explain what had happened at the October 1987 plenum and, second, might perhaps be my last chance to drag myself out of political 'exile' and once again to take an active part in public life. I was convinced, and still am convinced, that I committed no political errors in my speech to the October 1987 plenum of the central committee. And for that reason I felt sure that, by speaking from the rostrum at the nineteenth party conference to its delegates, to party members throughout the country and to ordinary people, everything would fall into place. If, therefore, I were not to be elected a delegate to the conference, this would be a crushing blow to me. No doubt that was why I did not even try to guess what I might do if the conference were to take place without me. Would I leave Moscow? Would I watch the conference on television? Would I ask Razumov for a ticket to the visitors' gallery? No, I could not contemplate the idea, even hypothetically. I had to become a delegate to the conference; no other alternative was possible.

Enterprises in Sverdlovsk, Moscow and other cities bestirred themselves and began putting forward my name among candidates for their delegations. But the *apparat* fought this tooth and nail, and it often had all the appearance of a farce in the tradition of the very worst years of Brezhnev's era of stagnation. Yet everywhere *perestroika* was apparently in full swing – at least, it was now three years since it had been officially launched.

The *apparat* had devised a system whereby the local party organisations would put forward a large number of potential candidates; this list would then be passed up to the district committee, where many of them would be weeded out; thence it went on to the city committee for further weeding, and finally to the provincial committee or the central committee of the Communist Party of the republic in question. There, behind closed doors, only those candidates were left on the list who, in the view of the *apparat*, would not play fast and loose at the conference, but would speak and vote as they were supposed to do. This system worked ideally, and the name 'Yeltsin' was duly thrown out at the very foothills of the route to the summit.

As I have already mentioned, the Muscovites showed great energy in putting my name forward at the party cells of many enterprises, but sometimes before even reaching the city committee, or in other cases at the city committee itself, my candidacy was vetoed. Many party organisations in Sverdlovsk also proposed me: the Uralmash; an electrical machinery factory; the Uralkhimmash; the Verkh-Isetsk works; the Pnevnostroimashina factory, and other large enterprises. And under such powerful pressure from these organisations, the Sverdlovsk city committee decided to let my candidacy go forward. But that was not the end of it: the next stage was a plenum of the provincial committee, and real passions flared up over the issue.

When the workers threatened to strike and the plenum still could not make the decision, the central committee, sensing that tension was rising fast and the situation might get out of control, decided to retreat. At virtually the last regional plenum in the whole country – which took place at Karelia – I was elected a delegate to the conference. My 'well-wishers' could not allow me to be a delegate from such big organisations as Moscow or Sverdlovsk. That was why, on practically the last day of the delegate elections, I found myself in Petrozavodsk, the Karelian regional capital. At the plenum I was warmly received and visited several of the local organisations. It is an interesting part of the country with interesting people, although like everywhere else it had many economic and social problems. So, in the end there I was, among the thirteen delegates to the nineteenth party conference representing the Karelian regional party organisation.

It was then that several more delicate situations arose. I have already mentioned that, during my political isolation, my name was taboo in the Soviet press; no such person as Yeltsin existed. Western journalists, however, were constantly asking me for interviews, one of which I gave to three American television networks, including CBS. I still do not understand why the Americans, when they transmitted the programme, found it necessary so to edit the video-tape that one of my answers was given out of context, but nevertheless they did so and thus precipitated a huge row. At one of his press conferences, Gorbachov said that he would sort the matter out with me, and that if I had forgotten what party discipline was and was still a member of the central committee, then I would have to be reminded of it, or something in that vein.

Apart from that, there was another unpleasant episode. Just before the start of the party conference, I was rung up, quite unexpectedly, by Alexander Radov, a columnist on the magazine *Ogonyok*, with the suggestion that he and I should have an extensive talk which would then be published in the magazine. Although I was glad that one of the most popular magazines in the country (I usually read it from cover to cover) was prepared to run the risk of publishing an interview with me, I nevertheless declined the offer. I told Radov that we would have to spend a long time talking to each other and that he would then have had to put in a lot of work editing the piece, with the only result being that he would not be allowed to publish it. Radov insisted, saying *Ogonyok* was a magazine with a lot of clout, that we should not have to show the piece to anyone and that the editor, Valery Korotich, would accept personal responsibility for any controversial material. In the end he persuaded me and I agreed to give the interview. And we did indeed put a lot of work into it; this was to be my first appearance in the Soviet press since the October 1987 plenum, and I therefore took this opportunity very seriously. But, of course, when everything was ready for publication, a crestfallen Radov came to me and announced that the interview could not be published in *Ogonyok* after all. Korotich had decided to show it to the central committee, where the officials had vetoed its publication in the magazine.

I was not greatly surprised, because I had been prepared for this, although it did upset me. It is psychologically extremely depressing to be gagged in one's own country, and to be unable to explain oneself or communicate with people except through the Western media. But most of all I was amazed when Korotich suddenly declared, in various interviews that he gave, that he had not published that conversation with me because it was apparently not very good and I had allegedly not answered the questions that interested the magazine; in particular I had said little about my new job, and that altogether the interview needed a lot more work. In short, the editor-in-chief had decided to assume full responsibility and thereby to cover up for the fact that the ban had been imposed by the senior officials of the central committee. Why did he do this? Didn't he realise that it was immoral not to allow someone to have his say who might think differently from, say, the general secretary? Who, if not he, a journalist, should be defending the universal principle of freedom of speech? But no; he had wriggled out of it and invented a lot of weak excuses rather than admit the real fact of the matter. If he had been afraid of the consequences, at least he could have kept his mouth shut, which would have been the more honourable course.

Thus I was in a state of nervous harassment as the start of the conference approached. Every day brought something new, little of it pleasant, until I had honestly forgotten that there was such a thing as good news. The nineteenth party conference opened in the Kremlin's Palace of Congresses. I was nervously excited as I drove to the opening session. After so many rumours, after the long 'conspiracy of silence' I was appearing in public for the first time and I was well aware how much people's reactions would differ. There were a lot of curious people who simply wanted to look at me, and it was these stares which irritated me most; I felt almost like an elephant in a zoo. Some of my old acquaintances averted their eyes in cowardly fashion, in case they might be infected by this 'leper'. In the circumstances I felt absolutely unnatural, almost persecuted, and therefore tried to stay in my seat during the breaks between sessions. There were, of course, others who came up to me quite calmly, asked me how I was, and expressed their support in words, smiles and looks.

The Karelian delegation was seated far at the back of the balcony – there was a space of only about six feet between our heads and the ceiling – and the presidium was barely visible. The speeches followed one after another and, as usual, some were bold and interesting, but the majority were a set of ready-made clichés that had been approved in advance by the *apparat*. Even so, the party conference was a big step forward. Probably for the first time in a party forum not everybody voted in favour of some of the resolutions, unlike the monotonous unanimity that had been the rule in the past. I had prepared a fighting speech, in which I had decided to put the question of my political rehabilitation.

Later, when the conference was over and I was deluged with letters of support, many of those who wrote only reproached me with one thing – the fact that I had asked to be politically rehabili-tated in my speech to the conference. They asked me if I didn't know what sort of people most of the delegates were, and how the delegate elections were carried out? How could I have asked any-thing of these people? One letter-writer, I think he was an engineer from Leningrad, wrote: 'Even Woland, the diabolical figure in Bulg-akov's *The Master and Margarita* said that one should never ask favours of anyone . . . And you forgot that sacred rule.'

Even so, I believe I was right to put the matter of my political rehabilitation to the delegates. It was important to state my position and to say aloud that the resolution of the October 1987 plenum of the central committee, which declared my speech to be a grave political error, was in itself a political error and should be with-drawn. I had no great illusions that this might happen, but I still had hopes. In the end, however, it was the people who pronounced my true rehabilitation. At the election to the Congress of People's Deputies, nearly 90 per cent of the Moscow electorate voted for me, and nothing is more precious to me than that, the most important form of rehabilitation. Whether the resolution of the October plenum is withdrawn or not, it no longer has any significance. That particular issue, it seems to me, is of much greater importance for Gorbachov himself and for the central committee.

But I run too far ahead. My first task at the conference was to obtain the right to speak. I knew that everything possible would be done to keep me away from the rostrum. The people who were organising the conference were well aware that my speech would be loaded with criticism and they did not want to hear it at all. And so it was. On the fifth and last day of the conference it was announced that three speakers would have the floor before the lunch-break and their names would be announced, and that after lunch, resolutions would be proposed and voted on. That was all. I kept thinking – how am I going to speak? The list of potential speakers was a long one, and from it they could always find those who could safely be allowed to speak – anyone, rather than allow me up to the rostrum. I sent a note to the presidium, to which there was no answer; I sent another, with the same result. Forty minutes before the break, the chairman announced that after lunch the conference would proceed to the adoption of resolutions and decisions. When I heard that my name was not on the list of chosen speakers, I decided on an extreme measure. I said to my fellow-members of the Karelian delegation that there was only one thing left for me to do – to take the rostrum by storm. They agreed. I went down the long staircase to the doors leading straight down the centre aisle to the rostrum and asked the KGB guards to open the doors. And since the officials of the KGB have always, generally speaking, treated me decently, they flung open the double doors. I took out my red conference mandate-card, held it over my head and firmly strode down the long aisle straight towards the presidium.

By the time I had reached the middle of that vast auditorium, everyone realised what was afoot, including the members of the presidium. The speaker – a delegate from Tadjikistan, I think – broke off in the middle of his speech. A sickening, deathly silence fell on the entire assembly. In that silence, with my red mandate-card held up in my outstretched hand, I walked straight forward, looking Gorbachov right in the eye. Every step reverberated within my soul. I could feel the breathing of over 5,000 people, every one of them staring at me. I reached the presidium, climbed the three steps, went up to Gorbachov with my mandate-card held out and, staring at him, I said in a firm voice that I demanded to be allowed to speak, or put my request to the vote of the whole conference. There was a moment or two of confusion, but I stood my ground. Finally Gorbachov told me to take a seat in the front row. I sat down there, immediately below the rostrum. I watched as the Politbureau members held a whispered consultation, then Gorbachov called up the head of the general department of the central committee, who went out after more whispering. Very soon one of his assistants came up to me and asked me to go to the presidium's ante-room, where they would like a word with me. I enquired who wanted to have a word with me? He replied that he didn't know, to which I countered that the arrangement did not suit me and that I should stay sitting there. He went away. Again the head of the general department conversed in whispers with the presidium, and there was some more nervous movement among its members. Once again the assistant approached me and said that one of the presidium members would come and see me in a moment or two.

I realised that I must not leave the hall; if I did, the doors would not be opened for me again. I said I would go, but would first wait and see which member of the presidium came to talk to me. As I tiptoed back up the aisle, people in the front rows whispered to me not to leave the auditorium. I stopped three or four yards short of the exit, turned and looked at the presidium. A group of journalists were seated near me, and they, too, advised me not to leave the hall. I was now quite sure that I must not go out. None of the presidium members stood up. The speaker went on with his speech. The same assistant came up to me again and said that Gorbachov had promised that I would be allowed to speak, but that I must first go back to the Karelian delegation. I realised that before I had gone back to the gallery and returned again, the time for speeches would have expired and I would not be allowed to speak. I therefore said that I would not go back upstairs, that I had formally taken leave of the delegation and so would not return; that I preferred to sit in the seat in the front row that had been offered to me. I turned sharply around and resumed my place in the front row on the aisle, directly facing Gorbachov.

Had he really meant to allow me to take the rostrum, or did he conclude, on second thoughts, that he would lose face if he put the matter to the vote and a majority chose to allow me to speak? It is hard to say. At all events, he announced my name as a speaker, adding that after the lunch-break the conference would proceed to the passing of resolutions. Later, I tried to guess what might have happened if the situation had developed differently. What if, for instance, the presidium had managed after all to persuade me to go back to the gallery, and the KGB men had then refused to let me back into the lower auditorium? Or if Gorbachov had exerted his authority to curtail the speeches before I had had time to mount the rostrum? What then? I remain convinced that somehow or other I would have contrived to have my say, having probably made a direct appeal to the conference delegates who, I felt sure, would have allowed me to speak. Even those who disliked me, who looked on me with suspicion or condemnation, had an interest in hearing what I might have to say. Having sensed the mood of the delegates, I am convinced they would have let me speak.

So I went up to the rostrum. Once again an absolute, almost oppressive silence fell on the hall. I began to speak and here I quote the text of the stenographic record of the conference:

Comrade delegates! First of all I must respond to the questions put in his speech by Comrade Zagainov, a delegate who spoke earlier, when he touched on a number of points concerning myself.

First question. Why did I give an interview to foreign television companies and not to the Soviet press? My answer is that the first to approach me was the Soviet news agency *Novosti*, and I gave their reporter an interview long before I spoke to the television companies, but *Moscow News* [for whom the interview was intended] was unable to publish it. Somewhat later, *Novosti* approached me again, but was unable to guarantee that the interview would be published. Even before that, the magazine *Ogonyok* also asked me to give them an interview; I spoke to their columnist for two whole hours, but that interview wasn't published either, even though there was an interval of six weeks [between the interview and its intended date of publication]. According to the statement made by Comrade Korotich, he was not allowed to print it.

Next question. Why were the remarks that I made at the

organisational plenum of the Moscow city committee so 'inarticulate?' To that I can only reply that I was severely ill at the time, confined to a hospital bed, without either permission or ability to get up. An hour and a half before the plenum I was summoned to attend and the doctors pumped me full of the necessary drugs. I sat through the plenum, but I could perceive almost nothing and was practically incapable of speech.

Further; I received a letter from the USSR state broadcasting committee (Gosteleradio) explaining that, in connection with this conference, the committee had been given the job of co-ordinating all interviews with foreign television companies, and requesting that I might give an interview to several of them.

By then, the number of such requests totalled fifteen. I told the first deputy chairman of Gosteleradio, Comrade Kravchenko, that I only had time to give interviews to two or three and not more. After that came a telephone message from Gosteleradio that three such foreign television organisations had been chosen: the BBC, CBS and ABC. I therefore named a date and time and gave an interview to these three networks in my office. One set of questions and answers was used for all three. I firmly rebuffed any unacceptable questions which might have been detrimental to the interests or prestige of our state or party.

The subsequent questions concerned my attitudes to Comrade Ligachov, to which I said that I shared his views at the strategic level, on the decisions of the [party] congress and the tasks of *perestroika*, although he and I did have certain differences of opinion on the tactics of *perestroika*, on questions of social justice and on styles of work. I did not go into detail on these points. I was also asked whether I thought that if someone else had been in Comrade Ligachov's place, *perestroika* would have progressed more rapidly, to which I replied, 'Yes'. Since what I said was distorted, the CBS broadcast my refutation of it and sent me a written apology for the error over the signature of a vice-president of the company.

I was then summoned by Comrade Solomentsev, who demanded an explanation. I expressed my indignation at being called to account on such an issue and replied verbally to every question about the interview that was put to me. The attempt to pin down my guilt by reference to the party statute failed. I regard myself as completely innocent in the matter. The original videotape with the full sound-track was translated for Comrade Solomentsev by our interpreter. I don't know what else may be done to me over this business, but it reminds me strongly of the shades of the recent past.

I shall now proceed with my speech.

Comrade delegates! The chief topic before this conference, as intended, is the democratisation of the party, bearing in mind that, over time, the party has become seriously deformed. In addition, of course, there is to be a discussion of today's burning questions of *perestroika* in general and of the revolutionary renewal of our society. The period of pre-conference preparation evoked unusual interest and hopes among party members and the whole Soviet population. *Perestroika* has given our people a thorough shaking-up. And it is evident that *perestroika* should have begun with a restructuring of the party itself; the party would then have drawn everyone else along behind it, as it has always done. Yet it is precisely in the matter of its own *perestroika* that the party has, in fact, lagged behind. Clearly, today's conference should have been held considerably earlier. That is my personal opinion.

Yet even so, the preparations for the conference were somehow hurried. The theses for discussion, compiled by the central committee's *apparat*, were published too late. No mention was made in them of the principal issue that emerged in the [chairman's] keynote speech. Not even a majority of central-committee members was brought into the process of drafting the theses. It will be impossible to incorporate all the suggestions that speakers have put forward, the whole storehouse of popular wisdom, into the resolutions to be passed by our conference.

Despite Comrade Razumov's attempt in the pages of *Pravda* to convince everyone that the selection of delegates was conducted democratically, that process was nevertheless conducted by many organisations along the old lines, and this showed yet again that the *apparat* of the party's upper echelon has not been restructured.

The discussion of ideas during the conference itself, however, has been interesting. Now the chief question is: What decisions will be taken? Will they satisfy our party members and society as a whole? Judging by what happened on the first day [of the conference], the impression created was one of caution – I would even call it depressing. But on each subsequent day the temperature rose, as the delegates' speeches became more and more interesting, and that will evidently be reflected in the resolutions that are adopted.

I would like to make a few comments and suggestions concerning the theses drawn up by the central committee, while also taking account of the speech made by Comrade Gorbachov.

On the political system, I regard it as essential that there should be a mechanism which functions, in the party and in society at large, in such a way as to exclude the repetition of errors even remotely resembling those of the past, which have put the country back by several decades; a mechanism which does not create 'leader'-figures and 'leaderism'; and which will create true popular sovereignty backed by firm guarantees of its permanence.

The proposal, made in [Gorbachov's] keynote speech to combine the offices of first secretary of party committees with chairmanship of the corresponding local or regional Soviets was so unexpected for the delegates that one worker, in his speech to the conference, said that he 'found it incomprehensible'. Speaking as a minister, I would say, 'So do I.' We need time to understand its implications. It is too complex a matter, and I propose that a national referendum on it should be held. (Applause)

Some suggestions about the elections: they should be universal, direct and secret, including elections to the party secretaryships, including the post of general secretary of the central committee and the party bureaux from bottom to top, from provincial level to the Politbureau, which should be elected by all party members under the same conditions (as in a two-tier electoral system). This should also apply to the Supreme Soviet, the trade unions and the Komsomol. The tenure of elective office should be limited to two terms, without exception – and especially in the case of the topmost echelon. Office holders should only be elected for a second term on the basis of concrete results achieved during their preceding term. A firm upper-age limit of sixty-five should be set for membership of all such bodies, including the Politbureau. The length of a term of office should be calculated from the date of the previous elections, and the age limit should be reckoned from the current year.

Our party, and society at large, have matured to the point where they can be trusted to decide such matters for themselves, and *perestroika* can only gain from that. In my opinion, all these suggestions that I have made – and not a two-party system, as some are proposing – will be an adequate guarantee against another 'cult of the personality', which will not take ten or fifteen years to emerge but can easily reappear at once if the soil is there in which it can flourish. I believe we should be on our guard against this now, since it has been the flouting of Leninist principles which has brought our people such calamities over recent years. Rigid barriers must be erected against it, and they must be upheld by the party statute or by the law.

In many countries it is established practice that when the leader steps down, his government steps down with him. With us, when anything goes wrong we habitually blame the dead – and that is no help at all in solving our problems. It now turns out that the only person to blame for the stagnation of recent years was Brezhnev. But what about those people who were in the Politbureau for ten, fifteen or twenty years under Brezhnev – and are still in it? They voted for any programme that was put in front of them. Why didn't they speak up, when one man alone, on the basis of projects fed to him by the central committee's *apparat*, decided the fate of the party, of the country, and of socialism? They voted 'yes' to the point of awarding one man his fifth star[1] – and to bringing society as a whole to a state of crisis. Why was the ailing Chernenko promoted to the general secretaryship? Why, when it was punishing people for comparatively minor deviations from the party's standards of behaviour, was the party commission afraid – and still is afraid – to prosecute the most highly placed leaders of certain republics and provinces for bribe-taking, for defrauding the state of millions of roubles? Yet the committee was undoubtedly aware that these offences were being committed. I must say that Comrade Solomentsev's liberal attitude to these millionaire bribe-takers does make one feel a certain disquiet.

I believe that a number of members of the Politbureau, as participants in the guilt of a collective body endowed with the trust of the central committee and the party as a whole, must answer this question: why were the country and the party brought to the state they are in today? And after that we must draw the necessary conclusion: they must be dismissed from membership of the Politbureau. (Applause) That is a more humane method than criticising them when they are dead, digging them up and burying them all over again!

I suggest that henceforth the following procedure should be adopted: when there is a change of general secretary, the Politbureau should be renewed, except for those who have only recently been elected to it; and broadly speaking the personnel of the central committee's *apparat* should also be changed. Then the nation will not be held, as in a trap, by a permanent, unchanging administration. Then people will no longer be criticised only after their death, knowing as they will that every one of them, including every member of the elective element of the central committee, is answerable to the party at large.

Further. At present, despite the general secretary's clear statement that there are no areas of policy, and no leaders – including himself – which are immune from criticism, in reality this is not the case. There is an area, there is a dividing line above which, at the first hint of criticism, there follows an instant warning, 'Hands off!' The result is that even members of the central committee are afraid to express their personal opinion to the leadership if it differs from an official statement of policy.

This does the greatest possible harm; it distorts an individual's personality and his party conscience, and trains him into the habit of instantly raising his hand with the 'ayes' – along with everyone else – whenever a vote is called, no matter what the issue may be. The present conference is, I believe, the first exception to what has become the rule. Until now it has been the case that the policies carried out by leading [party] bodies have effectively remained immune from criticism and beyond check or scrutiny by the mass of the people.

We must concur with the proposal in [Gorbachov's] keynote speech to create a commission, drawn from members of the central committee, to set long-term policy guidelines, and to ensure that without scrutiny and approval of this commission not a single central-committee resolution or directive may be implemented. As things stand at present, such directives are not the work of the central committee but of its bureaucratic *apparat*, and many of them are immediately stillborn. Major projects should be discussed by the whole party and by the country at large, including the holding of referendums. As a rule, the practice of issuing decrees jointly by the central committee and the USSR Council of Ministers should be abolished.

Yes, we are proud of socialism and proud of what has been achieved, but we must not rest on our laurels. In seventy years, after all, we have not yet solved the main problems: how to feed and clothe the population; how to ensure an efficient services sector of the economy; how to resolve social problems. It is the aim of *perestroika* to tackle all these, but its progress is being seriously held back, which means that each one of us is not putting enough vigour into working for it and fighting for it. But it is also true that one of the main obstacles to *perestroika* is its declarative nature. It was announced without adequate analysis of the causes of the stagnation that preceded it, without analysis of the current state of society, without a profound analysis on the historical plane of the party's shortcomings and past errors. As a result, after three years of *perestroika* we have not solved any of the real problems experienced by ordinary people, and still less have we achieved any [of the proposed] revolutionary transformations.

In putting *perestroika* into effect, we should not only set our sights on the year 2000 (to many people it is a matter of indifference whether they will get anything then or what they may get) but on each successive period of two or three years ahead, and within that span we should finally solve one or two specific problems for the good of the people. Without dissipating our efforts in other directions, we should concentrate everything – resources, science, human energy – on tackling those selected issues. Then – animated by a rapidly increasing faith that the restructuring of society is really under way; that it works; that it is irreversible – people will also resolve other problems at a significantly faster rate. As things are, people's faith in *perestroika* is liable to waver at any moment. So far, they are all still hypnotised by words, and that has saved the situation; for the future, however, there is a risk of losing both direction and political stability.

Now, about openness in the party. A multiplicity of opinions should be the normal state of affairs in the party, rather than colourless, standardised thinking. The existence of a distinct minority opinion will not destroy but only strengthen the unity of the party. The party exists for the people, and the people should know what the party is doing. This, unfortunately, does not happen. Detailed accounts of the proceedings of the Politbureau and the central committee's secretariat should be available, with the exception of topics involving state secrets. The public should also know about the lives and biographies of their leaders, about what they do, what salaries they receive, and the results achieved by each member of the top echelon in the sector for which he is responsible. There should also be regular appearances on television; announcement of the results of the entry of new members into the party; summaries of workers' letters addressed to the central committee, and so on. In general, there should be a comprehensive sociology concerning the moral health of the leaders of the party and the state. It should be open to all, and not kept secret.

And then there are the 'forbidden', 'secret' topics such as, for example, the financial details of the party's budget. It is stated in the party statute that the central committee decides on the expenditure of party funds – that is not the *apparat* but the central committee as a whole. But financial matters are not discussed at the plenary sessions of the central committee. I suggest that henceforth this should be compulsory. Because neither the members of the central committee nor still less other party members know anything of how the party's funds are spent – and they amount to hundreds of millions of roubles. The party audit commission never reports on this at party congresses, indeed the commission is not even allowed access to the books.

I know, for instance, exactly how many millions of roubles are transferred to the central committee from the Moscow city and the Sverdlovsk provincial party organisations. But how they are spent – I have no idea. I can only observe that, apart from rational and necessary expenditure, the party also spends its money on building luxurious houses, *dachi* and sanatoria on such a scale as to make one ashamed when the representatives of other [socialist] parties visit them. That money should instead be used for the material support of the primary, grass-roots party organisations, including the payment of decent salaries to their leading officials. And we are surprised when certain senior party leaders besmirch themselves with corruption, bribery and secret additions to their salaries; that they lose all sense of decency, moral purity, modesty and comradely relations with other party members. The corruption of the upper levels of the party under Brezhnev spread to many regions, and we must not underestimate or condone this. The rottenness has evidently gone deeper than many people suppose, and, as I know from my experience in Moscow, the mafia most definitely exists.

I now turn to matters of social justice. In broad outline, of course, we have dealt with these questions on socialist principles. But several problems remain unsolved which arouse people's indignation, lower the party's authority and have the most dire effect on the tempo of *perestroika*.

In my opinion, the principle should be as follows: if there is a lack of anything in our socialist society, then that shortage should be felt in equal degree by everyone without exception. (Applause) Differences in individual contributions to society in terms of labour should be reflected by differential payment; we must, at last, abolish the special 'rations' of otherwise unobtainable foods given to the 'starving' party establishment; we must eliminate élitism in our society, eliminate in both word and deed the epithet 'special' from our vocabulary, since there are no such creatures as 'special' communists. I believe this will greatly help party officials to work with the rest of the population and will also help *perestroika*.

Now, a few words about the structure and reduction in size of the party *apparat*. Lenin's call, 'All Power to the Soviets!' will never be realised given the existence of such a massive party *apparat*. I propose that we should reduce the *apparat* of provincial committees by two or three times, of the central committee by between six and ten times, including the complete abolition of those departments which at present deal with the various branches of the economy.

I would also like to mention young people. There is practically nothing about them in the theses for discussion at this conference. A lot was said about them, however, in [the general secretary's] keynote speech, and I would support the proposal to pass a separate resolution on young people. For it is they, and not we, who will have to play the main part in renewing our socialist society. We must boldly teach them how to direct this process at all levels, and hand over whole areas of leadership to them.

Comrade delegates! I now come to a ticklish matter. I would like to raise the question of my personal political rehabilitation after the October 1987 plenum of the central committee. (Noise in the hall) If you think that time will not permit it, then I have finished my remarks.

MIKHAIL GORBACHOV: Speak on, Boris Nikolayevich, they want you to have your say. (Applause) I think we should stop treating the Yeltsin case as secret. Let Boris Nikolayevich say whatever he thinks necessary. And if you and I feel the need, then we, too, can add a word or two after he has spoken. Go ahead, Boris Nikolayevich!

BORIS YELTSIN: Comrade delegates! Rehabilitation fifty years after a person's death has now become the rule, and this has had a healthy effect on society. But I am asking for my personal political rehabilitation while I am still alive. I regard this as a matter of principle and very appropriate, in the light of the calls made, in the keynote speech and in delegates' speeches, for socialist pluralism of opinions, for freedom to criticise and for tolerance towards opponents.

You know that by a decision of the central committee my speech at the October 1987 plenum of the central committee of the CPSU was declared to be 'politically erroneous'. But the questions that were raised at that plenum have since been raised on more than one occasion by the press and by party members. In the last few days practically all those same questions were voiced from this very rostrum, both in the keynote speech and in delegates' speeches. I consider that the only error in my speech was that I delivered it at the wrong time – immediately before the seventieth anniversary of the October Revolution.

Evidently we all need to master the rules of political discussion, to tolerate dissenting opinions as Lenin did; not to hang labels on people and not to regard them as heretics.

Comrade delegates! In the speeches made at this conference, including my own, the same questions that I raised at the October 1987 plenum have been fully aired. I resent what happened there very keenly, and I request the conference to withdraw the resolution about me which was passed at that plenum. If you consider it possible to annul it, you will thereby rehabilitate me in the eyes of party members. It is not only something personal; it will be in the spirit of *perestroika*, it will be democratic, and I believe it will help the cause of *perestroika* by increasing popular confidence in the party.

It is certainly proving hard to renew our society. But certain fundamental shifts, though small, have taken place, and life itself obliges us to take that road and no other. (Applause)

I finished my speech. To some degree my extreme tension had told on me, but even so I do believe that I got the better of myself and my nervous excitement, that I said everything I had to say and wanted to say. The reaction to my speech was good; at least they were applauding as I left the lower auditorium and started going upstairs to the balcony, where I rejoined the Karelian delegation. Just then the lunch-break was announced. My fellow delegates showed me the warmest attention, while others tried to show me their support with a smile or a handshake. I was keyed up and tense. I went outside, where I was surrounded by delegates and journalists who asked me a mass of questions.

Suspecting nothing, I rejoined my delegation after the break. According to the rules of procedure, the conference was supposed to start voting on resolutions and other decisions. But it turned out that the break had been used to mount a counter-attack on me and my speech from a whole battery of guns.

Ligachov's speech was memorable. Subsequently it was to be recycled in jokes, comedy sketches and satirical cartoons. His speech even had to be corrected for grammar and syntax in the published stenographic transcript, otherwise the Soviet Union's chief ideologist would have looked too incompetent. Despite all the labels he hung on me, despite all the nonsense he invented about me, and despite all his furious efforts, the whole thing was petty, vulgar and illiterate.

I think it was after that speech that his political career started to wane. He dealt himself such a crushing blow that he will never be able to recover from it. After the party conference he should have submitted his resignation, but he didn't want to. He didn't want to, but he will have to do so all the same. Since that speech, which reduced many delegates to embarrassed laughter, there is nothing else left for him to do.

The next speech was given by Lukin, the young first secretary of Moscow's Proletarsky district committee. He diligently showered me with mud, carrying out the noble task set him by the leadership.

I have often wondered how he could go on living with his conscience after that. In the end I decided that he would continue to get on splendidly with his conscience, because it has become so hardened. When these young careerists start climbing upwards they have to tell so many lies and do such things that in a case like his it is better not to mention his conscience at all.

Then came Chikiryov, general manager of the Ordzhonikidze works. It was he who concocted the story about the first secretary who allegedly threw himself out of an eighth-floor window on my account, in addition to spreading a lot more lies about me. As I listened to him I was not sure whether I was awake or having a nightmare. I had been to his factory, and had once even spent a whole day there with a minister, Panichev. As always, I spent some time in the canteen and the workers' rest-rooms, and after the visit I made some comments with which he appeared to agree. And now, suddenly, he poured out such invective against me that it is un-repeatable – it was nothing but lies and distortions of the facts. As may be imagined, this reduced me to a state of deep depression.

Then, to everyone's complete surprise, V. A. Volkov, a delegate from Sverdlovsk, came up to the rostrum and spoilt the pre-arranged scenario by saying a lot of kind words about me. I had never met Volkov before then. His sincere, impulsive speech was a natural human reaction to militant injustice. But after a few minutes the terrified first secretary of the Sverdlovsk provincial committee, Bobykin, sent a note up to the presidium. I will quote it:

The delegation of the Sverdlovsk provincial party organisation fully supports the decision taken by the October 1987 plenum of the central committee with regard to Comrade Yeltsin. No one empowered Comrade Volkov to speak in the name of our dele-gates. His speech has been thoroughly condemned. In the name of the Sverdlovsk delegation: Bobykin, First Secretary, Provincial Committe.

In fact, though, he did not consult his delegation before writing that note.

In conclusion Gorbachov also had plenty to say about me, but at least his remarks were not so crude and unrestrained.

All those around me were afraid even to turn and look at me. I sat motionless, staring down at the rostrum from the balcony, feeling that at any moment I might lose consciousness. Noticing my condition, several of the young stewards on duty took me to a doctor, who gave me an injection to enable me at least to hold out and stay in my place till the end of the conference. I returned to my seat, but it was physical and moral agony: I felt as if I were on fire inside, and everything was swimming in front of my eyes.

I found it very hard to recover from it all. I did not sleep for two nights in a row, agonising and wondering – what is happening, who is right and who is wrong? This, I felt, was the end. There was no other forum in which I could defend and justify myself. The session of the nineteenth party conference had been transmitted by television, live and in full, to the whole country. I felt that the 'establishment' was satisfied; they had beaten me to the ground and they had won. At that moment I was overcome by a certain state of apathy. I did not want to do any more fighting, any more explaining; I just wanted to forget everything, if only they would leave me in peace.

Then suddenly the telegrams and letters started coming to my office at Gosstroi from all over the country, from its most distant corners. It was a fantastic demonstration of popular support. People suggested honey, herbs, raspberry jam, massage, and so on and so forth to build up my strength and prevent me from ever falling ill again. I was advised to pay no attention to the idiotic things that had been said about me, since nobody believed them anyway. I was exhorted not to lose heart but to go on fighting for *perestroika*.

I received so many kind, touching, warm letters from total strangers that I could not believe it, and I kept asking myself – where does it come from? why do they write? for what reason? I did, of course, understand exactly where those burningly sincere emotions were coming from: our long-suffering people simply could not stand by calmly and watch dispassionately as a man was being pilloried. People were incensed by the obvious, rank injustice of it. In sending me those encouraging letters they were holding out their hands to me, and I was able to lean on them to get on my feet again. And to go forward once more.

9

Chronicle of the Election Campaign

27 March 1989

It is all over. The months-long marathon is finished. I don't know which is the greater feeling – exhaustion or relief. I have been told the precise results of the election: 89.6 per cent of the electorate voted for me. This is not quite a normal figure: in more 'civilised' elections, as it were, the number of votes for me should have been lower; but here people had been brought to such a state and such efforts had been made to discredit me, tell lies about me and prevent my election, that I might have collected even more votes.

Recently a new excuse for my success has been circulating: people did not vote for Yeltsin, they voted against the *apparat*. It is assumed that this remark will offend me, but I find it excellent if it means that my unequal struggle against the party bureaucracy was not fought in vain. If a protest against the *apparat* is associated with the name of Yeltsin, then there was some justification for my speeches at the October 1987 plenum of the central committee and at the nineteenth party conference.

I very much want to stop, look around me and have a rest; the election campaign has been so wearing and exhausting. But it is no good; new problems and worries are already overwhelming me. I have written a formal request to Nikolai Ryzhkov, chairman of the USSR Council of Ministers, asking him to release me from my ministerial post. According to the electoral law, a people's deputy cannot simultaneously be a minister, so as from today I am officially unemployed.

I have had telephone calls from Sverdlovsk congratulating me and saying that several progressive deputies were elected for their province, while Bobykin, the first secretary of the provincial committee of the party, was crushingly defeated. What is more, he had stood for a remote and, as he imagined, docile rural constituency, from which all other potential candidates had been eliminated at the selection meeting . . . yet even so the voters had thrown him out. At home there have also been hundreds of calls, all wishing me luck and sending the warmest greeting. Naya and I have arranged to leave Moscow for a few weeks and go somewhere where we can hide ourselves from everyone. I am, in fact, extremely tired and need a rest.

———

I sometimes feel that I have lived three different lives: the first, although not without its difficulties and tensions, was nevertheless much like other people's lives – study; work; family; a career as an industrial manager, then as a party official. It ended on the day of the October 1987 plenum of the central committee. Then began my second life – as a political outcast, surrounded by a void, a vacuum. I found myself cut off from people and had to struggle to survive, both as a human being and as a politician. Then, on the day that I won the election as a people's deputy, my third life began – it was my third birth, as it were. Less than a year has passed since then. And whereas little was generally known about the first two stages of my life, everything that has happened since the election – my work in the Congress of People's Deputies and at sessions of the Supreme Soviet; the creation of the Inter-Regional Group of Deputies; my trip to the USA and the attempts to compromise me – has taken place for all to see, and thus there have been no secrets and no blank pages. But since so many events have been crammed into these months, I must describe them.

After my convincing victory at the polls, rumours were going around that when the Congress of People's Deputies met I would challenge Gorbachov for the post of chairman of the Supreme

Soviet. I do not know how these rumours arose – whether it was among my supporters, who were in a state of euphoria after my election, or, on the contrary, among my enemies, frightened by such a powerful reaction from the voters of Moscow – but these rumours stubbornly persisted.

What did I feel about this? Practically nothing. I had a wholly realistic view of the political situation that had arisen in the country, and I had made a fairly exact prognosis of the make-up of the future minority and majority that would emerge at the Congress of People's Deputies, so that I had no illusions or ambitions on that score. I was, however, aware that my presence in the Congress would worry Gorbachov, and that he would want to know what my intentions were.

Approximately a week before the opening session, he phoned me and suggested that we meet for a talk. The meeting lasted for about an hour. For the first time in a long while we sat face to face. The conversation was tense and nervous, and I revealed to him much of the anxieties that had built up inside me over the past months. My own problems worried me least of all: what horrified me was that the country was falling apart. The bureaucratic *apparat* was playing the same old games as before, the chief one being to keep all power within its own hands and not to allow a scrap of it to pass to the Congress of the People's Deputies. I kept on trying to probe for the essence of his position: was he with the people – or with the system that had brought the country to the brink of disaster?

His answers were harsh and brusque, and the longer we talked the thicker grew the wall of incomprehension between us. When it became obvious that no human contact was going to be made, that no relationship of mutual trust could be built up, Gorbachov modified the tone and pressure of his remarks and asked me about my plans for the future: what was I going to do, what sort of work did I see myself taking up in future? I replied straight away that the Congress would decide everything. Gorbachov did not like that answer; he wanted me to give him some kind of guarantee, so he went on questioning me. What did I think of a job in industry? Would I be interested in a seat on the Council of Ministers? But I stuck to my line: the Congress would decide everything. I think I was right to do so; it was pointless to talk seriously about another job before the Congress had even started its work, but my reply irritated Gorbachov – he wanted to learn something more precise about my intentions, and he obviously thought I was concealing something from him. But I was quite sincere about not having made any premature plans; only after the session of the Congress would it be possible to start thinking about the future. On that we parted.

The very next day new rumours were being spread around Moscow. Oh, where is the poet or bard who will compose an ode to Russian rumours? Thanks to the chronic shortage of truthful (or even false) information, our people live on rumours. It is much the most important telegraph agency of the Soviet Union, of far greater importance than Tass itself. One would like to think that one day someone will make a study of our rumour-mill – how rumours arise and how they are circulated; it would make a fascinating book. This time the rumours announced that Gorbachov had met Yeltsin and offered him the post of first deputy prime minister, which Yeltsin had refused because he wanted to be chairman of the Supreme Soviet. This had then forced Gorbachov to offer him the office of first deputy chairman of the Supreme Soviet, but Yeltsin had again refused, to which Gorbachov had responded with an offer of the position of first secretary of the Moscow city committee of the party ... and this Yeltsin had accepted. Several people passed this story on to me, or variants of it, to which one could only shake one's head and marvel at the fertility of the human imagination.

Soon after that the Congress opened. I shall say very little about it, because anyone interested in it has been able to follow its progress in the minutest detail. Gorbachov took the important decision of principle that the entire session of the Congress should be broadcast, live, on national television. Those ten days, in which almost the whole country watched the desperate debates of the Congress, unable to tear themselves away from their television sets, gave the people more of a political education than seventy years of stereotyped Marxist-Leninist lectures multiplied a millionfold and flung at the Soviet people in order to turn them into dummies. On the day the congress opened, they were one sort of people; on the day that it closed they were different people. However negatively we may assess the final results of the Congress of People's Deputies, however much pain and regret we may have felt at the missed opportunities, the political and economic measures that were not taken in the right direction – nevertheless the most important thing was achieved: almost the entire population was awakened from its state of lethargy.

As usual, it did not pass off without some tense moments for me. During the discussions on the method of choosing the members of the new Supreme Soviet from among the people's deputies, I insisted categorically that this process should be a contested election. I honestly admit to hoping with all my heart that I would nevertheless be elected to the Supreme Soviet, though I also realised quite soberly that this particular body of people's deputies might well decide otherwise. The silent and obedient majority, which we had inherited from the recent past, would squash any proposal that displeased the leadership. And so it was. The first few calls to vote showed how successfully Gorbachov was managing to manipulate the Congress, and the elections to the Supreme Soviet only confirmed the fact that the cast-iron majority would block the path of anyone who was likely to step out of line. Sakharov, Chernichenko, Popov, Shmelyov, Zaslavskaya – all of them excellent, respected and highly competent deputies – failed to be elected to the Supreme Soviet. There were indeed so many who were not elected that it would be impossible to list them all. And I was among them. More than half the deputies voted for me, but I was still obliged to give way to those of my colleagues who received more votes than I did. I was not disturbed by this. I am not saying that to show how stoical I was; the fact was that the result was only to be expected. If that particular congress membership had voted me into the Supreme Soviet, that would have greatly surprised me. Events had taken their natural course, and I waited with interest to see how Gorbachov would wriggle out of the situation he had created for himself.

It was, of course, a scandal. Everyone realised that because of me this state of affairs might ultimately become explosive. The voters of Moscow regarded the outcome of the elections to the Supreme Soviet as a gross disregard of the wishes of several million people. That evening there began a series of spontaneous meetings, and here and there calls were heard for a political strike. As always in Soviet conditions, an individual emerged who had the sense to find a way out of this impasse. On this occasion the person who saved the situation was Alexei Kazannik, a deputy from Siberia. He was elected to the Supreme Soviet, but withdrew his candidacy in my favour. The Congress was obliged to approve this 'castling' move; when hands were raised in the congress hall and Gorbachov saw that the substitution would be approved, his face showed a look of unconcealed relief. Thus I became a member of the Supreme Soviet of the USSR and the question of my future employment automatically became redundant. A few days later I was elected chairman of the Supreme Soviet's committee on construction and architecture, and thus, *ex officio*, I also became a member of the presidium of the Supreme Soviet of the USSR.

I could spend a long time describing the proceedings of the Congress, which were marked by numerous dramatic, thrilling and tense situations. The whole country witnessed these events on television, as did the rest of the world, being by no means indifferent to what goes on in one-sixth of the inhabited globe. Therefore I will not dwell on these episodes in detail, for life has moved on again since then.

Generally speaking, the nearly two-months' work of the session of the Supreme Soviet, which included organising the committee on construction and architecture from zero, were marked by our traditional chaotic disorder: no offices for us to work in; no rooms in which to receive our constituents; incomprehensible instructions concerning a deputy's secretary or assistant; the dictatorship of the Supreme Soviet's permanent staff over the deputies. We will learn; at the moment we are still in the infants' class of the great parliamentary school, but I think it will take a long time before we reach university level.

Among the key episodes of the summer of 1989 was the miner's strike, which rocked the whole country. The day of the intimidated, obedient, puppet-like Soviet working class is past and I would like to believe it has gone for ever. A completely different worker has now stepped into the political arena – a worker who respects both himself and the value of his labour. As before, of course, there are plenty of frightened, weary people who regard their bosses with fear and trembling, but every day there are more of the other sort: men and women who have straightened their shoulders and hold their heads high. It was these workers who headed the strike committees and were followed by tens of thousands of their fellow miners.

Moscow's reaction was swift and precise. For a few days, it is true, the newspapers described the strikers' demands in the usual tone of irritated disapproval, then suddenly, all at once in every forum and in the columns of every newspaper there was total support for the miners' position. Naturally, if the strike had occurred in only one region, the reaction would have been the reverse, but the fact that all the miners in the country managed to unite determined the success of the strike. Unfortunately, Ryzhkov and his new team of ministers proved unable fully to exploit this situation. At that moment he had a real chance of breaking the backbone of our bureaucratically run command economy. Both the Supreme Soviet and public opinion were ready to accept radical economic reforms. But once again half measures were proposed, again it ended up as an attempt to solve the problems of only one branch of industry.

Another very important event, in which I took an active part, was the formation of the Inter-Regional Group of Deputies (I-RGD). I believe that 29–30 July 1989 will go down in the history of Soviet society. In the House of the Cinema in Moscow was held the first meeting of the Inter-Regional Group of People's Deputies. The epoch of monolithic unity was brought to an end. In spite of unprecedented pressure on the deputies to convince them that there was no room in the numerous halls of the Kremlin for such a meeting to take place, in spite of the attempt to label us schismatics, splitters and dictators – the words of abuse were unending – we nevertheless foregathered.

Why did we have to do it? Because what is happening to our country is bordering on catastrophe. The situation cannot be saved by half measures and timid steps. Only decisive, radical action can drag us back from the abyss. Everything that progressive deputies had announced in their electoral platforms, all the best ideas for getting us out of the blind alley were combined in the programme and platform of the I-RGD. Elections were held to choose five co-chairmen of the group; these were: Yuri Afanasiev [a historian]; Boris Yeltsin; Yuri Palm; Gavriil Popov; and Andrei Sakharov [since deceased]. I do not want to theorise much in this book, but perhaps the time has come to indicate, even if only in a few words, the programme for which I stand and which is shared by many of the deputies who have joined the I-RGD.

There are not many points of principle which divide the so-called 'rightists' and 'leftists' of the group. No doubt the main one is the question of property. If one accepts the private ownership of property, then this means the collapse of the main buttress which supports the state's monopoly of property ownership and everything which stems from that: the power of the state; the alienation of the state from the individual and his labour, and so on. The second point in our programme is probably no less important – the land

193

question. The slogan 'The Land to the Peasants!' is now even more topical than it was seventy-odd years ago. Only when the land is worked by the people who own it will the country be fed. Next comes the decentralisation of power, the economic independence of the republics and their genuine sovereignty. At the same time, this will go far towards solving the country's ethnic problems. We also call for the removal of all structural and financial limitations to the economic independence of enterprises and labour collectives. There must be a reform of the country's financial situation, which is directly linked to the measures referred to above (that is the proposals concerning property, land and regional independence), although special financial measures must also be taken to prevent the complete collapse of the rouble. I will not go into any greater detail on this point; the I-RGD includes several first-class economists, among them Shmelyov and Popov, who have drawn up a list of vitally urgent measures needed to save the country's finances. Yet even so their advice is not being followed.

Why have I always been one of those who have not responded to the calls for immediate adoption of a multi-party system? Because the mere existence of several parties does not in itself solve any problems. Several parties existed in Czechoslovakia and the GDR, but until very recently the socialism in those countries was of the Brezhnev-Stalin brand, albeit with certain specific local features. There are also several parties, by the way, in North Korea. My view is that we still need to grow and mature towards a real, civilised, multi-party system. And I would like to make another comment on this topic. So far we do not have several parties; but it is also an illusion to think that we have one party, united and unbeatable. In actual fact, if the CPSU membership can include Yuri Afanasiev and Viktor Afanasiev; Yeltsin and Ligachov; a deputy named Samsonov and a deputy named Vlasov [Yuri Vlasov is a former weightlifter], all of whom are poles apart in their political positions and in their actions, it means that our concepts have become completely muddled and we have altogether forgotten what a political party is. I therefore suggest, as a matter of urgency, that we pass a new law on the party, in which we give legal force to a situation in which the party is a part of society and not of the state, and which guarantees that citizens are free to combine in social organisations and parties. We should also delete Article 6 from the constitution, which legitimises the Communist Party's monopoly of power.

Another important issue is the relationship between church and state. As I see it, Stalin succeeded in creating the only state in the world in which even the church was brought to its knees and subordinated to it. Only now, and with great difficulty, has the church begun to recover consciousness after the series of crushing blows delivered to it over many decades. The facts of the recent past that we can now read in the press – of how priests informed on their parishioners to the party authorities and the KGB; of how the Greek Catholics [of the Ukraine] have still not been granted official permission to register as a religious organisation[1] – all bear witness not to the degeneration of the church but to the fact that when a society is sick, all its limbs become unhealthy too. Today the church has begun to recover its health, and I am convinced that the moment is coming when the church, with its message of eternal, universal values, will come to the aid of our society. For in these words – thou shalt not kill; thou shalt love thy neighbour as thyself – lie those very moral principles that will enable us to survive even the most critical situations. The principle of freedom of conscience is written into our constitution; but we know only too well how that principle has been observed in practice. And that article of the constitution will remain a dead letter until the economic and political reform of our country has been made a reality; until the worth of the human individual becomes the paramount value in our society. At present the opposite prevails: the paramount value of our system of rule by the party bureaucracy is the state. And we have to serve the state. I hope – at least I am doing and will do everything I can to this end – that it is only a matter of months, weeks, days before that service to the state comes to an end.

Now a word about the KGB, the army and the ministry of internal affairs [which controls the police and a large contingent of 'special troops']; here, of course, the situation is more or less clear. These organisations have always been the bulwark of state power. In totalitarian systems, their role and power are constantly being increased. The wind of change has not touched any of them; on the contrary – to everyone's surprise Vladimir Kryuchkov, the chairman of the KGB, was suddenly allowed to bypass the stage of candidate [that is, non-voting] member and was immediately made a full member of the Politbureau. This revival of the old tradition of merging the party leadership with the security organs naturally shocked everyone. In a time of *perestroika* and *glasnost*, if only out of tact and common sense, Gorbachov should not have turned one of the state committees into the senior and most important committee. But no; the thirst for power and the fear of losing it are stronger than any logic or common sense. The KGB has to be close at hand to stand guard over the party's interests, so let Kryuchkov be one of the 'inner circle'.

I can foresee that a fierce, hard struggle lies ahead over the future of the army and the KGB. We have not even begun to consider reforming these most important structures in the edifice of the state. And the reason is that we lack the strength to do so. It has become an almost unconscious reflex to jump to attention at the very mention of the words 'army' or 'KGB' – just in case. That feeling of fear lives in practically every Soviet citizen. That is why the leadership of both the army and the KGB quite calmly and, I would say, unceremoniously ignore the demands by deputies to decode the secret budgets of these organisations. They are not prepared to reveal any details of the activities and structure of these forces, and without such knowledge all talk of restricting and limiting their functions, of reducing their size and roles is so much hot air.

What do I hope for in this regard? First – and most important – I am relying on the development of society itself. Clearly the KGB and the armed forces are always going to lag behind in reforming themselves, but they are also going to have to adapt to the processes that are taking place in the country and they will be obliged to keep up with them. Second, I am putting my hopes on the men themselves. Neither the army nor the KGB are manned by lead soldiers, but by living people. A new generation of recruits is now being taken into the armed services, who will protest against the old image of the 'brutal and licentious soldiery', against blind obedience, against the lack of professionalism, and they are not going to accept the old ways.

The salvation of both the army and the KGB will be *glasnost*, openness. And every one of us who values *perestroika* will fight for this. As for the future of these forces, there is no need to invent anything new. Other societies have already developed smoothly functioning mechanisms for a proper relationship with the army and the security organisation, in which these are not above society but serve society and are subordinate to parliament. The army, in my view, must become a professional, volunteer force. Only then can it be qualitatively improved – but I am starting to go into detail.

I have moved far away from the story of the Inter-Regional Group of Deputies, and will now return to it because it is very instructive. While the co-ordinating council of the I-RGD was meeting in the rare hours that we could snatch from our limited spare time, and while we were frantically brainstorming in the attempt to put together a set of programmes that would offer the country a way out of the crisis, a storm of quite a different nature blew up: an organised attempt to discredit the members of the group. In the newspapers, at constituency meetings, at local party meetings, on every possible and impossible occasion, people were told that they – that is, we – were greedy for power; that we wanted to subject the country to a dictatorship; that we were an opposition; that we were a clique of intellectuals and bureaucrats removed from the people, that most of us had an obscure and shady past.

Once again, not for the first time in Soviet political life, the attempt was being made to substitute for the process of dialogue, the process of comparing different views and attitudes – to substitute for the processes, natural and necessary for a society that has renounced the artificiality of total unanimity – personal attacks on the people supporting and expressing those views and attitudes. All this has happened before in our history and has brought the Soviet people nothing but incalculable hardship and suffering. It is time to realise that our society – fortunately – is not homogeneous; that its different social groupings and strata have differing interests which do not altogether coincide. It is time to realise that the Inter-Regional Group of Deputies is not a 'collection of ambitious, power-hungry politicans'. The I-RGD expresses the interests of that significant proportion of our society which believes that *perestroika* is not being put through consistently and firmly enough; that our present troubles are not caused by trying to cure 'good' socialism with a dose of 'bad' capitalism. When encountering the first difficulties in the process of reforming our brand of bureaucratised 'barracks-socialism', we have tried to find solutions by the use of the same old methods of the bureaucratic state and the 'command economy'. But the main objective has nevertheless been achieved. The group exists and is working out the strategies and tactics needed to develop our society anew, and since it includes the best brains among the deputies, there will ultimately be no alternative: the people will follow the lead of the Inter-Regional Group of Deputies.

After the I-RGD had finished the first stage of its work came the short parliamentary recess, and in mid-September I went to America. That short trip, lasting no more than eight days, caused a considerable stir. I visited the USA at the request of several American organisations, universities and a number of politicians; altogether I received fifteen invitations. The trip was originally meant to last for two weeks, but the central committee of the party would only let me go for one week. This was a disaster for the people who were organising my visit, and they asked me not to disrupt the programme but to try and fit most of the planned engagements and lectures into one week. At school and later at the polytechnic, I had studied Marx's theory of the exploitation of man by man under capitalism. I now experienced that indisputable theory being applied to myself. Sleeping for only two or three hours in twenty-four, I flew from one state to another, attended meetings or made speeches six or seven times a day, and so on without let-up for a week, during which I visited nine states and eleven cities. After running that marathon at the pace of a sprint, I only came to my senses in the plane taking me back to Moscow, and it is now my dream to go back to America again, but this time not to see it like a speeded-up film but calmly and without haste, so that I can examine those details of the country for which on that occasion there was no time to spare.

A great deal was written about my trip to the States, both in the USA and in the Soviet Union, so for that reason I doubt whether it is worth dwelling on the overall results of the journey. I met many interesting people, starting with President Bush and ending with ordinary Americans on the streets of those eleven cities. No doubt it will sound banal, but what surprised me most were precisely those ordinary people in America, who radiated optimism, faith in themselves and in their country. There were, of course, shattering experiences of another sort – the supermarkets, for example. When I saw those shelves crammed with hundreds, thousands of cans, cartons and goods of every possible sort, for the first time I felt quite frankly sick with despair for the Soviet people. That such a potentially super-rich country as ours has been brought to a state of such poverty. It is terrible to think of it.

Under the terms agreed in advance with the organisers of my trip, I was paid fees for the lectures that I gave at universities. On the last day, it turned out that after deducting all expenses covering the costs of our four-man group, the sum remaining at my disposal was £100,000. I decided to contribute to the Soviet anti-AIDS campaign by acquiring a consignment of single-use throw-away hypodermic syringes, and only a week later the first batch of 100,000 one-time use syringes arrived in Moscow for distribution to eleven children's hospitals. The total order was for a million syringes, which accounted for the whole sum of money down to the last cent.

I only mention this because at the very moment when I was signing the document ordering my American earnings to be spent on acquiring those syringes, the first morning editions of *Pravda* were going on sale in Moscow's kiosks with an article reprinted from the Italian newspaper *La Repubblica*. It reported that throughout my time in America I had been hopelessly drunk; the journalist even quoted the exact quantities of what I had allegedly drunk during the whole trip (although here the Italian's imagination had clearly failed him, because only a weak-headed foreigner could have been brought to his knees by those amounts of alcohol). Apart from that, it also appeared that the Moscow hospitals would have to wait in vain for any syringes, because I had apparently spent all my money on video recorders and video cassettes, on presents for myself, consisting of suits, white shirts, shoes and other frippery; that I had hardly ever emerged from a series of supermarkets, where I had done nothing but say, 'I'll have that – and that – and that!' The article (translated and published by *Pravda* with quite uncharacteristic speed) made me look like the usual drunken, lumbering, ill-mannered Russian bear at his first encounter with civilised society.

I knew, of course, that my trip would provoke a fiercely negative reaction from the topmost level of the Soviet 'establishment'. I had suspected that there would be attempts to compromise me and discredit my visit to the USA. But to be honest, I had not expected that my ill-wishers would stoop so low and descend to such stupid and bare-faced lies. The reaction of the Muscovites and many, many people over the country, however, was unanimous. I received thousands of telegrams of support. Another provocation had failed in its aim.

But my invisible opponents did not let it rest at that. After a while, a ninety-minute programme about my trip to the USA was shown on central television, preceded by something very rare – a preliminary trailer on *Vremya*, the main current-affairs programme.

And the chief item in the programme, which was the reason for the whole elaborate set-up, was my meeting with the students and faculty members at Johns Hopkins University. I have already mentioned that in America I was subjected to an insane timetable, which, plus the change of time zones, the exhaustion and lack of sleep all combined to the point where, after a night flight, I took a sleeping tablet and immediately fell asleep. Two hours later, 6 a.m., I was awakened – there was another official meeting at 7 a.m. and at 8 a.m. I had to make a speech at Johns Hopkins. I was still completely knocked out and felt that I could not get up. I asked them to postpone the meeting. I was told that was impossible, there would be a scandal which my hosts would never survive. I said that I would not survive the day. And so, weak as I was, I summoned up all my will-power and attended the first meeting, then the second, and I gradually felt better – the enforced movement helped me throw off the lethargy and the effect of the tablet also wore off. Well, precisely that episode, of the dozens that could have been transmitted, was shown to Soviet television viewers, the video-tape having been acquired from goodness knows where – although one can easily guess from where and by whom.

What is more, certain experts had edited the video-tape, where necessary, by slowing down the image for fractions of a second and, where necessary, by slowing down my words as I spoke them. I was told this by the television engineers at the Ostankino studios, who even wrote a letter to the commission that was set up to investigate the biased presentation of my visit in the Soviet press. But of course no one was going to check and examine the scandalous fact of the video-tape having been doctored. In any case, the main objective had been attained; perplexed people – although they were few – were already wondering aloud whether I might have been really drunk? I considered it inappropriate to explain and justify myself.

Nevertheless, it was one more lesson for me. I could not relax or lower my guard for a moment when faced by this system which hated me, which tracked my every footstep and pounced on every movement that I might make, be it skilful or clumsy. And if I had known that over there, on another continent, I was being watched when I was almost asleep on my feet, I wouldn't have. What wouldn't I have done? Not taken the tablet? No, I couldn't have survived without some sleep. Would I have cancelled the meeting? That, too, was out of the question. Most likely I shouldn't have forced myself to take that trip at such a pace; I have taken note of that for the future.

Soon afterwards, however, another episode occurred which – literally – hit me much harder. Once again, it was an organised, premeditated act of provocation. It happened after a meeting with some of my constituents, when I was being driven to the village of Uspenskoye in the countryside outside Moscow to see an old friend of mine from Sverdlovsk days, who had a *dacha* out there. Not far from his house I dismissed the driver, as I almost always do, in order to walk the last few hundred yards. The car, a Volga, drove away; I walked a few yards. Suddenly another car appeared behind me and – I was in the river. I will not describe my emotions here, but what I went through in those few minutes is something I never want to experience again.

The water was terribly cold. I got cramp in my legs and was barely able to swim to the bank, although the distance was only a few yards. As I climbed up on to the bank, I collapsed and lay on the ground for some time to recover my senses. Then I got up, shivering with cold in an air-temperature of around zero. I realised that I would never make it to my friend's house on my own, and staggered to the nearby police station. The policeman on duty recognised me immediately. They asked me no questions, as I immediately told them not to tell anyone about this incident. While I was drinking the tea that the lads gave me, and while my clothes were drying out a little I cursed whoever had done this to me – 'How low can they sink?' – but I made no official statement. After a while my wife and daughter came to fetch me, and as I was leaving I asked the policemen to say nothing to anyone about what had happened.

Why did I do that? I foresaw the reaction of those people who have had great difficulty in tolerating the moral provocations directed against me, but would simply be incapable of taking calmly the news of a physical attack on me. Zelenograd, where the majority of the electronics and other factories work for the defence industry, and Sverdlovsk, where there are even more armaments factories, might have staged a protest strike, indeed half of Moscow might have downed tools. And then, as a result of strikes in the defence industries, martial law would have been declared, and a state of 'perpetual and ideal' order would have begun. Thus, as a result of Yeltsin giving way to a provocation, *perestroika* (of the wrong sort) might have been achieved in our country. Of course, I may be wrong. It is possible that my principle of always telling the truth might not have let me down then, too. For it was that which most surprised my constituents – the fact that I was hiding something, not telling the whole story.

I still think that people will nevertheless understand the incident and will work out the truth for themselves. Especially when Bakatin, the USSR minister of internal affairs, reported at a session of the Supreme Soviet that no attempt had been made on my life, and as proof offered some false information; this made me even more certain that people would guess at the truth. For some reason, Bakatin even misled his hearers over facts that can be easily checked. He said, for instance, that if the victim of an attack really had been knocked off the bridge, he would have been seriously injured, because the height of the bridge above the water is fifty feet. In fact, the distance from the bridge to the water is fifteen feet. So to make Bakatin's statement sound plausible, they should hastily build a new bridge – thirty-five feet higher than the previous one! But no one is going to do that, not even to discredit Yeltsin. Altogether I was certain that people would sense the numerous absurdities and inconsistencies in the version provided by the minister of internal affairs, and would realise that something really had happened to me. And that they would understand the most important point of all: the reason why he had announced to the Supreme Soviet that there had been no attempt on my life.

Nevertheless, I must honestly admit that this provocation had some success at the time. My many supporters announced in a panic that my popularity had fallen. Immediately, a lying rumour was then sown on the soil prepared for it, to the effect that I had been going to see my mistress at her *dacha*, who for some reason had thrown a bucketful of water over me! Although this is obvious nonsense, clearly the more improbable the concoction, the more likely it is to be believed. What is more, people often like hearing stories about the indiscretions of politicians. Even so, I reacted calmly enough to what sociologists would call a drop in my rating. I remain convinced that everything will fall into place again and that this stupid and pointless story will not for long undermine the confidence in me of those people who may have suddenly been given cause to doubt. After all, in the end people are judged by real achievements and concrete results and not by myths and rumours about them.

After my involuntary bathe in that ice-cold water, I was seriously ill for two weeks with a touch of pneumonia. For that reason, I watched part of the session [of the Supreme Soviet] on television. This turned out to be a very sorry spectacle, especially when one knew how serious was the situation in the country and how urgent it was to take certain decisions, since there was still a small chance that they might pull us out of the crisis. But those decisions were not being taken; the enactment of essential new laws was being put off to the indefinite future and we were clearly slithering downhill to the point where not even the boldest and most progressive legislation could save us.

I remember Yuri Afanasiev, at the first session of the Congress of People's Deputies, graphically describing the newly elected Supreme Soviet as being 'Stalinist-Brezhnevite' in make-up. For all my respect for the coiner of this phrase, I cannot agree with his assessment. Our Supreme Soviet is not 'Stalinist-Brezhnevite' – that is if anything too high, or perhaps even too low an evaluation of it. It is 'Gorbachovian', faithfully reflecting our chairman's inconsistency, timidity, love of half measures and semi-decisions. Everything the Supreme Soviet does is undertaken too late. Like our chairman, it is constantly lagging behind the march of events. And that is why so many urgently needed measures have not been passed into law.

On the evening of the autumn 1989 session, as though to teach us a lesson, the totalitarian socialism, forced on them by Stalin after the war, collapsed in three of the socialist countries [of Central and Eastern Europe]. And almost in mockery of our painful efforts at *perestroika* over more than four years, in a matter of days the GDR, Czechoslovakia and Bulgaria [and now Romania] have made the leap out of the past towards a normal, human, civilised society; it is not even clear whether we shall ever be able to catch them up. The opening of the Berlin Wall; new rules of entry and exit; new laws concerning the press and social organisations; the annulment of the articles in their constitutions guaranteeing the 'leading role' of the Communist Party; the resignation of the central committee; the summoning of extraordinary party congresses; the condemnation of the invasion of Czechoslovakia: all this should have happened in our country four years ago. Instead, we have been marking time all those years, terrified of taking a step forward and thereby jumping two steps backward.

I am very glad that these changes have taken place in the neighbouring socialist countries – glad for their sakes. But I also think that these changes will force us to think again and reassess what we so proudly call *perestroika*, and that we shall soon realise that we are practically the only country left on earth which is trying to enter the twenty-first century with an obsolte nineteenth-century ideology; that we are the last inhabitants of a country defeated by socialism, as one clever man put it.

The latest news is that rumours are going around Moscow that a coup is being planned for the next plenum [of the central committee], with the aim of dismissing Gorbachov from his post of general secretary of the central committee of the CPSU, but leaving him as chairman of the Congress of People's Deputies. I do not believe these rumours, but even if it actually happens, I shall fight for Gorbachov at the plenum. Yes, I shall fight for him – my perpetual opponent, the lover of half measures and half-steps. These, his preferred tactics, will also eventually be his downfall, unless of course he himself realises his chief failing in time. But for the present, at least until the next [party] congress, at which new leaders may perhaps emerge, he is the only man who can stop the ultimate collapse of the party. Our right-wingers, unfortunately, don't understand that. They believe that by the old mechanical method of voting by a show of hands they will succeed in turning back the clock of history. The fact that these rumours circulate is, of course, symptomatic. Our huge country is balanced on a razor's edge, and nobody knows what will happen to it tomorrow. It is slightly easier for the readers of this book than for me. They will already know what has happened tomorrow, will know where I am and what has become of me. They will already know what has happened to the Soviet Union. And to all of us.

Epilogue

Another year of my life has sped by. The questions I posed at the end of this book have been answered. What has happened to me in this past year seems clear enough, as is what has happened and is happening to our country. However, I believe it would be useful to add a brief comment on the events of the past twelve months, putting them into perspective. Yes, it would be useful . . . If only I were not under such tremendous, almost physical, pressure of time.

Is it really less than a year since I was elected Chairman of the Russian Federation's Supreme Soviet at the First Congress of Russian Republican People's Deputies? To me it seems as though this is something that happened oh, so long ago, somewhere in the distant past, in another era. And what about the wonderful '500 Days' programme, which offered real hope of bringing the country out of its economic crisis? Was it really not so long ago that we worked on it, believed in it . . .? That roseate period of hope also seems to belong to a long-vanished past.

Shevardnadze's resignation, the Bloody Sunday in Lithuania, the Black Berets' rampage in Latvia – these events are closer, but also from the past. And what does the future hold? Presidential rule by Gorbachov over the whole country, a rule reinforced by tanks and paratroopers, or civilised government by a new body – the Federal Soviet? The reader is probably in a better position to judge than I am: he already knows everything, whereas I can only analyse, feel, guess.

Would I have found it easier if I had taken no part in the drama called 'perestroika'? I could have remained on the sidelines, worried, complained, sworn in frustration, switched off in disgust when Central Television issued yet another stream of lies, knowing that I could exercise no influence on events. But what does one do when one does bear responsibility? And to a very considerable degree? It is truly a frightening, inhuman load to bear, knowing that the fate of millions of people today, as well as that of future generations, hangs upon your decisions, your steps, your deeds. Alas, these are not delusions of grandeur. It is our country's misfortune that she has not yet shed the mediaeval heritage, whereby confrontation between several individuals precipitated enormous changes in the fates of whole peoples and countries.

It depends upon the will of one individual – Gorbachov – whether tanks shall roll into the Baltic states, or whether their people shall be granted the right to self-determination. But some things depend upon me, too. Such as trying to prevent those tanks from moving in. And to do everything in my power to ensure that Russia, the Baltic states, and all the sovereign republics comprising the Soviet Union should be free to determine their own destiny.

I have just celebrated my sixtieth birthday. The Russian Supreme Soviet was meeting in session on that day, and before we got down to the day's business, the deputies offered their congratulations on my reaching this milestone. In reply, I found myself saying something that would have surprised me not so long ago: I said that I would devote all my energies to my work, and that if these were sufficient, I would be satisfied if I could achieve at least stability in Russia. No great leap forward, no extravagant flight, just stability.

This past year has put paid to many people's illusions, including mine.

I do not think I could be called a starry-eyed optimist, who harboured any naïve beliefs that the transition from totalitarianism to legal, civilised government could occur quickly and smoothly. I was always aware that the System representing the Party apparatus, and which is inextricably linked with the military–industrial complex and the KGB, would fight tooth and claw to survive. Yet I had faith in the power of logic and common sense. I realised, that Gorbachov the reformer was a representative of that apparatus, that he would be unswerving in his service to those who raised him to the top of the state and Party pyramid, that he would always be, first and foremost, the General Secretary of the Communist Party, and President in second place. I knew that he would strive to preserve himself and his power, that he is a shrewd politician; and that in order to assure his own well-being, he would try to maintain the balance between left and right forces.

Yet just within the period of a few months there was neither balance, nor well-being; we took steps towards each other, reached concessions and compromises – and then it all fell apart. It's like watching the death throes of some wounded animal. All the decrees, orders and directives issued by Gorbachov are hysterical outpourings which do nothing but add to the general tension and instability. One would expect him to try to take some measures to defuse the situation, to feed the people, to lessen the degree of confrontation, but instead, everything he does merely intensifies the overall atmosphere of fear and uncertainty.

Gorbachov's popularity rating has plunged to a new low – from 15 to 10 per cent. Mine, on the contrary, has never been higher, fluctuating between 60 and 70 per cent. I must say, however, that this brings me neither joy nor satisfaction. Rather, I feel burdened, tired and drained by this totally senseless conflict.

How can Russia be pulled out of her current crisis? That would seem to be our primary consideration. Lord, if only that were all! The most terrible thing, the whole paradox of the situation is that all my energies, the entire intellectual potential of the Russian Supreme Soviet, all the efforts and thoughts of numerous specialists and advisers are currently focused on a totally different issue – what can we do to avert interference in our attempts to save Russia? The situation could be depicted as follows: we are up to our throats in a swamp, and can go under at any moment; yet every time we find a branch to clutch and try to pull ourselves out, someone slaps our hand away, hits us on the head, saying – sit still! You'll get help when the Centre decides; helping yourself isn't permitted! Despite all our resources and wealth, we are in a much worse situation than any East European country which has also broken with Stalinism. At least, nobody tries to impede their progress. They are at liberty to create economic models with which one may agree or disagree, but which can be implemented.

All in all, our current situation is astounding. I am the legally elected leader of the legally elected parliament of the largest Soviet republic, with a population of over 150 million people, yet I have no idea as to what a President who enjoys only minimal popular trust, and a government which enjoys none at all, have in mind for Russia. I go to bed not knowing where, how and to what I shall wake in the morning. Who knows, maybe my money, and that of my fellow-citizens, will be confiscated under the guise of banknote reform, maybe our bank accounts will be frozen under the pretext of fighting inflation, maybe the Russian television centre will be seized during the night, or deprived of air time, maybe tanks, APCs and special troops will fill the streets . . .? All such matters are decided in the Kremlin, on the Old Square, in the KGB, in the Ministry of Defence, anywhere at all, except in the Russian parliament. We can only watch the latest agonised actions of the Centre in horror. And yet we are supposed to be a sovereign republic.

This past year has been a year of small, insignificant victories and huge, heavy defeats. The only comfort that can be drawn is the certainty that every defeat, no matter how great, and every victory, no matter how small, have not passed unnoticed. But the most significant thing is the existence of desperate, sincere, selfless support from the people, and with such support, one can undertake even the most difficult and demanding tasks. I feel this support all the time, I live with it and because of it, for without it I would have no hope at all for a better future. And I do believe in that future with all my heart.

Ever since the famous April 1985 Plenum of the Central Committee of the Communist Party of the USSR, it has been propounded as a Gospel truth that there is no alternative to Gorbachov, and, generally speaking, it was so until January 1991. After the tragic events in the Baltics in January, a new thesis was formulated for executive power in a renewed Union – the concept of a Federal Soviet (Council). I shall not, at this stage, go into details about the mooted mechanism of interaction between such a Soviet and the republics, who could lead it, the length of its term, with what responsibilities it would be charged by the constituent republics and so forth. At the moment this is not of cardinal importance. What is more important is that the whole country had finally realised that there can be a viable alternative to Gorbachov, and this alternative is much more attractive to the republics than presidential rule by the partocracy represented by Gorbachov. This new factor on our political stage may soon play a decisive role in the life of a new kind of Union. The republics will be drawn to a Federal Soviet which guarantees their independence and sovereignty, whereas the President will try to bind the republics even more firmly with the aid of decrees, Cabinet orders and resolutions, by legal and illegal means aimed at perpetuating the republics' subservience. This, I believe, is the scenario for the near future.

Gorbachov has frequently accused me of wanting to oust him and seize his place for myself. He has said as much to me in private meetings; I told him then, and I repeat here in writing, that I never coveted his place at any time or under any circumstances. Nor shall I seek to lead the Federal Soviet, or try to secure a predominant role within it for Russia. To create a new Centre in place of the old would be, in my opinion, a totally useless and self-defeating step. Nevertheless, I am tolerably certain that all the propaganda arsenal will be brought to bear on me quite soon, claiming that I want to gain power over the entire Union through the medium of the Federal Soviet. I am acutely aware of the changing mood in the republics, especially in the wake of the bloody events in Lithuania. The republican leaders understand full well that their territory could be subjected to the same kind of treatment at any moment. A national conflict could flare up in even the most 'obedient' republic, which would lead to the speedy emergence of yet another 'council of national salvation' which would seize power with the aid of weapons and military vehicles with the full approval of the Kremlin. It looks as though, for the first time, the desire for freedom of some, coupled with fear of the Centre of others, has united practically all the republics in resolute opposition to presidential power.

Before sitting down to write this epilogue, I re-read my book, millions of copies of which have spread across the country and the world. And I was amazed to see how quickly it has been overtaken by events. Many incidents, chapters and situations seem so different today from the way I perceived them in the not so distant past. Even now, as I write these lines about how I see and feel the present situation, I sense that much becomes outdated even before it is expressed. I am chasing after time, which has already flown ahead . . .

The First Congress of People's Deputies of the USSR brought about numerous changes in our country. Yet nowadays, the Congress, that obsolete tool of a crumbling empire, provokes nothing but irritation and boredom. Yet how many lines in my book were devoted to the Party, its Politbureau, its Plenums! And deservedly so. In that former existence the Party, which had seized all power in the country, rated that much attention. But these days, who cares about the Party, about the make-up of the Politbureau, about their plenums, about their discussions? Admittedly, they still exercise considerable control over much, they still have their hands on such major levers as the armed forces, finances, transport, communications; but the Stalinist Communist party is dying, disintegrating, and no amount of frantic effort by Gorbachov, Polozkov and their closest associates can save it. The Party may try to turn back the clock of history, and I think it may well attempt to recapture its lost positions with the aid of guns, tanks and truncheons. But its power, built upon fear and violence, is historically doomed.

So this is how I have spent the past year: battling the Communist Party for a free Russia. I have been totally immersed in tactics and strategies, completely enmeshed in this ceaseless struggle. Personal emotions and feelings have been relegated to some tiny, remote corner of my subconscious. I wish that I had time to pause, relax, look around me. It would be fascinating to be able to analyse my own reactions to the external changes which have affected me since I was elected leader of the Russian parliament. What were my feelings when I entered the office of the Chairman of the Supreme Soviet for the first time? Triumph, tiredness, personal importance? No, none of these: I remember that moment very clearly – I pulled out the chair behind the desk, and settled down to work straight away. Then there are the changes in those people who deserted me in my difficulties in October 1987: here they are, as though nothing had happened – 'A marvellous victory, Boris Nikolayevich! You can count on our support, we're with you heart and soul now, we're for you . . .' I was neither surprised nor offended, but I couldn't help feeling sad. But there are others, who volunteered their support and assistance when there was no prospect of success on the horizon, and I have included most of them in my administration. With them, we overcame fearsome obstacles, and with them beside me, I have nothing to fear.

Sometimes, when I can't sleep at night, my head fills with silly thoughts. Such as – is this all really necessary? Who wants to live like this? My family has been unlucky. I mentioned in my book that even earlier I was unable to devote as much time as I should to my wife and daughters. Now they never see me at all. Morning, noon and night, everything is devoted to the job in hand, anything else comes a long way behind.

These days I cannot afford the time to sit down and read a book or a magazine, go for a walk, see a film, phone a friend and invite him over for a cup of tea and a chat . . . I can't even spend an hour or two playing with my little grandson Boris, the way all normal grandfathers do at least once a week.

The trouble is that I'm not a normal grandfather, but a politician, the Chairman of the Russian Supreme Soviet, Boris Nikolayevich Yeltsin. But what's more important in life, when all is said and done?

To me, this is an abstract question. I have made my choice. I made it long ago. God grant that I have the necessary strength to carry it through.

Notes

Prologue

1   Refers to the first election, held on 26 March 1989, of deputies to the Congress of People's Deputies, the lower chamber of the new, reformed Soviet legislature, whose creation was enacted on 1 December 1988 by Mikhail Gorbachov in his capacity as chairman of the presidium of the Supreme Soviet of the USSR (see below, note 3). The Congress of People's Deputies is intended to be both a debating chamber and an electoral college for the election – from its own membership – of those deputies who will constitute the upper chamber, the reformed Supreme Soviet of the USSR. A majority (1,500) of the 2,250 members of the Congress of People's Deputies is elected in contested elections, on a territorial constituency basis, in secret ballot by universal adult suffrage. The remaining 750 seats in the congress are filled by members nominated by certain 'social organisations'; these include the Communist Party; the trade unions; the Academy of Sciences; the Writers' Union; the Theatre Workers' Union; and so on.

2   Since 1922, when other political parties were abolished and the country's official designation of 'Union of Soviet Socialist Republics' was adopted, the Communist Party (hereafter referred to for brevity as 'the party') has been the sole political party allowed to exist in the Soviet Union. Its status as such is enshrined in Article 6 of the 1975 Soviet constitution, which guarantees the unique 'leading role' of the party in the political, economic and social life of the USSR. Consequently, all policies are formulated and all major political decisions are taken by party bodies and party appointees. The two bodies

which constitute the apex of the Soviet Communist Party's organisational pyramid are the central committee and, above it, the Politbureau. Both are elected from senior party members at periodical party congresses, which are meant to be held at five-yearly intervals, although in the past the length of the interval has sometimes been longer.

There are other entities in the Soviet Union whose functions can be called 'political' in the broadest sense. These are:

i   The soviets (the Russian word *soviet* means 'council'): until the recent electoral reforms, the soviets were 'pseudo-elective', in that although the adult population dutifully went to the polls on 'election-day', only one party-nominated candidate stood for each ward or constituency and the voter's only form of choice was to spoil the ballot-paper – an inadvisable step, since the voting was not secret (no booths) and the process was monitored by security officials equipped with cameras. The soviets – largely powerless, rubber-stamp bodies – exist at each level of local and national government and their pyramidal structure culminates in the Supreme Soviet – or did so until the 1988 reform of the Soviet legislature (see above, note 1). The national sovereignty of the USSR is legally vested in the permanent presiding body of the Supreme Soviet – the presidium – and the chairman of the presidium is thus *ex officio* the constitutional head of state.

ii The government is constitutionally separate from the party and the soviets: it consists of the ministries, together with the 'state committees'; which are ministries in all but name. Apart from such classic 'ministries of state' to be found in all governmental systems (e.g. foreign affairs; internal affairs; defence), the great majority of Soviet ministries and state committees are really the central managing-boards of the various branches (in Russian: *otrasli*) of the country's nationalised economy (e.g. the ministry of coal; the ministry of iron and steel; the ministry of light industry; the ministry of culture). Of high ministerial status is the chairman of the state planning committee (Gosplan), whose senior position in the government's structure reflects Gosplan's importance in an almost totally planned, non-market, 'command' economy. Collectively, the heads of all the ministries make up the Council of Ministers of the USSR. Its chairman is Nikolai Ryzhkov, who, for want of a more accurate parallel, is often referred to as the 'prime minister' of the USSR. Unlike the Cabinets in other countries, however, the Council of Ministers does not originate policy; its function is to systematize, execute and administer the policies handed down to it by the top policy-making echelons of the party – the central committee and the Politbureau.

214

The structure and functions of the Communist Party of the Soviet Union

In 1989 the membership of the party is approximately 10 per cent of the USSR's population of 257 million. People can join the party at the age of twenty-five, usually after having first belonged to its young people's organisation, the Communist League of Youth (*Kommunisti-chesky Soyuz Molodyozhi*, a title invariably abbreviated to its acronym: Komsomol).

Within the party there is a functional distinction between the rank-and-file members, on the one hand, who pay their dues and occasionally attend meetings; and, on the other hand, the 'professional' members who make a career as *apparatchiki* in the party's large permanent administrative staff (the *apparat*) or who, if more ambitious, are promoted up the ladder of party officialdom, at the top of which are the powerful senior posts in the central committee and the Polit-bureau. The latter is the ultimate policy-making body and thus is effectively the country's real 'cabinet', chaired by the general secretary of the central committee – the post occupied successively by Lenin, Stalin, Malenkov (very briefly), Khrushchev, Brezhnev, Andropov, Chernenko (the latter two also very briefly), and now by Gorbachov. Both Yeltsin and Gorbachov pursued the politically significant part of their careers as party officials.

The organisational structure of the party is a pyramid-like pattern of 'committees', which correspond, at successive levels, to the administrative units into which the USSR is divided. Starting at the lowest unit and progressing upwards, these are: district (*raion*); town or city (*gorod*); province (*oblast*); region (*krai*); and union republic (*respublika*). Above them all is the central committee (*tsentralny komitet*), and, at the apex, the Political Bureau (invariably abbreviated to Polit-bureau). At the lower levels, from district up to region, to shorten their rather clumsy Russian designations (e.g. *oblastnoi komitet*), the title of each of these committees is compressed into one word, as follows: *raikom*; *gorkom*; *obkom*; *kraikom*. The official at the head of each committee at *raikom* level is titled 'secretary'; at the next four levels the title is 'first secretary'; from *gorkom* level upwards the party organisation is large enough to need a 'second secretary' and a 'third secretary' as well.

If the politbureau is the 'brain' of the party, the central committee is its 'heart', responsible for pumping the blood of policy *directives* downwards to the lower levels and the oxygen of *draft policies* upwards to the Politbureau. The elective central-committee membership varies between 250 and 300, but its total staff is much larger. As with the party as a whole, its gross complement is divided between the 'members' who attend each plenary session (plenum) and its permanent administrative staffs (*apparaty*). The senior members of the latter – known collectively as the secretariat, and individually titled 'secretary of the central committee' – also have *ex officio* seats at the plenums, which are held from twice to four times annually, according to need.

Each party congress elects (or largely re-elects) the full membership of the central committee, which in turn elects both the Politbureau membership and the heads of the central committee's two permanent bureaucracies (*apparaty*) – the secretariat and the central auditing commission; these *apparaty* respectively administer and monitor the day-to-day affairs of the party. The elective membership of the central committee is drawn from ten categories, some of whom are also senior officials of the central committee *apparat*. The categories are:

  i   the Politbureau (fourteen members);
  ii the central-committee secretariat (maximum of nine members);
  iii the section heads of the general central-committee *apparat*;
  iv the section heads of the central auditing commission;
  v all *obkom* first secretaries;
  vi all *kraikom* first secretaries;
  vii first, second and third secretaries of the Communist Parties of the fifteen Union Republics;
  viii representatives of the armed forces;
  ix representatives of the KGB;
  x workers and peasants (numbering five or six token figures, chosen by the cadres department of the central committee).

Although nominally elected by the free choice of the party congress, in practice candidates for election to the central committee are invariably chosen and put forward by the central-committee *apparat*, and their election is not normally opposed.

The central committee has four main functions:

  i It originates and drafts major policy proposals on matters right across the political spectrum, with the exception of defence and foreign affairs (but including relations with foreign Communist parties); the drafts are then submitted to the Politbureau for discussion, where they are either approved, rejected (very rarely), or sent back to the central committee for amendments.

ii It is responsible for seeing that all policy decisions, whether made by the Politbureau or by the plenary sessions of the central committee itself, are passed on to and implemented by the party committees and other party organisations all the way down the pyramid.

iii It directs and oversees the nationwide administration of the party in matters of organisation, finance and personnel.

iv It shadows the work of the economic or 'branch' ministries, right down the line to factory and collective-farm level. The aim of this function is for the party to monitor, and where necessary to correct and improve the performance of all branches of the economy. In practice it means that the work of ministry or other 'economic' officials is everywhere paralleled by the corresponding party officials, whose status and clout always override those of their 'government' opposite numbers. As this largely results in the duplication of senior managerial functions and can often confuse or retard the decision-making process in industry and agriculture, it is this aspect of the party's work which has come under the strongest criticism since the reforms proposed under Gorbachov's *perestroika* ('restructuring') first began to be widely debated in the Soviet media in 1986.

The full title of the Politbureau is the Political Bureau of the Central Committee of the Communist Party of the Soviet Union, and while standing above the central committee, the Politbureau is, as its name implies, an inseparable outgrowth of the central committee and is functionally very dependent on it. The Politbureau is the ultimate locus of executive power in the Soviet Union and takes all important political decisions. Nevertheless, every issue debated by the Politbureau and every executive act passed by it is first drafted by the central committee under the direction of the secretariat, and thus bears the stamp of the central committee's collective cast of mind. This tends to be strongly conservative, either for ideological reasons or from a more basic fear of losing some of the very great power that has accrued to the central committee over past decades – a tendency which has been a major factor in holding back the pace of reform envisaged in *perestroika*. Even such an adroit general secretary of the central committee as Gorbachov, the *ex officio* chairman of the Politbureau, is therefore to some extent in fee to the inbuilt conservatism of the central committee's *apparat*.

The Politbureau consists of fourteen members who are themselves drawn from the central committee secretariat and elected to the Politbureau by a plenary session of the central committee. Thus the minister of foreign affairs and the minister of defence, for instance, are elected to the Politbureau in their capacities as secretaries of the central committee rather than in their ministerial function (in the past, indeed, the minister of foreign affairs has not always been a Politbureau member). There are two classes of members: 'candidate' or non-voting members, and 'full' members who vote. It can take many years to be promoted from 'candidate' to 'full' membership; some (like Yeltsin himself) never reach the higher status. When a decision, resolution or decree is passed by the Politbureau, whether of an administrative or a more strictly legislative nature, it effectively acquires the force of law. Until the recent reform of the legislature, Politbureau decrees were simply rubber-stamped into formal legality by the docile and largely ornamental Supreme Soviet. Since the reform, however, it now seems as if the Politbureau will submit 'bills' to the legislature, where they will be debated and then either enacted, modified or rejected. It is so far (December 1989) too early to discern the precise relationship between the Politbureau and the new-style 'parliament'; the nature of that relationship may prove to be the most crucial aspect of Gorbachov's political reforms.

3   Intended as a means of keeping the number of candidates down to a reasonable minimum, the 'adoption meetings' were perceived by Yeltsin (and others)– as a device to eliminate candidates regarded by the party as likely oppositionists. Since the March 1989 election, however, the 'adoption meetings' have been abolished in all but two republics of the USSR.

4   Moscow, as the capital city (population: 9 million) of the Soviet Union, has the largest and, in many respects, the most important party organisation in the country. The size of the Moscow city committee of the party (*gorkom*) – bigger than the party organisation of several of the union republics and bigger than most provincial committees (*obkom*) – together with its close physical proximity to the central committee and the seat of government, combine to give it a special position in the party's national structure. The post of first secretary of the Moscow *gorkom*, which Yeltsin held from 1986 to 1988, carries with it automatic membership of the Politbureau (see above, note 2).

5   Born 1920. From 1965 to 1983, first secretary of the Tomsk (Siberia) provincial committee of the party. From 1983 to 1985, secretary of the central committee responsible for the personnel department; thereafter, secretary responsible for ideology. Full member of the Politbureau. A former protégé of Andropov (as was Gorbachov), Ligachov is also in the influential position of supervising the work of the central committee's secretariat (see above, note 2).

6   When Yeltsin was first secretary of the Moscow city committee, in the summer of 1987 he issued a directive allowing demonstrations to be held, provided the organisers gave the police advance warning of the venue and the likely number of demonstrators. Ligachov (who was

chairing the Politbureau during Gorbachov's absence on holiday) was indignant about this directive, which he regarded as far too liberal. With Gorbachov away, he used his position to set up a committee of inquiry into Yeltsin's handling of affairs in Moscow, using the demonstrations as a pretext. Yeltsin interpreted this move as an attack on his authority as first secretary.

Chapter 1

1   When in 1928 Stalin decreed the wholesale appropriation of all individually owned peasant landholdings and their enforced consolidation into large collective farms, the Communist Party divided the peasantry into three categories, as part of a policy of enlisting the support of a majority of peasants for a difficult, unpopular piece of ruthless social engineering. The three categories, which roughly reflected the differentiation in land ownership, efficiency and prosperity that had developed over the years, were as follows:

   i   the most successful peasants, labelled '*kulaki*'; *kulak* is an expressive and intentionally derogatory Russian word meaning 'fist';

   ii the average or moderately successful peasants, designated as *serednyaki*, a term derived from the Russian word for 'medium' or 'middling'; and

   iii the unsuccessful, often landless peasants, characterised as *bednyaki*, from the Russian word meaning 'poor', most of whom worked as hired labourers for *kulaki*.

The political significance of this categorisation was to identify those peasants who had a lot to lose from collectivisation – namely the *kulaki* – and who would therefore resist the process. Those who did resist were either shot or deported, together with their families, to remote and inhospitable regions of the Soviet Union, where those who had not already succumbed to the hardships of the journey often died of starvation, disease and overwork under conditions of forced labour. The commonest form of resistance to collectivisation was for a peasant farmer to destroy his stocks of grain and to slaughter all his livestock. Another kind of protest was to run away and band together with other dispossessed peasants, who would then turn to murder and theft for survival – and revenge; hence Yeltsin's reference to 'gangs of outlaws'.

The *bednyaki*, or poor peasants, who had nothing to lose and everything to gain by joining a collective farm, were seen as the party's natural allies in imposing collectivisation, and they formed the greater part of those who voluntarily joined collectives. Unfortunately for the future of Soviet agriculture, they were also by and large the laziest, least intelligent and most shiftless of the peasantry.

In political terms the *serednyaki*, who usually owned some livestock and farmed with enough success not to fall into the 'poor' category, were the doubtful factor in Stalin's equation: here, the party's tactics were either to persuade or to terrorise them – depending on circumstances – into accepting collectivisation. From Yeltsin's description of his family's position during that period, they seem to have been *serednyaki*, or 'middling' peasants, and the official policy applied to them at that time and in that region ('all peasants were treated as *kulaki*') seems to have been one of coercion rather than persuasion. The 'very bad harvests and no food' were a direct consequence of the disruption caused by collectivisation, which led to such a drastic fall in agricultural output that rationing had to be introduced. In some parts of the Soviet Union the scarcity of food amounted to a famine, which claimed between two and three million victims.

2　The uniform method of awarding marks throughout the Soviet education system is a survival from pre-revolutionary practice. Marks are graded numerically on a scale from '1' to '5', with upward or downward modifications by adding pluses and minuses; thus each unmodified numeral represents the lower end of a 20-percentile. Zero is not used, therefore '1' is the lowest possible mark, while '5 + +' effectively corresponds to 100 per cent. '1' is practically never given, and is not supposed to be given at all for 'behaviour' for which the lowest mark is '2'. For scholastic performance in tests and examinations, '2' is a fail; '3' is normally the first pass mark; '4' is classified as 'good'; '5' is 'excellent'.

3　40°C is equivalent to 103°F. Normal body temperature on the Celsius scale is 36.6°.

4　The outdoor wooden bathhouse of rural Russia – sometimes private, sometimes communal – houses a steam-bath similar to the Scandinavian sauna.

5　*Burá* (the stress is on the second syllable) is a card game, a primitive form of poker favoured by criminals and prisoners. Each player is dealt three cards and is allowed to exchange one card for another from the pack. When all hands are shown, the player with the lowest score loses his stake, which goes to the player with the highest score.

6　The 'Golden Ring' is the name given to a group of the most ancient and beautiful cities of central Russia, in which much of the country's finest medieval architecture, ecclesiastical and secular, has been preserved. The cities which make up the Golden Ring are: Vladimir, Suzdal, Rostov the Great, Uglich and Yaroslavl.

Chapter 2

1 Official reprimands by the party authorities to an errant member are of two degrees of severity: 'without entry' and 'with entry' in the offender's personal party record.

2 The 'exchange of party documents' is a procedure undertaken at irregular intervals in the Soviet Communist Party, whereby all members have to surrender their membership cards and only get them back if they satisfy a scrutinising board as to their suitability for further membership. Since a certain number of members are 'weeded out' of the party by this process, its practical effect is that of a minor purge. Equally, entries recording any misdemeanour or reprimand are erased from a member's party record at this point.

Chapter 3

1 Born 1908. Politbureau member from 1952 until he was retired in 1983. He was latterly responsible for ideology.

2 The provincial executive committee (PEC) is the permanent executive body of the soviet, responsible for local government. It carries out orders of the soviet and local party committee and it functions permanently, even when the soviet is not sitting.

3 ZIK is an abbreviation for the name of the Kalinin factory.

4 At province level of the party machinery, the bureau stands in relation to the provincial committee (*obkom*) as does the Politbureau to the central committee at national level, i.e., it is the senior decision-making body. The members of the *obkom* bureau are:

> First secretary of the *obkom*
> Second secretary of the *obkom*
> Two other *obkom* secretaries
> Head of the KGB for the province
> Commanding officer of the military district
> State prosecutor of the province
> Chairman of the executive committee of the provincial soviet
> General managers of the major industrial enterprises in the province

5 *Ty* (pronounced 'tea') is the familiar, second-person singular form of the Russian words for you equivalent to the French *tu* or the German *du*. This form of address is normally only used to relatives, to close friends – or by a superior to a very junior subordinate. To someone in

Yeltsin's position, therefore, Gorbachov's use of it in addressing him carried implications either of excessive familiarity or of condescension by someone standing higher on the ladder of the party hierarchy.

6 Born 1924. Holds the ranks of colonel-general in the KGB; head of the KGB since 1986; member of the Politbureau. As part of the recent reforms of the Soviet legislature, ministers and chairmen of state committees (e.g. the KGB), who rank as ministers, must now be confirmed in their appointments by a vote of the Supreme Soviet.

7 This was not a normal outbreak of anthrax among cattle, but a leak of the anthrax virus from a secret factory, which was producing it as a biological weapon of war. As a result of the leak, a number of people were infected with anthrax and died.

8 Born 1904. Chairman of the Council of Ministers of the USSR from 1964 to 1980. He shared power for most of that period with Brezhnev. In 1965 he attempted a reform of the soviet economy, which proved abortive. Politbureau member 1948–52 and 1960–80. Died December 1980.

Chapter 6

1 Memorial is a voluntary organisation, headed by a number of distinguished public figures, including academics, writers and others prominent in the arts and sciences, with the aim of establishing monuments and cultural institutions dedicated to perpetuating the memory of the tens of millions of victims of Stalin's murderous policies of purges, imprisonment, torture and massacre over the twenty years from the early 1930s until his death in 1953.

2 This prediction has come true; while this book was being prepared for publication, the central committee of the CPSU held its September 1989 plenum, at which Shcherbitsky was pensioned off. I was wrong about one thing: he was not dismissed in disgrace but with honour, and what's more he was thanked for his excellent work in the job. (Author's note.)

Chapter 7

1 These remarks are an attack on Ligachov in his capacity of chairman of the central committee's secretariat; his aggressive, coercive

methods of inducing compliance with party orders reverberated all the way down the hierarchy to the lowest levels, such as party committees in factories or other enterprises.

Chapter 8

1 This refers to the gold star, the insignia of the titles of 'Hero of the Soviet Union' and 'Hero of Socialist Labour' which Brezhnev, with Politbureau compliance, awarded to himself.

Chapter 9

1 Since this passage was written, the Soviet authorities have granted recognition to the 'Uniate' or Greek Catholic church of the Western Ukraine, which worships according to the Eastern Orthodox rite but recognises the supremacy and infallibility of the Pope.

Charles Higham
Wallis £5.99

Secret Lives of the Duchess of Windsor

The astonishing truth behind the most talked about woman of the century

The well-documented romance of the Duke and Duchess of Windsor has been called the greatest love story of the century. But new research has uncovered a darker side to their forty year long affair. (WALLIS throws new light on the abdication saga and the Duchess's consuming passion for fabulous jewels.)

Centering on her unprecedented rise to social supremacy with neither beauty, money nor background, it reveals how her extraordinary talents reawakened the Duke's notoriously feeble virility. And, most sensationally of all, it discloses Wallis's previously undocumented involvement in international espionage – from her early spying missions to China to her treacherous moves to bring about the fall of Britain to Hitler.

Here at last is a true insight into a woman who left scandal in her wake – from faked jewel robbery to murder: a woman whose scheming ways earned her the wrath of the House of Windsor like no-one else before or since.

'An absorbing and at times outraging account of the Duchess' complex, ruthless and undeniably self-serving life' WOMAN'S JOURNAL

Patrick Cosgrave
The Lives of Enoch Powell £7.99

Enoch Powell has provoked more extreme reaction than any other MP since the war. For some, the 1968 'rivers of blood' speech marked him as an unforgivable racist; for others he remains the greatest Prime Minister Britain never had.

In *The Lives of Enoch Powell*, Patrick Cosgrave explores a highly complex figure. A brilliant academic and inspiring orator, Powell was also a politician of unflinching principle – and was destined never to achieve the heights of power his gifts demanded.

But from Westminster and the north of Ireland to the wilderness years outside his beloved Parliament, he always remained committed to his country. And his country remains compelled by him.

'Patrick Cosgrave's biography is almost everything we could expect when the life of a contemporary political giant is recounted by a talented political journalist' NORMAN TEBBIT, THE SUNDAY TIMES

'Enoch Powell is perhaps the most poignant figure in contemporary life. He is certainly the classic example of the flawed Shakespearian hero in public life and, as such, deserves the kind of serious treatment that he receives in this biography' ANTHONY HOWARD, THE INDEPENDENT

'Gaunt, cerebral, complex and melancholy, he has been a voice in the wilderness for the last 40 years. *The Lives of Enoch Powell* explains why. Cosgrave's masterly book . . . has done him justice'
JULIAN CRITCHLEY, TODAY

Edwina Currie
Lifelines £4.99

'One of the secrets of political success is the resilience normally only seen
in cartoons. Drop them, eat them, electrocute them, trample on them, kick
them over cliffs and they – the cartoon characters and the politicians –
are indestructible. I found it impossible to dislike Edwina Currie. She is
professional, chatty, confidential, disarming, genuinely caring, and
indefatigable' LESLEY GARNER, THE DAILY TELEGRAPH

'On the occasion I sat next to Mrs Currie at dinner I must say I warmed to
her. The party lost some of its entertainment value when its agricultural
lobby decided that she was, after all, not quite fit for human consumption.
Now she has written a book which, coming as it does in the twilight of the
Thatcher years, might serve as a valuable postscript to that period'
JOHN MORTIMER, THE SUNDAY TIMES

'Who will not remember the political storm, the writs, the fury of the
farming industry, the gloating jibes from her own party as well as the
Opposition? What she went through – even if much of it was self-inflicted
– was enough to traumatise even the strongest'
ANNE de COURCY, EVENING STANDARD

'Underneath that bright'n'breezy exterior is an essentially well meaning
politician . . . as an attitude shifter and leader in public opinion, none can
deny the part that Edwina Currie has played in building a more health
conscious Britain' DERBY EVENING TELEGRAPH

'No beating about the bush with Edwina . . . in telling her version of events
we are left in no doubt that she is still smarting'
VAL HENNESSEY. DAILY MAIL

Martin Bauml Duberman
Paul Robeson £15.99

'A superb biography . . . History written in the grand narrative tradition . . .
The glorious and tragic life of Paul Robeson is a poignant, gripping story
from beginning to end' THE NEW YORK TIMES BOOK REVIEW

'Among the finest biographies of any twentieth-century American. I could
not put it down' NATHAN I. HUGGINS, HARVARD UNIVERSITY

Paul Robeson is one of the most significant black figures in American
history. The son of an ex-slave, he was a brilliant scholar and athlete.
He became world famous as an actor and singer, but drew establishment fury
because of his political activism. At the height of his career, he was a prime
target of McCarthy's witchhunts, was hounded by the FBI, and spent his
old age plagued by illness, living virtually in internal exile.

Martin Bauml Duberman, who had exclusive access to the Robeson
archives, describes in detail Robeson's complex personal life, his stormy
marriage, numerous affairs, and the public turmoil of this enigmatic
personality.

'Gripping and powerfully moving. He has put Robeson back where
he belongs, both a hero and a victim in the sad, ugly story of
twentieth-century racism and political confusion' THE SPECTATOR

'Anyone who wants to understand the hidden histories of America since
the First World War will find this biography essential reading'
BEN OKRI, OBSERVER

'Triumphant and overwhelming' GEOFFREY MOORE, THE GUARDIAN

'The definitive work' STUDS TERKEL, CHICAGO SUN-TIMES

John Costello
Mask of Treachery £6.99

'In 1979 I cornered and flushed out the then Sir Anthony Blunt, a smooth, tough and seasoned spy if ever there was one. Now, MASK OF TREACHERY causes my heart to miss a beat or two . . .'
ANDREW BOYLE in THE DAILY TELEGRAPH

'New and explosive material about the activities of Anthony Blunt. Costello shows how the old spy became a homosexual mole for Stalin inside Buckingham Palace, when he carried out a secret mission in the American occupation zone of Germany on behalf of King George VI. Blunt recovered royal family papers and among the documents was hard evidence about the dangerous political flirtation between the Duke of Windsor and Hitler. As a reward Blunt became Keeper of the King's Pictures and allegedly used his position to provide Stalin with information from the pinnacle of the British establishment.
This fascinating book asserts that Blunt's knowledge provided him with a gold-plated insurance policy. For years his threat to reveal the royal secret saved him from exposure' THE DAILY MAIL

'Costello's assertions about Blunt and Britain's band of upper-class traitors . . . raise questions about the incompetence, self-protectionism and curious sexual habits that were rife among the British ruling elite' INTERNATIONAL HERALD TRIBUNE

Researched from British Intelligence files available in America but classified in Britain. *Mask of Treachery* could not have been written under the government's new official secrets act.

All Pan books are available at your local bookshop or newsagent, or can be ordered direct from the publisher. Indicate the number of copies required and fill in the form below.

Send to: **CS Department, Pan Books Ltd., P.O. Box 40, Basingstoke, Hants.   RG21 2YT.**

or phone: 0256 469551 (Ansaphone), quoting title, author and Credit Card number.

Please enclose a remittance* to the value of the cover price plus: 60p for the first book plus 30p per copy for each additional book ordered to a maximum charge of £2.40 to cover postage and packing.

*Payment may be made in sterling by UK personal cheque, postal order, sterling draft or international money order, made payable to Pan Books Ltd.

Alternatively by Barclaycard/Access:

Card No. | | | | | | | | | | | | | | | | | | | |

Signature:

Applicable only in the UK and Republic of Ireland.

While every effort is made to keep prices low, it is sometimes necessary to increase prices at short notice. Pan Books reserve the right to show on covers and charge new retail prices which may differ from those advertised in the text or elsewhere.

NAME AND ADDRESS IN BLOCK LETTERS PLEASE:

....

Name———————————————————————————————

Address———————————————————————————————

——————————————————————————————————————

——————————————————————————————————————

——————————————————————————————————————

3/87